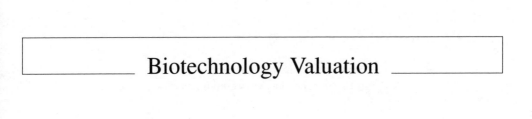

Biotechnology Valuation

For other titles in the Wiley Finance series
please see www.wiley.com/finance

Biotechnology Valuation

An Introductory Guide

Karl D. Keegan

A John Wiley and Sons, Ltd., Publication

Copyright © 2008   John Wiley & Sons Ltd, The Atrium, Southern Gate, Chichester,
West Sussex PO19 8SQ, England

Telephone   (+44) 1243 779777

Email (for orders and customer service enquiries): cs-books@wiley.co.uk
Visit our Home Page on www.wiley.com

Other Wiley Editorial Offices

John Wiley & Sons Inc., 111 River Street, Hoboken, NJ 07030, USA

Jossey-Bass, 989 Market Street, San Francisco, CA 94103-1741, USA

Wiley-VCH Verlag GmbH, Boschstr. 12, D-69469 Weinheim, Germany

John Wiley & Sons Australia Ltd, 42 McDougall Street, Milton, Queensland 4064, Australia

John Wiley & Sons (Asia) Pte Ltd, 2 Clementi Loop #02-01, Jin Xing Distripark, Singapore 129809

John Wiley & Sons Canada Ltd, 6045 Freemont Blvd, Mississauga, ONT, L5R 4J3, Canada

Wiley also publishes its books in a variety of electronic formats. Some content that appears in print may not be
available in electronic books.

Library of Congress Cataloging-in-Publication Data

Keegan, Karl D.
  Biotechnology valuation : an introductory guide / Karl D. Keegan.
    p. cm.
  Includes bibliographical references and index.
  ISBN 978-0-470-51178-7
  1. Biotechnology industries—Valuation.   2. Pharmaceutical
industry—Valuation.   3. Investment analysis. I. Title.
  HD9999.B442K44 2008
  332.63′221–dc22   2008040293

British Library Cataloguing in Publication Data

A catalogue record for this book is available from the British Library

ISBN 978-0-470-51178-7 (H/B)

Typeset in 10/12pt Times by Aptara Inc., New Delhi, India
Printed and bound in Great Britain by CPI Antony Rowe, Chippenham, Wiltshire

For TB and DJ
All my love
Mutley

Contents

Acknowledgements

This book arose from trying to answer many questions regarding the difficulties of valuing biotechnology stocks. The questions came from institutional clients, company management teams and colleagues. After trying to answer the questions and more importantly, trying to answer consistently, I was prompted to write this book.

In the course of writing the book, I would like to thank my colleagues at work at CanaccordAdams especially Guilluame van Renterghem and Lala Gregorek who provided excellent feedback and support. Neil Maruoka in our Toronto office was also a great sounding board for ideas.

Finally I would like to thank Catherine for putting up with me as I worked on this book over weekends and evenings and for her assistance in collating it all together.

1

Introduction

The aim of this book is to help ascertain the value of biotechnology assets whether they are drugs or companies. As with any investment, it's better to be well informed ahead of making the investment decision. This requires preparation as the potential for value differences arises partly because of differing expectations among different buyers and sellers. This book should provide a background to the principles of valuation and a toolkit to establishing the value of a biotechnology company. Valuation is important to people performing different roles in the pharmaceutical, biotechnology and investment industries such as venture capitalists, investors, and business development staff. Appropriate valuation metrics put buyers and sellers together whether they are investors assessing a stock or a biotechnology company's management team assessing an out-licensing opportunity. The key aim of the industry is to transform financial resources into new drugs. In this book I try and ascribe a value to that transformation.

I started my career as an academic scientist, followed by a period in industry before moving into a commercial role at a pharmaceutical company. This gave me my first encounter with valuing drug assets, both for internal purposes and also as part of a team that assessed in-licensing and out-licensing opportunities from a commercial or valuation perspective. I was also fortunate to work on drug projects at different phases of their development and commercial life cycles, which gave me an insight into the different factors that impact valuation, as the asset moves through the drug development value chain.

The sector can be viewed as quite technical which can be off-putting for some. However in my view it is a mistake to get overzealous about the science, to the extent that it handicaps your assessment of value. Although some of the science underlying the drugs is extremely cutting edge and exciting, the basic business models employed by the majority of companies are relatively straightforward. I have included a glossary of the more frequently encountered scientific and technical terms but my advice is to use the standard metrics included in this book to assess chances of success and focus on the cash flows.

Over the past 11 years I have had a career as a sell side analyst with a number of investment banks. Sell side refers to an analyst that works for brokerage houses/investment banks where sales people sell stocks based on analysts' recommendations. In recent years this job has come in for a lot of criticism, especially post the Global Settlement on April 2003, which was an enforcement agreement reached between financial services regulators in the United States, and ten of the largest investment banks to address issues of conflicts of interest. These conflicts in essence stemmed from the investment banking divisions potentially having too much influence on the research department's publications and compensation. As trading commissions declined, the costs of the sell side research department were offset by banking fees.

Post the Global Settlement, analysts in all banks have fewer interactions with their investment banking counterparts and when those interactions occur, they are carefully monitored by management and the compliance department. One of the consequences of these events is that sell side analysts are moving their coverage universe (companies they write research on) towards larger, more liquid (heavily traded) companies. This decline in the number of analysts covering a stock can mean a dwindling exposure to investors.

Whilst I acknowledge that the sell side has been justifiably criticized in the past, I do believe that the sell side has a very important education role in more abstruse sectors such as biotechnology. Most people can understand the market for a new version of a cola drink or a novel technology widget that increases the functionality of their mobile phone but understanding how a novel cancer treatment fits into the current market is a much more difficult task. Thus I see the sell side fulfilling this broader educational role that is perhaps not required in other traditional sectors.

Typically analysts have either a scientific or a medical background plus business experience. The key priority is to provide objective, timely and value-added research to help institutional investors make profitable decisions. Analysts review financial statements of the companies, read industry news, use trading history and industry information databases, meet management and attend conferences.

Analysts form their opinions using multiple sources to understand and monitor their recommendations, including:

- macro-interest rate, business cycle
- industry newsletters
- company interaction and published information
  - management
  - press releases
  - financial statements
- clinical-trials, initiation, design and interpretation
- real time input from the markets
  - LSE, AiM, Euronext, SWX, NASDAQ, AMEX, TSX

Sell side analysts seek to develop, and communicate to investors, insights regarding the value, risk and volatility of a stock and thus assist the investor to decide whether to buy, hold or sell stocks. Valuation is an important component in this job but with a number of caveats. Analysts generally put a price target per share as part of their recommendations but valuation can never be so precise. As an analyst publishing research notes there is a danger of becoming fixated with the one year price target which is the value per share that the analyst believes the stock should rise (or fall) to. Thus the notion of valuation range must be incorporated into the analysis, coupled to where the stock may be trading now. Furthermore some of the inputs are subjective and this is where the "art" of the valuation comes into play. Each individual must make their own assessment of certain facts. I encourage readers to look beyond the confines of the valuation issue at hand and seek a variety of ways of approaching the problem. Even how the problem is addressed or the framework in which it is positioned is important and relies significantly on the individual's creativity in problem solving.

This is probably the hardest element to capture correctly in a valuation analysis. Experience does help, which is a key driver of what prompted me to write this book. However drug development has huge uncertainty involved, as one tries to predict what a biological or chemical molecule will do within the physiological system of a human. Therefore even experience can only be a guide and we, as individuals, will get analyses wrong. A key aim of this book is to impart my experience and try and help get you up the learning curves as quickly and as easily as possible.

I was fortunate to be an analyst during the recent biotechnology boom in 2000 and it was the experience of marketing to institutional investors over that time period that first triggered

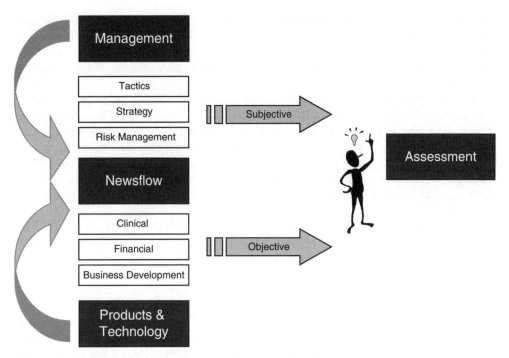

Figure 1.1   Analysis is a combination of subjective and objective assessments

my interest in the broader aspects of biotechnology valuations. During the biotechnology boom, the valuations of biotechnology companies rocketed as companies and investors sought to capitalize on the furore surrounding the outcome of sequencing the human genome.[1,2,3] Media hype also played its part. However the lesson I learned from that exciting period was that investors looking at a stock used a variety of metrics. Furthermore when investors wanted to talk about a valuation, they really want to know the assumptions underlying the model, not the exact outputs that are derived. This prompted me to focus on applying a consistent and transparent methodology to biotechnology company and asset valuation. I believe that this is a really important point and in essence is what I am trying to do in this book. Hopefully when you have finished reading this book, you should have developed a consistent approach and have a useful toolkit to tackle the valuation of a biotechnology company or individual drug, with confidence.

As in all books of this nature, there is no standardized reader. Thus, I have included chapters addressing the regulatory and technical hurdles that define drug development. Furthermore I have tried to share some of my experiences, highlighting some of the potential pitfalls when attempting to value biotech companies. This is not comprehensive but merely consists of some of the most common errors which I have succumbed to in the past.

In this introductory chapter I focus on defining the task ahead, namely trying to value healthcare-focused biotechnology companies which are trying to develop new therapeutics. This segment of biotechnology is one of the most dynamic in terms of investment, capital raised and number of companies, both public and private. Biotechnology assets are generally composed of drugs, patents and people, all of which are difficult to value in a traditional sense.

However currently there is no consistent way to value drug assets and the methodologies that are generally used in other sectors need modification in order to apply to the technically focused and regulation bound world of drug development. This book demonstrates the areas where the practitioner will need to use skill and judgement in order to get a meaningful valuation from the analysis.

Over the subsequent chapters I briefly review traditional valuation techniques so that all readers can tackle the remainder of the book with a suitable level of financial understanding. This is not meant to be a book steeped in financial theory, more a practical guide for the interested individual who wishes to ascribe value to drug assets. I have included a bibliography which includes some general finance textbooks and a selection of other books that provide interesting perspectives on the biotechnology industry. Whilst there are many books on valuation methodology, there are not too many on biotechnology valuation. This book is my attempt to remedy this issue.

One of the features of both the pharmaceutical and biotechnology industries is that both are heavily regulated, not just in the United States but across the globe. Whilst providing a framework for analysis and a (relatively) clear pathway to take drugs to the market, the drug development process also poses many hurdles and each phase is associated with probabilities of success. In Chapter 3 I attempt to provide an overview of the process and highlight some tips and potential pitfalls for the unwary investor.

In Chapter 4, I move on to valuing biotechnology companies and again provide a framework for the valuation with an emphasis on discounted cash flow analysis, comparable company analysis and product pipeline assessments using a probability weighted net present value model. This latter approach is very important as the majority of biotechnology companies are loss-making and thus investors need to ascertain value in the absence of earnings. The key point is that no single methodology can provide all the answers and thus the use of multiple approaches to addressing the problem in hand is a far better approach.

Chapter 5 takes the analysis further by looking at individual net present values (NPV) of drug assets, a useful technique when one's estimated valuation suggests that one or two drug assets comprise the majority of the value being determined. Although the methods discussed in Chapter 4 are useful and can be successfully applied to biotechnology valuation, there are an increasing number of papers and books advocating the use of decision trees and real options analysis to capture the value inherent in management decisions through the development phase that is not captured in a straightforward discounted cash flow analysis. In this chapter I go through the mechanism and some of the theory underlying these approaches. However in my view, the use of real option analysis is more appropriate for insiders in a company. By that I mean access to management accounts and business plan, including the costs timings and expected commercial potential of the drug. The need for these "real" figures curtails the use of such analyses for those external to the company as they have to rely on publicly disclosed information on estimates.

Chapter 6 provides a guide to investing in the biotechnology industry and looks at some of the approaches that successful investors apply. This builds on the toolkit of valuation approaches discussed in the previous chapters and incorporates more of the art with an emphasis on other non-valuation driven metrics that are useful for biotechnology investing.

In Chapter 7 I review concepts applicable to the valuation of early-stage or venture backed biotechnology companies, thereby completing the valuation of all types of biotechnology companies: private venture backed, loss-making public and profitable public companies.

BIOTECHNOLOGY BACKGROUND

Biotechnology is a general term describing the directed modification of biological processes and has been defined as "the application of biological organisms, systems and their components to industrial products and processes".[4] This may be accomplished by introducing new genes into organisms, breeding organisms to form new variants, or treating organisms with specific compounds. Thus, biotechnology in its broadest sense is about the use of living organisms with the aim of developing new products or processes to improve our health, environment or agriculture.

Biotechnology is not a separate science but rather incorporates expertise from a wide range of scientific disciplines. As the realization of the power of biotechnology has become more widespread, the biotechnology industry has in itself become global in nature. Biotechnology is being used to develop crops and breed animals with special characteristics. In addition biotechnology tools and techniques are being applied in the development of new industrial enzymes. In the business sense biotechnology could refer to the use of biological processes to make money! This also refers to the historical aspects of biotechnology when natural processes were used to improve crops and animal husbandry and to provide foodstuffs such as wine and cheese.

However the scope of the industry in this sense is way beyond the boundaries of this book. This book will restrict itself to trying to value the companies that make up the biotechnology industry involved with the discovery and development of new medicines. As such, it should be called the discovery industry because it now employs far broader technology than its original focus on recombinant DNA and monoclonal antibodies.[5] The discovery of the structure of DNA in 1953 and the identification of DNA as the genetic material in all life allowed for great leaps in our understanding of life forms from bacteria to plants to humans. However, the biotechnology industry is generally accepted to have originated in the 1970s, based largely on a new recombinant DNA technique whose details were published in 1973 by Stanley Cohen of Stanford University and Herbert Boyer of the University of California, San Francisco. These scientists had successfully extracted DNA from a toad and then inserted this DNA into a bacterium. As the bacterium multiplied, the new bacteria produced the protein encoded by the toad DNA. This technique utilizes recombinant DNA technology and today is a method of making proteins – such as human insulin and other therapies – in cultured cells under controlled manufacturing conditions. In 1974, the industry got another technological boost when Cesar Milstein and Georges Kohler discovered how to fuse an antibody-producing cell with a cancer cell, allowing the resulting combination (hybridoma) to produce large amounts of identical antibodies (termed monoclonal antibodies) essentially forever. In 1976 the healthcare-focused biotechnology industry as we know it today was born when Boyer agreed to start a company (Genentech) funded by Bob Swanson. The excitement of the new industry was attracting new capital and in 1980, Genentech went public on October 14 at US$ 35/share, raising US$ 35 million.

In my view the successful financing of independent biotechnology start-ups has been a hugely significant achievement, especially as the funds raised are raised on the basis of potential rewards rather than current cash flows or operations. This success is to be applauded but it does raise questions on how to ascribe value to the potential rewards.

I have focused on the pharmaceutical sector and the issues facing companies trying to develop new drugs, irrespective of whether these drugs are derived using biotechnology methods or not. Furthermore I have used the term biotechnology to encompass the broad range of technologies that are used in drug discovery and development rather than the more narrow view of focusing only on biotechnologically derived drugs.

Within this restricted definition of the application of biotechnology to medicine, I have attempted to provide the layperson, or interested amateur, with a guide as to the investment potential of biotech companies, which in themselves cover a broad spectrum of technologies and business models. I do not differentiate between the technologies used to discover drugs (chemical or biotechnology) and indeed a more proper definition would be to class all of these companies as small to medium-sized emerging pharmaceutical companies.

Historically biotechnology companies could be differentiated from pharmaceutical companies by their use of biotechnology techniques (in essence a comparison between recombinant engineering and synthetic chemistry). It initially appeared that the biotechnology industry could enforce a paradigm shift in drug development that would leave traditional pharmaceutical companies obsolete. However the large pharmaceutical companies did not succumb to the introduction of the biotechnology techniques but instead learned rapidly from the new start-ups. Thus this easy categorization is no longer appropriate and companies in both biotechnology and pharmaceutical sectors utilize all of the tools available. In my view, it is more important that the term biotechnology company refers to the philosophy underlying the business model rather than the actual scientific and technical means of developing a drug.

The global biotechnology industry is an exciting investment arena because it seeks to integrate the cutting edge of science with the world of finance in order to bring us the medicines of the future. Biotechnology offers investors an exciting entry point, where the business world meets the world of scientifically driven healthcare research. Thus the investor has the opportunity to potentially add to the development of new medicines and also to capture economic value from the endeavour. Biotech companies are small to medium-sized companies operating in the pharmaceutical research and development industry (R&D) with the development of a new drug as their primary focus. A very dynamic environment and high levels of technical and commercial uncertainty are typical features of the biotechnology

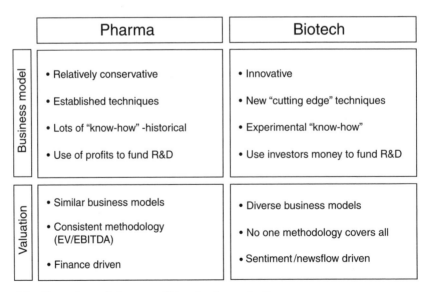

Figure 1.2   Comparison of pharma and biotechnology valuation

Table 1.1 Global biotechnology at a glance 2005

	Global	US	Europe	Canada	Asia-Pacific
Revenues ($m)	84 872	68 400	13 352	2 692	3 970
R&D expenses ($m)	31 806	30 000	6 309	915	488
Net Income (loss) ($m)	−2 694	−3 600	−2 645	−722	−6
Number of companies					
Public	798	386	181	82	149
Private	3 616	1 502	1 563	322	615
Total	4 414	1 888	1 744	404	764

Source: Ernst & Young. Beyond Borders Global Biotechnology Report 2008, reproduced with permission

sector. Many companies have significant valuations many years before they earn any profits from selling their products.

Key difficulties in biotechnology are the long timeframes and high development costs to bring one product to the market along with the challenges of high risk and technical uncertainty. This means that a lot of money is needed for a long period of time until the investors get any compensation for their investment. Meantime, the odds against them succeeding are fairly high.

However, biotechnology-derived products have the potential to positively change our society, from improving health care and increasing agricultural products to producing a cleaner environment. The public markets recognize this potential and a lot of money has flowed into biotechnology companies. Sales, revenues and market capitalization all more than doubled during the period from 1993 to 1999. The year 2000 saw more money invested in biotechnology firms than the previous five years combined. The business models have matured and the tools of biotechnology research are refined to the extent that the industry is ready for unprecedented growth.

In this book, I have focused on product-based biotechnology investments. I believe that the structure (stages) of the product development process, the consequent predictability of news flow timing and the possibility of assigning real value to the compounds has captured investor interest in the product-based stories. In 2000, the world was focused on the hype surrounding the sequencing of the human genome (The Human Genome Project), driven for the most part by the accompanying media frenzy. However, this interest waned and with it investors' acceptance of platform technologies. In truth, it is difficult to truly differentiate among a plethora of technologies that all claim to offer drug discovery nirvana to the pharmaceutical industry. A key metric for these companies was the number of partnerships they could sign and in most cases, management was found wanting.

Unless a technology platform company is broad enough to support many deals, this model remains limited, and companies should be valued with this in mind. In addition, both management and investors often underestimate the time needed to complete a deal, and this alone limits the number of deals a company can do in any one year. Platform technology companies have been perceived as lower risk than product companies, and as the nascent European biotechnology industry emerged in the late 1990s, this model initially appealed to investors. However it is worth remembering that while platform companies are not exposed to the specific technical risks associated with drug development, commercial risk can be higher and potentially more limiting. Drug development is the driver of both opportunity and risk. Many management teams have glossy presentations providing copious detail on the minutiae of the science but as an investor, none of this matters unless the company is either bought out or brings a drug to the market. Even then the valuation depends upon how well the management team can identify and manage development and commercial risk.

Successful investing in any product company requires a true understanding of the risks in bringing products to market. I categorize these risks as:

- Technical – Successfully taking the drug through the complete clinical trials and regulatory process and on to the market. Technical risks relate to the stage of clinical trials that a drug is in, but also the extent to which a concept and any drug based on that concept, is proven in man. Ultimately technical risks can be reduced to a binary decision; is the drug approvable or not?
- Commercial – Recognizing and realizing the true market potential of a drug and the associated commercialization hurdles, e.g. marketing, partnering. Thus the commercial risks are much broader and consist of a spectrum of possible outcomes. Is there room for five such products on the market? The later products, without the first-to-market advantage, are likely to have to show real advantages over established products (or be better marketed) to get more than a relatively small share, albeit of a potentially big market.

Commercial risks are equally as important as technical, yet are often neglected by analysts and investors alike. It is potentially possible to create enormous opportunities for drugs to treat stroke. However, the standard probabilities of success ought to be modified according to the specific hurdles associated with drug development in a particular therapy area. Most biotech companies lack a GP sales force or the resources to create one. Equally licensing a cancer drug to a company lacking any presence in this market may be less than ideal. Investors need to focus as much on commercial success as technical probabilities.

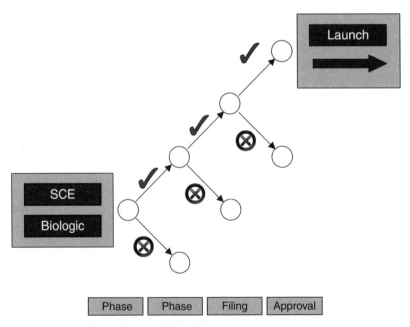

Figure 1.3   Schematic technical risk decision tree

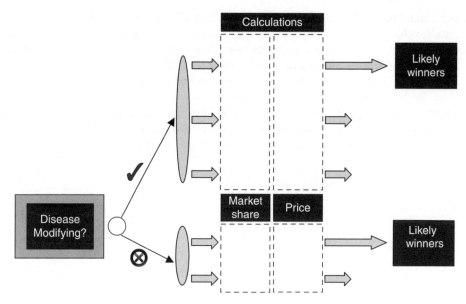

Figure 1.4   Schematic commercial risk decision tree

Commercial risk must be considered as it impacts over the entire product life cycle, and I believe that the pressures on the pharmaceutical industry are squeezing these life cycles into narrower timeframes.

In summary innovation drives the biotechnology industry, including both the drugs and the companies formed to develop and commercialize them. Not all will succeed but there will be

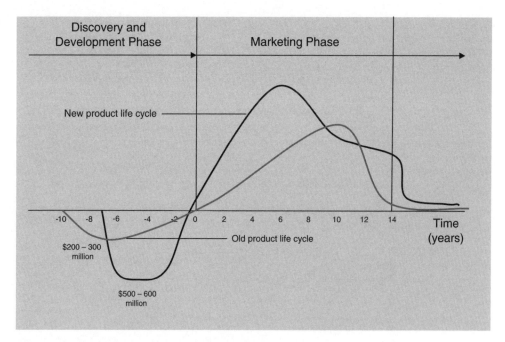

Figure 1.5   Schematic of typical pharmaceutical product life cycle

winners, and some of these drugs, companies and investors will win on a huge scale. That is the attraction for the investor in my view. However it is not an easy path to become a successful biotechnology investor. My view is that an appropriate understanding of the potential risks and rewards can facilitate astute investment. I also believe that astute investment is driven by a knowledge and understanding of value, both relative and absolute.

I love the biotechnology industry, the wonderful fusion of science and business and the fact that I am constantly learning, unable to accept that my knowledge of the drivers of this industry have peaked. I hope I have captured some of that excitement in this book and have in some small way, better prepared you for assessing the value of biotechnology assets and companies.

2
Traditional Valuation Methods

Valuation is as much an art as a science and is composed of reaching a judgement regarding a company's growth prospects and related financial projections. As such it is a blend of subjective and objective assessments of all aspects of the company, including the management team. In this chapter, I will review, briefly, some traditional valuation methodologies including discounted cash flow (DCF) analysis and relative valuation metrics. These will be reviewed assuming that the company in question has a traditional format, i.e. the company is in a mature phase of its evolution and has measurable profits and cash flows. This chapter is designed to give a flavour of valuation methods that are used widely and highlight some of the accounting concepts that one should be aware of before embarking on a valuation. For a more in-depth appraisal of accounting and valuation please refer to some standard textbooks.[1,2,3]

For those readers who are familiar with financial statements, this chapter can be skipped as it is intended to be a basic guide to those with scientific knowledge but little formal financial experience.

THE VALUE OF A COMPANY

The value of a company tends to be composed of the following components:

- Operating businesses: biotechnology companies may have operating businesses selling drugs or services but the vast majority will be purely research and development-focused entities.
- Capital structure for early stage companies: this is usually cash but can include convertible securities and some debt.
- Management: a key driver of value creation in any business.
- Opportunities: the uses of cash through R&D expenditure to create future value. The cash balance and the cash burn are important metrics when evaluating biotechnology companies.

A popular model of traditional company valuation suggests that the value of a firm should be based on its cash flows plus the net present value of its growth opportunities. Any given company valuation should be approached using multiple valuation techniques to see the range of values suggested by each. Such an approach prevents over-emphasis on one technique at the expense of others, which are perhaps equally relevant. Sensitivity analysis should be used to identify parameters that impact the valuation significantly. Additional research can then be focused on these key drivers of value.

Valuation techniques focus on a specific part of a company's financial performance. Three categories of techniques may be used:

- income statement multiples
- balance sheet analysis
- discounted cash flows

Rather than yielding a single estimate of a company's worth these techniques will lead to a range of values that are the function of many assumptions.

I mentioned above that management is a key driver of any business but is that true and how does one start assessing the management team? Unfortunately there is no textbook approach to evaluating management teams. At the level of investment into private companies many venture capitalists state openly that they are backing the management team as the quality of the management team is arguably the best predictor of success.

As biotechnology companies evolve through their maturity cycle, the consistent objective of management should be to secure the resources that enable the research to continue, facilitate business development and communicate the company's strategy to external investors. From the perspective of the sell side analyst, a good management team "under promises and over delivers". The key component of this aspect is that the management team are able to concisely express their strategy with a corresponding lack of jargon. In essence, one should be able to understand what the company is trying to do.

Too many management teams consistently get this the wrong way round, thereby undermining investors' faith in the strategy and sometimes leading to what has been described as a "management discount" being applied to the share price. Although this discount is difficult to ascertain, it can be more evident when things go wrong. Many companies that have management teams that are perceived as being poor get severely punished by the market when disappointing results (clinical or financial) are announced. For public companies, it is worthwhile checking whether the management team are buying or selling shares. One should look for management to hold shares for significant periods, thereby aligning their interest with those of shareholders. That is not to say that management cannot sell shares in order to diversify their wealth but large sales of shares should be questioned thoroughly.

Management teams can make very positive contributions to valuation. If business development such as out-licensing a drug in clinical trials is important to the business strategy, good management teams can add value by striking better deals (better economics with better partners). In assessing management teams of public companies, it is worthwhile accessing company presentations from the start of the year (usually found on the web site under the investor relations section). These will usually have key goals and/or objectives set out for the coming year. It is important that the potential investor should make note of these and monitor progress. Some adjustments are bound to occur, usually in my experience to clinical trial slippage of timelines. It is important to reality check these statements and assess their impact on valuation. For example if a company says that a clinical trial has been delayed due to difficulties in recruiting patients and that they are expanding the number of trial centres from 10 to 50, is there an explanation of how this will impact the company's expenses over the coming year and is there a new timeline provided for the trial to complete?

However past failures should not automatically taint a management team and in many instances, the experience of failure can be more informative than success. This is a more subtle assessment of management that can only come from meeting them and observing their responses in a public forum such as a conference or analyst meeting.

Accounts – Providing the Data for Valuation Analysis

All corporate annual reports include three financial statements:

- Income statement or profit and loss (P&L). This statement summarizes the revenues and expenses over a period (usually one year)

- Balance sheet. This statement is prepared at the close of business on the last day of the income statement period and thus represents the business at one particular point in time.
- Cash flow statement. This statement reports the cash receipts and the cash payments of an accounting period.

The financial statements are prepared according to financial standards, the two most common being Generally Accepted Accounting Principles (GAAP; typically in the United States) and International Financial Reporting Standards (IFRS). One should note at this stage that accounts are compiled according to the accruals concept. This means that revenues and costs are recognized as they are earned or incurred, not as money is received or paid.

The most important point regarding the three accounting statements is that they interlock with each other (similar to a three piece jigsaw!). I will explain what to look for in the three statements and then show how they interlink with each other.

The Income Statement

The income statement is where the revenues are stated and where costs are deducted to generate the earnings number over the accounting period. The typical accounting period is one year, and this fiscal year usually ends on December 31, to coincide with the calendar year. However some companies end the fiscal year in other months. For example to calendarize earnings for a company with a May year end use the following formula: May 2006 earnings* (5/12) + May 2007 earnings* (7/12) = December 2006 earnings.

The income statement reports the results of the firm's operating activities. The preparation of the income statement is governed by the matching principle which states that revenues and related costs are accounted for during the same time period. A typical layout of the income statement is depicted in Table 2.1.

The key terms are:

Sales/revenues: the total amount received from the sale of products or services during the period. Note that sales revenue is reported as a net figure, meaning that discounts or other amounts taken off the list price are taken prior to reporting this number.

Cost of goods sold (COGS): the total cost of goods sold during the period. It is worthwhile to try and gauge the impact of COGS for biotechnology companies. For a small chemical molecule, the cost of goods is usually <10 % of the selling price but for drugs that are biologically derived (for example monoclonal antibodies and protein drugs) the cost of goods may be a significant cost. In addition there is deemed to be a current shortage of biological manufacturing capacity available globally and thus management should be questioned regarding their strategy on this point.

Gross profit/margin: revenues less COGS.

The next step is to subtract operating expenses from the gross profit. In summary operating expenses includes all expenses other than the costs of goods sold, interest expenses and income tax. Usually these are split into three categories:

1. Selling expenses
2. General and administrative expenses
3. R&D expenses

Table 2.1 Sample income statement

Profit & Loss	2006A	2007A	2008E	2009E	2010E
Product Sales	5.28	7.08	9.69	10.54	27.46
Royalties	0.00	0.00	1.53	5.37	8.38
Milestones	0.00	2.58	3.87	5.16	0.52
Others	0.00	0.00	0.00	0.00	0.00
Revenues	**5.28**	**9.66**	**15.09**	**21.08**	**36.35**
CoGS	1.24	1.42	1.45	1.58	5.72
Gross Profit	**4.04**	**8.25**	**13.64**	**19.49**	**30.63**
Gross margin	*77%*	*85%*	*90%*	*92%*	*84%*
G&A	1.07	1.34	1.72	1.99	2.17
Sales & Marketing	2.90	4.04	5.91	6.32	11.67
R&D	3.69	4.43	3.77	4.64	7.27
– of which share-based compensation	0.00	0.08	0.19	0.33	0.57
Other op ex	0.07	0.00	0.00	0.00	1.28
EBIT	**(3.70)**	**(1.56)**	**2.23**	**6.55**	**8.24**
EBIT margin	*Nm*	*nm*	*15%*	*31%*	*23%*
Depreciation	0.11	0.17	0.23	0.29	0.44
Amortization Intangibles	0.00	0.00	0.00	0.00	0.00
EBITDA	**(3.59)**	**(1.39)**	**2.46**	**6.83**	**8.67**
EBITDA margin	*Nm*	*nm*	*16%*	*32%*	*24%*
Non operating expenses (income)	0.00	0.82	0.00	0.00	0.00
Net Financials	0.10	(0.04)	(0.09)	0.00	0.12
EBT	**(3.60)**	**(2.42)**	**2.14**	**6.55**	**8.35**
EBT margin	*Nm*	*nm*	*14%*	*31%*	*23%*
Provision for taxes	0.25	0.35	0.48	1.02	1.89
Net Income	**(3.86)**	**(2.77)**	**1.66**	**5.53**	**6.46**
net margin	*Nm*	*nm*	*11%*	*26%*	*18%*
NoSH	24.76	25.80	25.80	25.80	25.80
EPS – basic (p)	**(15.58)**	**(10.73)**	**6.42**	**21.43**	**25.03**
Dividends	0.00	0.00	0.00	0.00	0.00
Net to retained earnings	**(3.86)**	**(2.68)**	**1.85**	**5.86**	**7.03**

Subtracting the operating expenses from the gross profit yields Earnings Before Interest, Taxes, Depreciation and Amortization (EBITDA). EBITDA differs from the operating cash flow in the cash flow statement primarily by excluding payments for taxes or interest as well as changes in working capital. Although not defined by GAAP, EBITDA is widely used by analysts as a proxy for operating cash flow.

Depreciation spreads the cost of fixed assets over their useful life and thus in any accounting period, the depreciation expense is the "cost" for using these assets in that period. Note that depreciation is not a cash expense and thus there is no cash outflow associated with depreciation in the accounting period.

Amortization of intangible assets is similar to depreciation of fixed assets. Examples of intangible assets with identifiable useful lives include past and current R&D investments and the company's patent portfolio. In contrast to physical assets it is impossible for all the components of intangible capital to be accurately described.

> Earnings Before Interest and Taxes (EBIT/Operating profit) is calculated as EBITDA less depreciation and amortization.
> Interest income details the amount received from investing for the period.
> Interest expense is the amount of interest on debt for the period.
> Tax expense is the amount owed by the business to the government during the period.
>   = Net Income

Dividends are payments made by a firm to its shareholders. When a firm earns a profit, that money can either be reinvested in the business or it can be paid to the shareholders as a dividend. Many corporations retain a portion of their earnings and pay the remainder as a dividend.

Net to retained earnings is the amount of money that is reinvested in the business after a dividend has been paid to shareholders.

In start-up and early growth stages, the revenue and expenses generated by a firm's assets in place are expected to be more transitory than in later growth or mature stages, when income is more predictable. In the biotechnology industry, the assets in place used for development of products and research early in the firm's life cycle, generate few if any revenues and income is negative. As these companies mature, the nature of the revenues and expenses changes to include more production and sales-related activities which become more predictable and permanent as the firm matures.

Most biotech companies are loss-making and thus report a loss. However there are some components of the P&L that should be scrutinized carefully. In my view these include

- Revenue recognition
- Operating expenses – use of common size
- Cash earnings

Many biotechnology companies seek licensing agreements and partnership with other companies, especially large pharmaceutical companies. These deals are usually structured as a combination of upfront payment, milestone payments and royalties on sales. It is important to note that many of these upfront payments will need to be amortized over an appropriate period. For example, a company may receive a US$ 150 million licence fee but whilst the company receives the cash straight way, the income statement records the revenue over an appropriate period based on factors such as the length of the deal and milestones that need to be achieved.

Operating expenses are always worth an extra bit of attention, especially the level of spending on R&D, and I find it useful to analyse what one company is spending against a peer group, using common size analysis. This technique is simply a standardization of line items to eliminate the effect of size by expressing the items in proportion to some size-related measure. All line items are expressed as a percentage of the reference item (i.e. if revenue is the reference item, the revenue line equals 100 %). Common size ratios are used to compare financial statements of different companies or of the same company over a time period.

It is often insightful to compare a firm to the best firms in the particular industry. As with most accounting-based metrics, care must be exercised to adjust for the impact of different accounting policies. In biotechnology it is useful for the profitable companies but less so for

Table 2.2 Common size analysis

	Income Statement	Common Size Income Statement
Revenues	85 102	100.0%
CoGS	25 002	29.4%
Gross profit	60 100	70.6%
R&D	21 000	24.7%
SG&A	11 489	13.5%
Other operating expenses	2 012	2.4%
EBIT	25 599	30.1%
Net financials	1 000	1.2%
Net income	26 599	31.3%

the non-profitable companies as many do not even have a consistent revenue base to perform a common size analysis. Nonetheless a comparison of absolute spending should be performed to gain a sense of how long the company can continue spending before requiring additional cash resources.

The first step in conducting a common size analysis is to review the common size statement and to look for changes and trends that warrant further review. Once the trends are identified explanations should be sought. This provides a link to the comment I made on good management. A company that is spending significantly more than its peers on R&D may have valid reasons for doing so but management should be able to explain the strategy behind the spending. It is also useful to compare spending patterns between comparable companies to try and assess the underlying differences.

Net income is given on a dollar/pound basis and on a per share basis. Earnings per share (EPS) refers to net income divided by outstanding number of shares. Appearing on income statements, it shows the earnings of the company after all expenses have been paid off and adjustments made for depreciation of assets. Basic earnings per share is net income available to ordinary shareholders divided by the weighted average of ordinary shares outstanding during the period (usually a year but may be a quarter). The weighted average is used to accommodate changes in shares outstanding from share issues and repurchases.

Diluted earnings per share is based on the total amount of ordinary shares that would be outstanding if holders of contingent claims on shares (i.e. convertible bonds, warrants and stock options) were to exercise their options and hold ordinary shares. There are two recommended ways of calculating fully diluted number shares outstanding:

1. The treasury stock method is used to include the effects of options and warrants.
2. The "if converted" method is used to include the effects of convertible securities.

The treasury stock method affects the denominator of the EPS equation. The method assumes the proceeds from exercised options would be used to repurchase outstanding stock, therefore the net number of shares added to the denominator is less than the additional shares that would be outstanding from exercised options. To illustrate, assume 10 000 options are outstanding to purchase shares at £ 2.40 per share. Shares have been selling at an average of £ 3.00 per share. Using the treasury stock method, we would compute an incremental number of shares to be added to the denominator. The proceeds from the exercise of the options would be £ 24 000

Table 2.3 EPS reconciliation

	Q3 07 $m	Q3 07 cents/ADS	Q3 06 $m	Q3 06 cents/ADS
Net income for diluted EPS (ADS)	**34.7**	**19.9**	**97.2**	**51.3**
Fair adjustment		6.7		3.9
In-licensing payments	75.0	39.0	30.5	18.3
Gain on disposal of product rights	−7.1	−3.6	−63.0	−37.5
Legal settlement provision	27.0	13.8		
Intangible asset amortization	31.1	15.9	14.6	8.7
SFAS 123 R	11.7	6.0	9.1	5.4
Taxes on above adjustments	46.2	−23.7	0.6	0.3
Non GAAP net income / EPS (ADS)	**126.2**	**66.3**	**85.7**	**50.4**

(10 000 × £ 2.40). Using the proceeds of £ 24 000 to purchase stock at £ 3.00 per share would result in the purchase of 8000 shares (£ 24 000/£3.00).

The incremental number of shares would be:

Shares under option 10 000
Shares repurchased 8000
Incremental shares 2000

Using the numbers, it can be seen that if the average market price per share were less than the option price, the incremental number of shares would be negative, indicating a non-dilution. The impact of non-dilution is ignored in EPS calculations.

When calculating fully diluted EPS, shares are repurchased at the average or year-end market price, whichever is higher. If the year-end market price is higher, fewer shares can be repurchased from the proceeds, thereby increasing the incremental number of shares to be added to the denominator. Therefore, the higher year-end price further dilutes the EPS statistic.

The if-converted method assumes convertibles are converted during the period of time they are outstanding. This method affects both the numerator and the denominator of the EPS calculation. If bonds were converted, interest expense (less applicable taxes) would be avoided, therefore net income would increase. If preferred stock were converted, no dividends would be paid, therefore dividends would not be deducted from net income in the numerator. Conversion of either bonds or preferred stock would increase the denominator number of shares.

However there are a number of distortions that can occur through the accounting rules and thus many companies offer an alternative analysis of their operating results to try and demonstrate the true cash generating capabilities of the operations of the company.

Balance Sheet

The balance sheet is a snapshot at a given moment in time (usually the company's year end) that indicates all the assets owned by the company and all the claims against those assets. This position is usually summarized by the following equation:

$$\text{Assets} = \text{liabilities and shareholders' equity}$$

Table 2.4 Sample balance sheet

Balance sheet	2006A	2007A	2008E	2009E
Assets				
Cash and cash equivalents	1.60	0.00	0.00	3.59
Accounts receivable	0.32	0.58	0.91	1.26
Inventory	0.79	1.45	2.26	3.16
Other current assets	0.00	0.00	0.00	0.00
Current assets	**2.71**	**2.03**	**3.17**	**8.01**
Net PPE	0.22	0.35	0.46	0.57
Intangibles	0.00	0.00	0.00	0.00
LTA	0.32	0.58	0.91	1.26
Total assets	**3.24**	**2.95**	**4.53**	**9.85**
Liabilities				
ST notes	0.00	0.00	0.00	0.00
Accounts payable	**0.53**	**0.97**	**1.51**	**2.11**
Other current liabilities	0.00	0.00	0.00	0.00
Current Liabilities	0.53	0.97	1.51	2.11
Debt 1	0.00	0.00	0.00	0.00
Deferred income	0.82	0.82	0.82	0.82
Other long-term liabilities	0.00	0.00	0.00	0.00
Total Liabilities	**1.34**	**3.74**	**3.47**	**2.92**
Shareholders' equity				
Common Stock	0.22	0.22	0.22	0.22
Retained earnings	(12.04)	(14.73)	(12.88)	(7.02)
Other equity accts	13.72	13.72	13.72	13.72
Total SH equity	**1.90**	**(0.78)**	**1.07**	**6.92**
Total Liabilities & SH equity	**3.24**	**2.95**	**4.53**	**9.85**

A typical balance sheet layout is depicted above. Note that both sides of the equation "balance". Note that whereas the income statement is a record covering 12 months, the balance sheet is a one point in time record.

Assets

Assets are generally grouped into two types, current and non-current. Current means that they have a horizon of less than one year, meaning that they can be easily converted into cash:

Cash: cash is cash

Marketable securities: these are short-term securities held as investments. They are convertible to cash at a moment's notice. A company may have them when it has excess cash and wishes to produce a higher interest income from the holdings.

Accounts receivable: monies owed by a company's customers for services billed but not paid for. It is important that a company collect on these as quickly as possible. It is a loan which the company makes to its buyers. Note that the accounts payable section in the current liabilities section is the reverse: it is a loan that a company gets from its suppliers.

Inventory: raw materials and other supplies needed for production, and goods waiting to be sold.

Other current assets: anything else that is an asset and is not a long-term asset.

The above equals Total Current Assets.

Fixed assets: generally any long-term asset used for production. This is often called plant, property and equipment.

Accumulated depreciation: this is the total amount of cost that has been used up or depreciated over the life to date of the fixed assets.

Net fixed assets: fixed assets less accumulated depreciation. As you work with different models for different analytical needs, you may find that you need to show only this line and not (gross) fixed assets and accumulated depreciation on the balance sheet. This line is often called net property plant and equipment (PPE).

Investments in affiliates: this shows the investments held by the company under the equity method. When a company holds between a 20 and 50 % interest in another company and has significant influence (but not a controlling interest) over that company, that investment is shown in this category.

Goodwill: when a company buys another company using the purchase accounting method and pays a price that is higher than the net assets (the value of the assets less the value of the liabilities) the difference is held in this account. There is no identifiable asset to this account – it's just a place to note that the purchase price was more than the value purchased. Such goodwill used to be required to be amortized over a set period of years, up to 40 years, depressing the earnings figure. From a cash flow point of view, there is no effect, as the amortization is a non-cash expense. However, this rule was changed in 2001, and goodwill has to remain unamortized, subject only to a period test for impairment.

Intangibles: though similar to goodwill in that its amortization is a non-cash expense, intangibles represent identifiable assets such as patents, trademarks and proprietary technology.

Other long-term assets: these are other assets that are non-current. Depending on your modelling needs, you can include more than one long-term assets account.

The above section plus total current assets equals Total Assets.

Liabilities

Liabilities refer to the financial obligations that the company owes to third parties. They can also be split into current and non-current, reflecting a time horizon of less than or greater than one year:

Short-term debt: debt payable within one year. There is another account in the current liabilities that is also debt, and that is "Current portion of long-term debt". This is the portion of the long-term debt that is known to be payable within one year because of the amortization schedules.

Accounts payable: represents the amounts owed to suppliers for products or services that the company has purchased. An important point to make here is that accounts payable is like an interest free short-term loan from a company's suppliers. The longer a company can delay in paying off the suppliers, the longer it holds on to "free money".

Accrued expenses: expenses that the company has incurred, but has not paid yet.

Other current liabilities: represent any accounts that the company has to pay off within one year, such as taxes or dividends.

Debts: these can include bank debt, bonds and subordinated debt, to name but a few.

Long-term liabilities: any other obligations that are non-current.

The above section equals Total Liabilities.

Shareholders' Equity

Shareholders' equity is the initial amount of money invested into a business. If at the end of the fiscal year, a company decides to reinvest its net earnings into the company (after taxes), these retained earnings will be transferred from the income statement onto the balance sheet into the shareholders' equity account. Therefore shareholders' equity is what the company would be worth if accounting rules were perfect. However the shareholders' equity as recorded in the balance sheet almost never corresponds to the market value of any company. In biotech, the situation is worse because almost all the assets and liabilities do not appear on the balance sheet. For example, the intellectual capital of scientists, especially "star" scientists, has been found to be an important determinant of the ultimate success of biotech firms. These scientists do not appear on the biotech's balance sheet nor does the output of their intellectual curiosity. This is a result of the immediate expensing of the intangible R&D asset each year.

Common stock: lists the amount of common stock issued at par. Common stock pays dividends if a dividend policy exists.

Additional paid-in capital (APIC): lists the differences between the proceeds of the common stock issued and the par value of the common stock.

Preferred stock: another kind of stock that has priority in dividends and has priority claims on assets if a company goes into liquidation. Preferred stock pays preferred dividends.

Treasury stock: stock that has been issued but has been later reacquired by the company. Treasury stock can be written off.

Retained earnings: is capital that increases through earnings. This is the connection point between the income statement and the balance sheet: the net income after dividends flows into this account.

Total Liabilities and Shareholders' Equity equals Total Assets.

The points to note from the balance sheet are that the valuation of assets is at historic cost and therefore the balance sheet value does not necessarily reflect what those assets are worth today (market values). Furthermore one should note that the equity (shareholders' funds) is listed with the liabilities. This highlights the distinction between the owners of the firm (shareholders) and the management. To the shareholders the firm is part of their assets but to the management of the firm these same shareholders are an obligation due to the equity they own.

Cash Flow Statement

Cash flow is the after tax cash from operations that is available to pay dividends to shareholders and interest to creditors in traditional firms. It records how much cash is coming in and how

Table 2.5 Sample cash flow statement

Cash flow statement	2006A	2007A	2008E	2009E
Net Income	(3.86)	(2.77)	1.66	5.53
Depreciation	0.11	0.17	0.23	0.29
Amortization	0.00	0.00	0.00	0.00
Share-based compensation	0.00	0.08	0.19	0.33
Operating cash flow	(3.75)	(2.51)	2.08	6.14
(Inc) in Accounts receivable	0.00	0.00	0.00	0.00
(inc) in Inventory	(0.79)	(0.66)	(0.81)	(0.90)
(Inc) in Other current assets	(0.05)	(0.26)	(0.33)	(0.36)
Inc in Accounts payable	0.00	0.00	0.00	0.00
Inc in other current liabilities	0.00	0.00	0.00	0.00
(Inc) in Operating working capital	(1.11)	(0.48)	(0.60)	(0.66)
Cash from operations	**(4.85)**	**(2.99)**	**1.48**	**5.48**
Capex PPE	(0.26)	(0.30)	(0.34)	(0.40)
Other (inc)/dec in net PPE	0.00	0.00	0.00	0.00
Intangibles Capex	0.00	0.00	0.00	0.00
Other (inc)/dec in intangibles	0.00	0.00	0.00	0.00
(inc)/dec in LTA	(0.32)	(0.26)	(0.33)	(0.36)
Cash from Investments	**(0.58)**	**(0.56)**	**(0.67)**	**(0.75)**
Inc (dec) in ST notes	0.00	0.00	0.00	0.00
Inc (dec) in NTF	(0.27)	0.44	0.54	0.60
Inc (dec) in debt 1	0.00	0.00	0.00	0.00
Dividends	0.00	0.00	0.00	0.00
Inc (dec) in LTL	0.00	0.00	0.00	0.00
Inc (dec) in common stock	0.00	0.00	0.00	0.00
Inc (dec) in other equity acc	0.00	0.00	0.00	0.00
Cash from financing	**0.82**	**1.96**	**(0.81)**	**(1.14)**
Change in cash & equivalents	**(4.62)**	**(1.60)**	**0.00**	**3.59**
Cash & equivalents	**1.59**	**(0.00)**	**(0.00)**	**3.58**

it is being used within an accounting period. Importantly the cash flow statement is the key to most valuation methods. The typical cash flow statement has three sections:

1. operations
2. investments
3. financing activities

The cash flow statement looks at the income statement for the year and the balance sheet at two points in time: the end of the current year and the end of the prior year (or beginning of the current year, if you prefer to think of it that way). One should understand that the cash flow statement is nothing more than a reconciliation of the flows in the income statement and the changes in the balance sheet. The elements of a cash flow statement are depicted above.

Cash flow from operations includes any flows from the income statement, and thus it is useful to start this section with operating income. However this figure also includes non-cash charges such as depreciation which are required to be added back. This section also includes any changes in the balance sheet that are related to operations. Thus in practice this usually means that most of the current assets and current liabilities (e.g. change in stocks, change in debtors and change in creditors) are included with the notable exceptions of cash and debt. These latter flows are included in the financing section.

The key component of the investments section is capital expenditure and also includes any changes in the balance sheet that are related to investments. Financing activities are an important part of the cash flow statement and reflect any changes in the balance sheet that are related to debt or equity financing. Dividends are also included as are changes in the cash balance. Their primary purpose is to allow ongoing operations to grow and for the company to invest in new opportunities that earn more than the cost of capital. This is the prime reason why one invests in companies i.e. investors hope companies can earn a significant return on their investment.

If new money needs to be raised it can be done through the issuance of new debt or equity. This is detailed in the financing section but note that only the principal amounts involved are included. Associated interest payments appear under the category returns on investment and servicing of finance.

Free cash flow equals operating cash flow less related capital expenditures. It is independent of financing and in the absence of debt, it is what would be available to the company and its shareholders for investment or distribution. Free cash flow is the most common basis for valuing businesses.

In the next two diagrams I highlight how the three accounting statements are interlinked.

Income Statement Multiples

In addition to having some historical financial data, the prospective investor should also determine a list of comparable companies. This list should be comprised of two sections, the first containing companies that operate in the same or similar therapeutic area on a global basis and another section with companies in the same geography with similar market capitalizations. This list will be used in compiling a comparable company valuation.

Much of the relative valuation metrics used for analysing traditional stocks makes use of the income statement. In relative valuation, the value of an asset is compared to the value assessed by the market for similar or comparable assets. To do relative valuation, one needs to identify comparable assets, the most difficult aspect of which is finding truly comparable companies. There are many factors that one can look at when determining comparability, including financial performance, growth stage, size and many others.

However in applying this technique the investor must take care on a number of issues. First, an investor should look at the multiples of companies in the same industry, of approximately the same size of sales and with similar performance histories. Second, the ratios need to be applied consistently and one needs to be especially careful to distinguish between trailing and forward looking multiples. Trailing results are best used to determine the value of a company today whereas forward looking results should be used to estimate the value of a company in the future. Nonetheless comparison companies and corresponding multiples are often difficult to find so the investor will have to incorporate a certain amount of "art" in the valuation.

Earnings per Share and Price/Earnings Ratios

The most common way to value a company is to compare its price to earnings power. To allow meaningful comparisons across companies, most people look at earnings per share (EPS), calculated by dividing the dollar or pound amount of the earnings reported by the number of shares outstanding.

Table 2.6 Link between income statement and balance sheet

BALANCE SHEET

Assets	End of Year	Start of Year
Cash	$ 7 997 607	$ 750 000
Accounts Receivable	1 000 000	825 000
Inventory	1 690 000	1 250 000
Prepaid Expenses	160 000	185 000
Total Current Assets	$ 10 847 607	$ 3 010 000
Property, Plant & Equipment	3 000 000	2 250 000
Accumulated Depreciation	(790 000)	(540 000)
Total Assets	$ 13 057 607	$ 4 720 000

Liabilities and Owners' Equity	End of Year	Start of Year
Accounts Payable – Inventory	$ 520 000	$ 450 000
Accounts Payable – Operating Expenses	120 000	85 000
Total Accounts Payable	$ 640 000	$ 535 000
Accrued Operating Expenses	$ 240 000	$ 185 000
Accrued Interest Payable	17 167	12 500
Total Accrued Expenses	$ 257 167	$ 197 500
Income Tax Payable	23 940	36 000
Short-Term Notes Payable	625 000	600 000
Total Current Liabilities	$ 1 546 107	$ 1 368 500
Long-Term Notes Payable	750 000	600 000
Capital Stock (200 000 shares)	775 000	725 000
Retained Earnings	9 976 500	2 026 500
Total Owners' Equity	$ 10 751 500	$ 2 751 500
Total Liabilities and Owners' Equity	$ 13 047 607	$ 4 720 000

INCOME STATEMENT FOR YEAR

Sales Revenue	$ 20 000 000
Cost of Goods Sold Expense	5 000 000
Gross Margin	$ 15 000 000
Operating Expenses	6 000 000
Depreciation Expense	250 000
Operating Earnings	$ 8 750 000
Interest Expense	100 000
Earnings Before Tax	$ 8 650 000
Income Tax Expense	500 000
Net Income	$ 8 150 000
Earnings Per Share	$ 40.75

Table 2.7 Link between cash flow statement and balance sheet

BALANCE SHEET

Assets	End of Year	Start of Year
Cash	$7 997 607	$750 000
Accounts Receivable	1 000 000	825 000
Inventory	1 690 000	1 250 000
Prepaid Expenses	160 000	185 000
Total Current Assets	$10 847 607	$3 010 000
Property, Plant & Equipment	3 000 000	2 250 000
Accumulated Depreciation	(790 000)	(540 000)
Total Assets	$13 057 607	$4 720 000

Liabilities and Owners' Equity	End of Year	Start of Year
Accounts Payable – Inventory	$520 000	$450 000
Accounts Payable – Operating Expenses	120 000	85 000
Total Accounts Payable	$640 000	$535 000
Accrued Operating Expenses	$240 000	$185 000
Accrued Interest Payable	17 167	12 500
Total Accrued Expenses	$257 167	$197 500
Income Tax Payable	23 940	36 000
Short-Term Notes Payable	625 000	600 000
Total Current Liabilities	$1 546 107	$1 368 500
Long-Term Notes Payable	750 000	600 000
Capital Stock (200 000 shares)	775 000	725 000
Retained Earnings	9 976 500	2 026 500
Total Owners' Equity	$10 751 500	$2 751 500
Total Liabilities and Owners' Equity	$13 047 607	$4 720 000

CASH FLOW STATEMENT FOR YEAR

Cash Flows from Operating Activities

Net Income		$8 150 000
Accounts Receivable Increase	$ (175 000)	
Inventory Increase	(440 000)	
Prepaid Expenses Decrease	25 000	
Depreciation Expense	250 000	
Accounts Payable Increase	105 000	
Accrued Expenses Increase	59 667	
Income Tax Payable Decrease	(12 060)	
		$ (177 393)
Cash Flow from Operating Activities		$7 972 607

Cash Flows from Investing Activities

Purchases of Property, Plant & Equipment	$ (750 000)

Cash Flows from Financing Activities

Short-Term Debt Borrowing	$25 000	
Long-Term Debt Borrowing	150 000	
Capital Stock Issue	50 000	
Dividends paid Stockholders	(200 000)	$25 000

Increase (Decrease) in Cash during Year	$7 247 607

The price/earnings ratio is a simple comparison of a company's current share price and its EPS. Analysts and investors compare a company's P/E ratio with other similar companies, the overall stock market or relative to the company's historical P/E range. Companies with high P/Es typically have a high growth rate or are highly regarded. In general, the P/E ratio is not useful for biotechnology companies given that most firms have net losses (negative earnings) making the ratio meaningless.

The use of P/E stems from its ease of use, calculation and communication, thereby allowing comparison of stocks to be conducted effortlessly. Yet the use of such ratios can, in isolation, allow investors to ascribe a value to a stock without being explicit about their assumptions. The P/E ratio is very subjective and is susceptible to differences in accounting policies. The ratio also ignores different levels of business risk and growth as well as capital structure. Firms with higher gearing (increased debt on the balance sheet relative to comparators) will increase the risk for equity shareholders. P/E ratios are also much more likely to reflect market moods but this can be problematic when sectors are out of favour. One can try and factor out these potential issues but the hassle involved suggests that a cash-based valuation may be better to start with.

Price/Earnings to Growth Ratios

One can also compare P/E ratios to the expected growth rate to identify under- and overvalued stocks. Firms with P/E ratios less than their expected growth rate are viewed as undervalued. However there is no basis for believing that a firm is undervalued just because it has a P/E ratio less than its expected growth.

In a more general form, the ratio of P/E growth is used as a measure of relative value. Using the assumption that a stock's P/E ratio should be equal to its projected long-term earnings growth rate, a stock trading a P/E of 17 with expected earnings growth of 17 % annually would appear to be fairly valued. Such a stock would have a PEG of 1. A P/E lower than the projected growth suggests an undervalued stock and such a stock would have a PEG less than 1.

If company A has a current P/E of 16 and the long-term growth rate is 8 %, then the PEG is 2. If company B has a P/E of 16 and a long-term growth rate of 12 %, then the PEG is 1.34. This relative comparison of the PEG ratios would suggest that company B is undervalued.

All of the shortcomings of the P/E ratio are relevant for the PEG ratio. In addition the estimate of future earnings growth can either be estimated by oneself or obtained from an analyst's report but then the investor has to question whether the projections used are in line with the markets. Again a certain level of "art" is required to make the appropriate assumptions.

Other Income Statement Multiples

The following income statement items can be substituted for earnings:

- sales
- profit before tax (PBT)
- profit after tax (PAT)
- earnings before interest and taxes (EBIT)
- earnings before interest, taxes, depreciation and amortization (EBITDA).

These multiples use either the current share price or enterprise value, which encompasses the value of its stock market equity value plus the company's debt minus its cash.

In most circumstances it is best to use EBIT or EBITDA since these two measures most closely approximate the true cash generating potential of the business. Price/sales is not a measure of profitability and thus has the advantage of being susceptible to accounting distortions. Yet it does reflect the economic realities of the business by ignoring gearing, risk and growth prospects. PAT and PBT are affected by the company's financial structure since they are a calculation of earnings after debt interest expenses. Profit after tax creates additional complications since tax rates often vary among companies, even within the same industry.

EBIT and EBITDA are measures of profitability that are not affected by existing financial structure or taxes. EBIT is a pre-tax, pre-interest figure and thus overcomes many of the accounting issues with the previous financial statement ratios. EBITDA is a preferable measure to EBIT as it additionally excludes the effects of depreciation and amortization. Accounting practices for depreciation often do not reflect the real utility of the items being depreciated and therefore distort the cash flow being returned to the equity holders.

However in shifting the emphasis away from earnings per share (the earnings available to shareholders) to EBIT or EBITDA (these are a measurement of earnings available to both equity and debt holders in the company), the investor needs to look at the value of equity and debt combined. This is termed the enterprise value (EV) and can be calculated as the market value of equity plus total debt less cash. Enterprise value is sometimes referred to as firm value. Equity value represents the value of the enterprise to equity shareholders; it is calculated after deducting the values of debt, preferred stock and minority interests from firm value.

The most important lesson from this section is that there is no correct valuation multiple. All multiples, including EV/EBITDA and P/E have their uses in the process of valuation. P/E ratios are comprehensive in that they take account of differences in capital intensity and taxation but often are not really comparable because of accounting and capital structure differences. Although EV/EBITDA multiples are less comprehensive they do resolve many of the accounting and capital structure comparability problems.

Balance Sheet Multiples

Balance sheet valuations attempt to calculate the worth of the underlying assets of a business as recorded in the accounting statements.

Book Value

Book value is calculated as the assets minus the liabilities on the company's balance sheet. Book value is after debt and preferred financing is taken into account and therefore multiples of book value should be based on the value of the equity only. For various reasons the book value of a company's assets rarely equals the true market value of the corresponding assets. Book value is an overall measure of how much liquidation value a company has if all of its assets were to be sold off. Price/book value highlights the relationship between the market value of a share and the book value of a company's assets. A low price/book ratio may indicate that the company is undervalued or is not earning sufficient return on its assets to satisfy its shareholders.

Adjusted book value is an attempt to reconcile the accounting values with the market values by assuming that the company will continue operating as an ongoing concern and approximating the replacement value of each asset and liability. Liquidation is an estimate of the worth of the assets and the liabilities, assuming that the company will cease its operations and the assets will be auctioned off immediately. The usefulness of a liquidation value is limited since most buyers intend to continue operating a business as a going concern. However a liquidation value can set a floor below which a seller will be unlikely to accept.

Cash per Share

A company's cash and cash equivalents per share is a quick measure that indicates how much of the current share price that current company has on hand. As mentioned in the introduction, investors should assess how much cash a company has and how long that cash will continue to keep a company going.

Summary

The valuation technique most frequently used is income statement multiples since it is the easiest to use and to communicate. Multiples are simple approximations of discounted cash flows. They are forward looking in stable environments where future cash flows are expected to be similar to current ones. However the use of such multiples gives rise to certain disadvantages which the investor should be aware of. In a future where the economic and industry conditions are not expected to mirror their historical counterparts, the use of income statement techniques is questionable. In addition, this technique only accounts for the risk of an opportunity to the extent that the comparable company has similar characteristics to the target company.

Discounted Cash Flow Analysis

The concept of discounted cash flow (DCF) and the time value of money is a crucial component of the valuation of stocks. However the fact that these future returns are uncertain mandates that the investor uses a significant amount of judgement. Thus the use of the DCF shifts us away from an accounting model of valuation towards an economic model of valuation. The main drawback of accounting approaches to valuation is that they do not consider the investment required to generate earnings or its timing. The DCF model allows for the difference in value by factoring in the capital expenditures and other cash flows required to generate earnings. However the accounting approach has little to offer investors looking at biotechnology companies. When earnings reflect cash flow the accounting approach provides a reasonably good proxy for DCF. It is when earnings and cash flow diverge that the accounting approach comes up short. It should be remembered that the true objective of an investor is to buy a stream of cash flows for less than what they are worth.

Net Present Value

The first step in understanding net present value (NPV) is appreciating the time value of money. The premise is that a pound received tomorrow is worth less than a pound in your wallet today. The reason is that an investor can invest her pound today and receive more than a pound tomorrow. This is a familiar situation to those who have savings accounts. Thus a person investing £100 today in a bank account could receive 5 % interest. It is important to note that this interest is compounded annually. The future value (FV) of this sum invested can be calculated using the formula

$$FV = PV \times (1 + M)^n$$

where PV is the sum invested (£100), M is the interest rate (5 %) and n is the number of years that the money is invested. If for example, one put £100 into an account paying 5 % interest for five years, the amount of money in the account at the end of that period would equal £127 if the interest were allowed to accumulate.

The issue with trying to ascribe value to an investment is that the present value of the investment is unknown. However investors can use a similar approach to discount back an estimated future value to determine how much it is worth today. The difference is that M becomes the hurdle rate that investors want this particular investment to achieve rather than being the interest rate on offer. The formula is

$$PV = \sum P_n / (1 + M)^n$$

where P_n represents cash inflows in year n.

The NPV is the present value of a stream of future cash flows (Pn) less the initial investment (Io).

$$NPV = -I_0 + \sum P_n / (1 + M)^n$$

I_0 initial investment made today
P_n stream of cash flows received over n years
$(1 + M)^n$ discount factor for any given year n

There are four points to keep in mind:

1. The NPV is meaningless unless one knows the discount rate.
2. If a project or investment has a positive NPV at the given cost of capital (discount rate) then it will be acceptable.
3. A negative NPV means that the project is not earning the cost of capital required.
4. The internal rate of return (IRR) is the rate of return of the investment and is equal to the discount rate that produces $NPV = 0$.

Net present value or intrinsic value can be defined as the discounted value of the cash flows that can be taken out of a business during its remaining life. As such NPV is an estimate and differs according to the assumptions and thus the calculated NPV can differ depending upon who is doing the calculation.

Constructing the DCF

In order to understand the process of valuing biotechnology stocks it is essential to start with how one values what could be referred to as traditional stocks. What one is trying to do is to buy stocks that one believes will go up in value. The value of a firm is based upon its capacity to generate cash flows and the uncertainty associated with these cash flows. Generally speaking, more profitable firms have been valued more highly than less profitable ones.

Most analysts rely on the fundamental building blocks of stock value – the dividends and earnings of firms – to make stock valuation decisions. Stocks have value because of the potential cash flows (dividends) which a stockholder expects to receive from ownership of the firm. Stocks also have value if, in the future, other stockholders may decide that the valuation of these future dividends is not fully reflected in the future share price. It is by forecasting and valuing potential future dividends and earnings and deciding whether someone will, in the future, value these differently, that enables one to judge the investment value of shares.

Most DCF analyses use one of two approaches, the free cash flow to the firm method (FCFF) and the free cash flows to equity (FCFE) method. The FCFF DCF model values all of the cash flows generated by the firm, regardless of whether the cash flow is used to pay interest to debt holders or dividends to equity holders. The value of operations is calculated by estimating cash flows and discounting them at a rate that reflects the riskiness of these cash flows. After determining the total value of all of the cash flows (also termed enterprise value) the value of debt currently outstanding can be deducted to arrive at the equity value.

The free cash flows to equity method of valuation relies on much the same logic as the FCFF method with some modifications to take into account a changing capital structure. I will return to this method later in the chapter.

The FCFF valuation approach has a very established position in the financial world. As long as the discount rates are selected properly to reflect the riskiness of each cash flow stream, the entity approach will result in exactly the same equity value as if one directly discounted the cash flow to the shareholders. Furthermore two main variables, cash flows and the discount rate, have to be estimated.

The theory behind discounted cash flow is that the value of the business is equal to the future expected cash flows discounted at a rate that reflects the riskiness of the cash flow stream. Four steps are required:

1. Project the cash flow stream
2. Chose a discount rate
3. Determine a terminal value at the end of the projections
4. Apply the discount rate to the projected cash flow stream and the terminal value.

The investor should remember that the model used to calculate the DCF requires inputs and estimations of the company's growth patterns and that these should be consistent with the company's positioning within the marketplace.

Projecting the Cash Flow Stream

The valuation of a company is based on two prime components:

1. the explicit forecasting period
2. the terminal value.

The free cash flow of a company is the cash not required for operations (working capital) or reinvestment (capital expenditure). The valuation horizon that is chosen typically reflects the time period over which the company's growth rate is expected to stabilize, usually within 5–10 years. A common mistake in constructing DCF models is that the analyst or investor feels uncomfortable about forecasting more than 1–2 years into the future. Yet an explicit forecast period of 5–10 years is appropriate for most companies. Indeed by curtailing the explicit forecast period, with its implicit transparency, means that the value within that period is shunted from the transparent portion of the model into a more opaque element, the terminal value. It should be clear that the longer the estimation period, the greater portion of the value that can be explained by forecast cash flows. However the longer the explicit period, the more difficult it is to make accurate assumptions about the future. Realistic assumptions should be made regarding sales growth and margin improvements.

This task always includes some uncertainty and subjective assumptions. Problems arise when firms may be lacking cash flows, profits or turnover which is a frequent occurrence when trying to value the majority of biotech companies. Even if the companies produce cash flows, they do not necessarily follow the same patterns as in some other industries but are determined by industry specific factors (e.g. patenting). A normal assumption made about the discount rate is that the risk does not change during the life of the project, a fact which is not plausible in a very dynamic environment that features long-term projects. It is also worth noting that the DCF methodology does not call for accurate forecasts, but rather for the accurate assessment of the mean of possible outcomes.

Free cash flow to the firm is calculated as follows:

$$\text{FCFF} = \text{EBIT}\,(1\text{-tax rate}) + \text{depreciation \& amortization} - \text{increase in net}$$
$$\text{working capital} - \text{capital expenditures} + \text{other non-cash items}$$

Free cash flow to the firm is defined as the cash flow prior to making any payments to investors in the firm, being primarily equity, preferred stock and debt investors. The first step in calculating free cash flow is to take the "operating income" or EBIT from the income statement. Then adjust this number for any tax that needs to be paid. Once the after tax EBIT is calculated the number undergoes a series of adjustments to reconcile the accounting figures to a cash-based value (operating cash flow). This figure reflects the cash actually generated by the company much better than EBIT which is an accounting term.

Depreciation is added back (as it is a non-cash expense that is subtracted a part of the calculation of EBIT in the income statement) to get gross cash flow. Gross cash flow includes cash tied up in investments. Thus capital expenditure is deducted (these cash outflows are not part of operating expenses in the income statement and can be found in the cash flow statement) as are the changes in net working capital. Net working capital is calculated as current assets less current liabilities and can either be a positive or negative number. An increase in net working capital means that more capital is tied up in the business than the previous year and is denoted as a cash outflow. The gross cash flow figure is also adjusted for any increase in non-interest bearing liabilities (added back as it has an opposite effect to net working capital) in order to get free operating cash flow.

An important point to note is that although, as a potential investor, one is trying to value the equity in a company, firm or enterprise value has an important part to play in the valuation process. The reason for this is that it ignores the level of gearing (leverage) and other financial factors when calculating the value of a company. The equity value can subsequently be calculated by adjusting for the value of other sources of finance (cash on hand and debt). The value of the equity free cash flow to the firm is divided by the number of shares outstanding to get the fair value of the company's share.

Choosing a Discount Rate

An investor who is considering the purchase of a common stock must assess its risk and, given its risk, the minimum expected rate of return that will be required to induce the investor to make the purchase. This minimum expected return, or required rate of return, is the opportunity cost.

Firms usually target a ratio of debt to equity in their total capital structure and will from time to time adjust the capital structure as costs of financial instruments change in the market place. It is more appropriate not to use these short-term decisions to calculate a cost of capital but rather to use a weighted average cost of capital (WACC) where the weights relate to a broad mix of debt and equity. The choice of a capital structure is critical in the FCFF model. The model assumes that the capital structure is constant over the entire life of the investment. Thus it is important to choose a capital structure that reflects the most likely long-term structure. This is termed the target capital structure and may differ significantly from the company's actual capital structure at the time of the valuation. The target structure can be estimated by looking at comparable companies.

Market values should be used for both debt and equity. For debt this is usually a minor distinction but valuing equity at book rather than market can make a hugely significant difference. Generally speaking only long-term debt is used in the calculation of WACC and one should note that short-term debt from lines of credit may be regarded as working capital.

To derive a discount rate, an investor may use WACC which accounts for industry risk, company specific risk and the financial risk of the target company.

$$WACC = K_E (E/(E+D)) + K_D (D/(E+D))(1-t)$$

E = amount of equity in the company
D = target amount of debt in the company
K_E = cost of equity
K_D = cost of debt
t = corporate tax rate (because debt is tax deductible)

The WACC is an overall combined cost of capital for the company reflecting all sources of finance. This number is the discount rate that we seek to use in discount cash flow analysis. If we have underestimated the discount rate (i.e. too low) this will have the effect of making projects more attractive than they really are. Too high a discount rate will have the opposite effect, penalizing projects with too high a hurdle rate. It is important to remember that getting the correct free cash flow estimates will usually have a much larger impact on the final value than obtaining the correct discount rate. There have been a number of reports from academia that suggest the appropriate discount rate is the opportunity cost of capital and various estimates suggest a range between 9 % and 15 %.[4,5]

Calculating the Cost of Debt

The cost of debt is the rate of return that the firm must offer creditors to induce them to provide funds. For a traditional firm, the cost of debt is a blend of many rates negotiated by the firm. Only long-term debt is used in the calculation of WACC and because of that the short-term debt that is available to companies can be viewed as working capital.

Within long-term debt, different interest rates apply, depending upon whether the debt is secured or unsecured. Debt that is secured by physical assets such as land or buildings will be less expensive. Unsecured debt will become increasingly costly as a function of the seniority and creditworthiness of the firm. The terms senior and junior debt refer to which holders of debt get paid first. Thus junior debt gets paid after the firm has met the obligations of the senior debt holders. As a consequence junior debt becomes increasingly more expensive as the company becomes more highly leveraged.

Although the WACC formula uses a constant debt to equity ratio, the free cash flow to the firm approach is flexible enough to allow for debt ratios that change over time. It is important in this situation to use a cost of debt that is likely to reflect the long-term capital structure. One of the biggest strengths of the model is the ease with which changes in the financing mix can be built into the valuation through the discount rate rather than the cash flows.

So if the cost of debt is cheaper than the cost of equity, why do we not see many debt laden biotech companies? As the leverage increases, debt holders demand higher and higher rates as the percentage of debt increases. Thus a company will be reluctant to issue more debt at the point where the marginal cost of debt financing approaches the cost of new equity.

Cost of Equity

Estimating the cost of equity is more challenging than estimating the cost of debt. The cost of equity is higher than the cost of debt because the equity's claim on the firm is junior. As the providers of debt financing get prior claims to fixed cash flows, equity investors get residual claims to the remaining cash flows. Thus there is no simple method to estimate the cost of equity. To determine the cost of equity, investors can use various models, one of the most widely used being the capital asset pricing model (CAPM) shown below. The CAPM states that a company's cost of equity equals the risk-free rate plus the product of the equity risk premium and beta. However a simple way to view this is that the cost of equity to the firm is the same as the returns of investors in the firm.

$$K_E = R_F + B_L {}^* (R_M - R_F)$$

where

    R_F = risk-free rate
    R_M = market risk premium
    B_L = levered beta of the comparable company.

A point to keep in mind is that although the above formulas suggest a certain level of plug and play, an amount of art or judgement is required. For example, how does one pick the risk-free rate and the excess return on the market? Government issued notes generally provide a good proxy for the risk-free rate but estimates for the equity risk premium and beta prove more challenging.

Conceptually the return on equity is a function of the risk-free rate or return (i.e. the base rate that the investor would choose to lend to a risk-free entity, usually assumed to be a stable government (UK/US) and a premium (also termed excess return) for business and financial risk, appropriate to the level of risk involved. The interest rate on government treasury bonds can be used for the risk-free rate, trying to keep the same time horizon as the investment; for example for long-term projects use the long-term treasury rates. The market risk premium (R_M-R_F) varies over time but historically has been four to six percentage points. Arguments have been made that the risk premium has been contracting over the past 20 years as the perceived risk of investing in equities has diminished. However at the time of writing (early 2008), the perceived risk of equities is definitely increasing.

The total risk in a stock can be measured in statistical terms by noting how widely its value fluctuates about a mean, i.e. the variability of its returns about its expected return can be measured by its standard deviation. Both the mean and standard deviation can be calculated for any stock from historical share price data. The total risk can be split into two components:

1. market or systematic risk
2. specific or unsystematic risk.

Market risk measures the variability in the investment returns which are caused by general market fluctuations and cannot be diversified away by an investor. Specific risk is the remaining risk which reflects factors specific to the investment or the industry in which the company operates. It is this element of an investor's risk that can be diversified away within a well diversified portfolio.

Thus the relevance of the above to the well diversified investor is that specific risk is irrelevant and that the required returns depend upon market risk. The systematic risk in the market is not the same for each stock in the market. Utility companies which pay regular dividends and whose earnings may be regulated are far less vulnerable to market decline than biotechnology stocks. The relationship between the stock price movements and that of the market as a whole can also be calculated statistically from historical price data.

The term that defines the relationship between an individual stock's moves and the markets is called beta. Beta attempts to reflect the sensitivity of a stock's price movement, relative to the broader market. In statistical terms beta is proportional to the covariance of the stock's return to the market return. By definition, the beta of the market as a whole is set at 1. Thus if a stock has a beta of 1, we know that its share price movements have been about the same as the movements for the market as a whole. A beta below 1 suggests a stock moves less than the market, while a beta above implies moves greater than the market but ought to be associated with greater risk. In essence, financial theory suggests that a higher beta is associated with higher risk and reward. Intuitively, this makes sense. Think of an early-stage biotechnology stock with a price that bounces up and down more than the market. It's hard not to think that this stock will be riskier than, say, a mature utility industry stock with a low beta. Nonetheless it is worth remembering that past price movements are very poor predictors of the future.

Betas are calculated essentially by measuring the correlation of stock movements with respect to a benchmark index over a meaningful time frame. There are also variations on beta depending on the market index used and the time period measured. Please note that the calculated beta for individual stocks differs depending upon the particular financial data provider (Bloomberg and Ibbotson are examples of beta providers) used to access the beta and the methodology used for calculation. Yet as with many of the financial theories covered so far, the investor has to use judgement. For example, although we ideally want a forward looking beta, the services provide a historic figure. Thus a level of assessment of the figures is required rather than blithe acceptance.

Using the formula above the cost of equity for a firm with a beta of 1.2 can be calculated as follows:

$$K_E = R_F + B_L{}^* (R_M - R_F)$$

where

$R_F = 5\%$ obtained from UK gilts
$B_L = 1.2$ chosen for this example but obtained from Bloomberg
$R_M = 6\%$

$$K_E = 5 + 1.2^* (7-5)$$
$$K_E = 5 + 2.4$$
$$K_E = 7.4\%$$

The beta is a function of both the business risk and the degree of leverage. If the beta of the target company in question is derived from a comparable company and the comparator has a different financial structure (different levels of debt), the use of beta will yield a bias. It is for this reason that the beta should be adjusted to reflect the projected amount of debt the target company will utilize.

The beta for a comparable company can be unlevered using the following equation:

$$B_{U/L} = B_L/(1 + D/E^*(1-t))$$

where

$B_{U/L}$ = unlevered beta of the comparable company
B_L = levered beta of the comparable company
E = amount of equity in the comparable company
D = amount of debt in the comparable company
T = corporate tax rate

The unlevered beta can then be relevered using the parameters of the target company as in the formula below:

$$B_L = Bu/_L/(1 + D/E^*(1-t))$$

The second important input into the CAPM is the equity risk premium, the return above and beyond the risk-free rate an investor expects to earn, as compensation for assuming greater risk. Again investors ideally want a forward looking estimate but in practice historical risk premiums are used which differ depending upon the time frame. For example the geometric average equity risk premium was 1.9 percentage points from 1982–2005, 3.7 percentage points from 1962–2005 and 6.2 percentage points from 1926–2005. In my view, an equity risk premium in the 4–6 percentage point range seems reasonable.

There are other approaches to calculating the risk premium but I do not have the scope to cover them here. However none of the theories takes into account factors that are unique to a company – new risks and opportunities. The CAPM and other theories tend to assume that the marketplace averages out these unique or unsystematic risks. This assumption is made because an individual investor can eliminate almost all unique risks by diversification of her portfolio.

Terminal value

Terminal value is critical to the task of assigning a value to a technology or a business using the DCF method. Most of the net present value of projects, especially those with high revenue growth rates (including many biotechnology companies) is found in the terminal value. The most important take away is that the market value of a security is the present value of the future expected cash receipts discounted at the investor's required rate of return.

Terminal values are calculated in a distant year (10+ years into the future) where it no longer makes sense to project independent estimates for the individual factors (markets, margins, depreciation) that create value. In my view detailed estimates cannot be made by outside investors 10+ years into the future and instead, a mathematical extrapolation is a better way of capturing longer term value creation.

Terminal values must be discounted back to the present, and although they can be significant, they will be much smaller in today's dollars owing to discounting over many years.

Zero Terminal Value

The most conservative method of dealing with terminal values is to assign them zero value. This approach assumes that the assets will no longer be productive at the end of a stipulated time, operations will cease and the project will be liquidated.

Multiple Derived Terminal Value

Terminal values can also be derived using a multiple of EBIT, EBITDA or P/E. The appropriate multiple or ratio can be based on actual merger and acquisition (M&A) transactions involving similar businesses or using derived multiples from comparable public companies. Anticipated growth rates in the horizon year are likely to be an important factor: other factors being equal, PE ratios are higher for more rapidly growing businesses. Typically single digit PE ratios are applied to companies that experience low or negative growth; large multiples (30+) can occur in aggressive growth situations; whereas a large band of companies with moderate growth cluster at multiples in the 12 to 25 range. Remember that if a multiple of earnings is used (P/E), then one needs to calculate the earnings in the final year, not cash flows. In my view this approach may be useful if the investor is trying to assess a sale transaction and is using multiples of recent deals. Otherwise the multiple implies little about financial performance.

Terminal Value as Perpetuity

The cash flow in the final year can also be treated as a perpetuity and therefore divided by the chosen discount rate. A perpetuity is a security that pays out a fixed sum forever. The value of a perpetuity is determined as follows:

$$\text{Value} = \text{annual payment}/\text{cost of money}$$

Some of you may be bothered by the improbability that any business can survive in perpetuity. However owing to the time value of money, most of the net present value would be earned in the earlier years so that the extension of time to infinity is not nearly as extreme an assumption as it may seem. For example approximately 90 % of the value of the perpetuity is paid back in the first twenty annual payments if a 12 % discount rate is used.

Growth in Perpetuity Terminal Value

Perpetuities are useful as a conceptual financial instrument but in a competitive business, companies will either grow or perish. If the business manages to carry on, it will grow and the key question investors must ask themselves is "at what rate?"

The growth in perpetuity terminal value is based on direct valuation of extrapolated future cash flows in the terminal year. This method estimates future growth but also targets the issue of whether that growth is valuable to the investor. Hence it is a more reliable guide to valuation that PE ratios or multiples (EBIT or EBITDA).

This method requires the investor to input three assumptions:

1. the annual cash flow estimated in the terminal year (CF_0)
2. the discount rate (r)
3. the rate of growth into perpetuity (g)

$$TV = (CF_0 \times (1+g))/(r-g)$$

Please note that this method should only be used when the growth rate is several per cent less than the discount rate. Unless this condition is met, unrealistically large values will be generated.

The mathematics are predicated on the assumption that in any given year the cash flow will be larger than the cash flow in the previous year. This difference between one year and the next is expressed as a percentage and is the rate of growth.

If we call next year (P_1) and assume growth (g) of 5 %,

$$P_1 = P_0(1+g), \text{ which equals } P_1 = P_0(1+0.05)$$

However the value of Y_1 (one year from now) must be discounted back to the present. In these examples we are using a discount rate of 15 %:

$$PV_1 = P_1/(1+i)$$

where i equals the discount rate (15 %).

In the next year, both factors are applied again:

$$P_2 = P_1(1+g)/(1+i) = P_0(1+g)^2/(1+i)^2$$

Note that in selecting a growth rate to perpetuity, one should choose a growth rate that is modestly higher than the underlying growth rate for the economy with an adjustment for inflation. The investor should also check that depreciation, networking capital and other cash flows are consistent with the growth rate he has chosen.

To obtain the NPV of the firm, the forecast cash flows and the terminal value are discounted back to the present using the WACC. Discounting these amounts will provide the enterprise value of the company. In order to determine the value of the equity of the company, it is necessary to subtract from the enterprise value the market value of the debt in the company's current capital structure.

Free Cash Flows to Equity

The key limitation of the FCFF model is its assumption that the debt level of the company being valued is constant throughout the life of the company. Four steps are required

1. Project the cash flow stream to the equity holders
2. Calculate the equity cost of capital for these cash flows
3. Determine a terminal value for the equity at the end of the projections
4. Apply the equity cost of capital to the projected cash flow stream and the terminal value and discount back to the present.

Free cash flow to equity is calculated as follows

FCFE = ((EBIT − interest)(1-tax rate)) − debt repayments + debt additions +
depreciation & amortization − increase in net working capital −
capital expenditures

Thus in contrast to the FCFF approach additional adjustments for interest and debt principal additions or repayments must be included. The anticipated debt level must be estimated each year and in this manner the effect of capital structure is incorporated by including it within the forecast cash flows.

In order to discount these cash flows, the cost of equity is used instead of WACC. However each year a new cost of equity must be calculated for each forecast year by levering the beta by the appropriate amount each period. The terminal value is calculated as before. Note that there is an implicit assumption that the cost of equity (and thus the capital structure) will be constant. As a result it is appropriate to calculate a terminal value only for the period following the significant changes in debt levels.

Other Thoughts

Once the basics are grasped, investors can begin to experiment with their assumptions and use scenario analyses to fine tune their inputs. Discounting valuations is common when dealing with issues of illiquidity or control, for example when evaluating private companies. I will discuss this in Chapter 7. Non-public companies where investor liquidity is not guaranteed generally trade at a discount (20–35 %) to their public counterparts. Minority shareholders in a company that is majority owned by another party often get a 10–20 % discount; conversely investors sometimes pay a premium for control.

Once the valuation is complete, the investor should do a sensitivity analysis check, even going so far as redoing the valuation with other discount rates. For potential investments in public companies, it is important that investors compare their valuation estimate to the market value. If there is a significant difference, investors should try and understand why this is the case. Remember the importance of correctly estimating the free cash flows. The model deriving the valuation should be adjusted until the estimate approaches the market value. Then the investor can check whether the assumptions he has used seem sensible compared to the assumptions that the market seems to be using. The key point that I am trying to make here is not that the goal of modelling is to match the market price but that each investor should try and understand where the market is potentially wrong while also checking his own model for gross errors.

Valuation is a critical skill of any successful investor. Hopefully as one may have garnered in this chapter there is a significant degree of art in deriving a valuation and it is certainly not just a matter of plugging numbers into a spreadsheet. This chapter should have provided the basics of putting valuations together. In the next chapter I go through the drug development process in order to provide the technical and regulatory backdrop to the biotechnology industry. In Chapter 4, I endeavour to put the valuation framework into the context of this regulatory framework and begin to start valuing biotechnology companies.

3
The Drug Development Process

In this chapter I will explain the basic process of R&D in the pharmaceutical and biotechnology industry. While it is virtually impossible for any one individual to have a working understanding of all the cutting edge science that biotech companies are involved with, the processes that all companies have to go through to get a drug approved are remarkably consistent. Furthermore there are peer reviewed papers which outline the statistics of drug development including probabilities that any one drug will fail at a particular stage of its development. In fact there are many excellent web sites which provide overviews of many diseases and clinical trials information.

For the investor who wishes to attempt to value a biotechnology company, the first step is to understand what the technical hurdles are in terms of drug development. The basic building blocks of drug discovery and development will be summarized along with a discussion of the probabilities associated with each phase. This knowledge should provide the investor with a roadmap as to the company's strategy and also provide a "balance sheet" view of how near to commercialization the drug assets are and the cash expenditure required reaching the next decision point.

Thus while I am not advocating a crash course in a pharmacology PhD, the informed investor who understands the basic regulatory processes (i.e. the technical and clinical hurdles that a potential drug must overcome) has significant advantages over one who just fancies a quick punt on a biotech stock. I also believe that there is an element of "avoidance" in biotech investing. For every biotech company that becomes a biotech bellwether and makes many people lots of money, there are many, many more that fail.

Therefore an important next step before we begin to put the valuation together is to get a sense of how well these trials are designed and how well management can answer your questions. This chapter aims to provide an overview of what constitutes a good clinical trial

Table 3.1 Some web resources for disease and clinical trials information

Link	Description
cochrane.org	Up to date information about the effects of healthcare
clinicaltrials.gov	Information regarding current clinical research
jameslindlibrary.org	Evolution of fair tests of medical treatments
gpp-guidelines.org	Encourages responsible publication of clinical trials
ncbi.nlm.nih.gov/entrez/mcclurenet.	PubMed: includes over 14 million citations for biomedical
com/ICHefficacy.html	articles
	Efficacy guidelines
controlled-trials.org	Access to peer reviewed biomedical research
fda.gov	Access to information on regulations, upcoming advisory meetings and events
nih.gov	Access to information on diseases, research and ongoing trials
biomednet.com	Access to MEDLINE data base of scientific articles

and some of the questions that should be asked of the company. I believe that investment research (and valuation) is a process and by adopting a rigorous approach to valuation, many of the simple (and common) errors can be avoided.

I hope therefore to be able to give the investor a framework that provides an overview of the process, highlights how far this stage is from potential commercialization (i.e. when the drug begins to generate revenues) and discuss the risks associated with each developmental phase. This latter point is probably the most important!

THE DRUG DEVELOPMENT PROCESS

R&D encompasses the processes by which drugs are discovered, tested and brought to market, and has traditionally been seen as the core competency of pharmaceutical companies. Indeed one could say that R&D represents the life blood of the pharmaceutical and biotech industries. It is only through innovation and the successful commercialization of new therapeutics that the industry can continue to grow. The amount of money invested into R&D has grown considerably over the past decade.

According to the Tufts Center for the Study of Drug Development,[1] it takes an average of 15 years for a new drug to move from the discovery phase, into animal testing through clinical trials, past the regulatory authorities and into the marketplace. Recent statistics released[2] show that R&D investments in new medicines by the Pharmaceutical Research and Manufacturers of America (PhRMA) biotechnology and pharmaceutical research member companies reached a record estimated $ 43.0 billion in 2006 (up from $ 39.9 billion in 2005), according to PhRMA's Annual Member Survey. The increased investment in biomedical R&D in 2007 continues 25 years of strong growth in R&D investments by America's research-based pharmaceutical companies – up from $ 2 billion in 1980. When factored together, the total investments in biotechnology and pharmaceutical R&D by both PhRMA member companies and non-PhRMA members reached a record estimated $ 55.2 billion in 2006, according to a Burrill & Company analysis for PhRMA.[3] If the historic growth rates are maintained, biopharmaceutical research could exceed $ 70 billion globally by 2010.

The discovery and development of a novel therapeutic agent requires a huge investment of time and money and the process is very risky. Industry estimates suggest that of the 5000–10 000 molecules screened in the discovery process, only one will make it to the market as an approved drug. In an interesting paper, Dimasi and colleagues[4] estimated the cost of drug discovery and development to average in excess of $ 800 million (in year 2000 dollars). This number includes the costs of failures and time costs. Not surprisingly, the mean cost per investigational drug entering a phase increases substantially by clinical phase, particularly for Phase 3, which is typically characterized by large-scale trials. This has risen from an estimated US$ 300 million in the 1990s driven in part by the increasing complexity of new drug molecules and an ever increasing regulatory burden.

In a follow-up paper,[5] the same authors looked at the costs of developing biotech drugs. The null hypothesis was that biopharmaceuticals are less costly to develop because biotechnology firms need to be more nimble and creative and that fewer safety issues arise for many biopharmaceuticals because they replace substances that already exist in the body. The study found that the cash outlay costs were higher but adjusting for the time differences in the data suggest that the capitalized costs are the same.

It is important to note that these estimated values of the cost of drug development include all costs, including the costs of all failures, the cost of capital and the opportunity cost (i.e. the

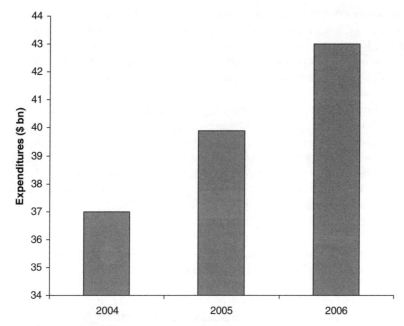

Figure 3.1 Increasing investment in Research and Development
Source: Burrill & Co., analysis PhRMA 2007 and PhRMA Annual Member survey (Washington DC; PhRMA 2007), reproduced with permission

estimated revenue that might have been generated if the cash associated with R&D expenditure had been invested in the equity market). Thus the $ 802 million value is a capitalized cost. This adjustment almost doubles the $ 403 million cost estimate for the drugs in their sample. It is also worth noting that the sample of drugs chosen were new molecular entities (no other versions of these drugs were on the market) and all were developed in-house by the pharmaceutical companies. It is therefore unlikely that the average cost estimates for these drugs would be applicable to the average new drug because it is undoubtedly cheaper to in-license a drug or make an improved version of an already marketed drug. A final point to keep in mind is that the estimate is in pre-tax dollars whereas in real life, R&D expenses are tax deductible, thereby lowering the actual cash cost of R&D to the company. In the remainder of the book when I refer to costs I will be looking at direct cash costs and specific risks and explicitly will be discounting for the time value of money.

It is also reported that biotechnology drug development took an average of 97.7 months (over 12 years) to complete clinical development, an increase of 8 % over pharmaceutical development times and that the mean clinical costs were 14 % higher than for pharmaceutical development. These trends reflect the factors affecting growth in clinical trial costs including the regulatory requirement for more clinical trial subjects to be enrolled, especially as safety concerns become more of a focus and the fact that many of the new investigational drugs are targeted at chronic disease or diseases associated with an ageing population and therefore require longer trials.

The sector is also prone to a large degree of volatility, especially on an individual stock level driven in part by the large amount of press releases that biotechnology companies tend to publish. However some of these press releases contain important data on how drugs are doing in the development process and a key to successful investing is to understand, at a minimum, the regulatory hurdles that all drugs must overcome before they can be launched on the market. A key skill to develop which I will highlight in more detail later is the ability to see clearly what the issues facing a company really are and not necessarily what the headline of the press release says.

The discovery and development process can be subdivided into five distinct stages, during which the drug company gathers evidence to convince government regulators that it can consistently manufacture a safe and efficacious form of the compound for the medical condition it is intended to treat. At the end of each stage, the company uses the technological and market information revealed up to that point to decide whether to abandon or continue development of the compound. It is important for investors to be generally familiar with these stages because the risks associated with the different stages are very different.

The five stages I would like to highlight are:

- Drug discovery: The aim in this phase is to identify a candidate drug, also termed a "lead" candidate by conducting initial tests on a variety of compounds.
- Preclinical development: The preclinical phase refers to a variety of animal studies that form part of the filing package, the bulk of which are completed before the drug ever enters humans. The key objective is to ensure that the drug is safe to be given acutely (for a short period) to humans.
- Early clinical phase incorporating Phase 1 and 2 studies: These studies assess the drug's properties in healthy volunteers and then in relatively small numbers of patients.
- Phase 3 trials: To determine statistically significant efficacy and safety in patients. This late stage of clinical development is sometimes pooled in with the other phases of clinical development.
- Post-marketing surveillance studies: These monitor the ongoing safety of marketed drugs.

On average it takes 14.2 years for a new drug to come to market.[6] Over the past four decades drug development timescales have grown, rising from an average of 8.1 years in the 1960s to 11.6 years in the 1970s to the current timescale. In 2001, a study[7] demonstrated that the preclinical phase in the decade of the 1990s took approximately six years, the clinical phase 6.3 years and the approval phase 1.8 years. These timelines are in line with the PhRMA's estimate of 10–15 years to complete the discovery and development stages. All pharmaceutical and biotechnology companies are actively striving to reduce the length of these timescales.

Investors should note that the drug development process is both complex and lengthy. At the start of the chapter I highlighted the huge amounts of money that are required for drug development. The data below shows how the R&D budget is typically allocated across functions, with the cost dramatically rising as the drug enters clinical development. According to data from the Centre for Medicines Research (CMR),[8] the clinical functions together accounted for the majority of total R&D expenditure in 2005.

As can be seen from the data, once the potential drug begins to be evaluated in humans, the costs go up dramatically. An important point to note for investors is that the cost of Phase 3 trials in certain indications (e.g. cardiovascular disease) can be prohibitively lengthy and expensive for biotechnology companies to contemplate on their own, necessitating them to seek a partner post the end of Phase 3 trials. These indications require seriously large-scale clinical trials and even if successful, require significant marketing resources behind them.

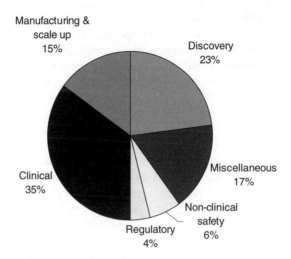

Figure 3.2 Proportion of total R&D expenditure by function
Source: CMR International 2006/2007 *Pharmaceutical R&D Factbook*, reproduced with permission

Thus, when assessing potential investments, investors need to be able to estimate when a particular drug might make it to the market, even if all trials and associated timelines go according to plan. Another reason why investors ought to focus on timelines concerns the old adage that "time is money" and the impact is two-fold. For every day that the drug is in development, it is not generating revenues (or generating positive cash flow) for the company. Thus for a blockbuster drug which sells $ 1 billion annually, this equates to approximately $ 4 million per working day (assuming 252 working days per year).

Secondly for every day that the drug is in development, it loses a day of its patent life. The owner of a patent is given a 20-year period of monopoly rights from the date of filing. Post this period there is no protection on the intellectual property rights for the drug and generic drugs can enter in the market. However because patents are normally filed long before the drug is marketed they tend to be effective for only 7–12 years.

To compensate for the short effective patent life which pharmaceuticals inevitably have, an extension of the period of legal protection (patent term restoration) has been possible in the USA since 1984 and in Japan since 1988. Europe has accordingly introduced Supplementary Protection Certificates (SPCs) for pharmaceuticals which provide a maximum of 15 years' legal protection after the first marketing authorization in the European Union, subject to a maximum SPC term of five years. In the pharmaceutical and biotechnology industry, there may be extensions available through management of the drug life cycle using alternative delivery forms but essentially the "composition of matter" patent is lost. This patent covers the chemical composition of the drug. Companies can also try and extend the life cycle of a given drug by applying for additional patents that cover new uses, indications, doses and changes in formulation.

The drug industry also benefits from marketing exclusivity which is the granting of exclusive marketing rights. Exclusivity runs independently from patent coverage, and has different expiration times (e.g. paediatric exclusivity lasts for six months while an incentive for the treatment of rare diseases (typically those affecting less than 200 000 in the US), called orphan drug status, lasts for seven years in the US and 10 years in Europe). A five-year period of exclusivity is granted to new drug applications for products containing chemical entities never previously approved by FDA either alone or in combination. A three-year period of exclusivity is granted for a drug product that contains an active moiety that has been previously approved, when the application contains reports of new clinical investigations. For example, the changes in an approved drug product that affect its active ingredient(s), strength, dosage form, route of administration or conditions of use may be granted exclusivity if clinical investigations were essential to approval of the application containing those changes. It is important to note that a drug can have a patent, exclusivity, both or neither.

Loss of exclusivity can be very costly as it allows the entry of generic competition. A generic medicine is an equivalent version of an originator pharmaceutical product containing the same active drug substance but is typically 20–80 % less expensive. When generic versions of Lilly's antidepressant Prozac (fluoxetine) were introduced in 2001, Prozac's volume fell precipitously – losing 73 % of its share of new prescriptions within two weeks.

Generic drugs counted for 60 % of total drugs dispensed in 2006 but accounted for less than 20 % of the pharmacy spend.[9] The rise of generics is set to continue and there is data to show that generic competition has intensified over the 1995–2005 period. In the case of blockbuster drugs with sales over $ 1 billion, the situation is worse. In 1995–2001 the market exclusivity period for these drugs was 13.8 years but had fallen to 11.2 years in the 2002–2005 period.[10]

DRUG DISCOVERY AND RESEARCH

An ideal drug is potent, efficacious and has specificity for its target in order to minimize unwanted side effects. However the reality is that no drug is 100 % effective and free from side effects. The first stage of the drug development pathway is drug discovery in which the pharmacology of a potential new drug is characterized using *in vitro* and animal models in an attempt to obtain data on the safety and effectiveness of the potential drug. At this point, the drug company is hoping that the compound or class of compounds can influence a disease process and thus ultimately has the potential to offer a therapeutic benefit in humans.

In this phase the company tests many hundreds of thousands of chemical entities, searching for those that produce a pharmacological effect. Depending on the disease in question and the level of prior knowledge regarding the potential new drug, drug discovery can take from two years to many years to complete. This discovery stage is estimated to cost between $ 30m and $ 50m and on average only 40 out of an initial 10 000 compounds (0.4 %) are taken onto the next stage, preclinical development. This cost estimate includes all the screening of the tens of thousands of chemicals that goes into identifying a lead compound and the subsequent modifications and safety assessments that make it more "druggable" i.e. suitable to be taken into clinical trials. Typically drug discovery accounts for approximately 23 % of the cash cost of getting a successful drug to market.

The discovery function also includes some preclinical development work such as Absorption, Distribution, Metabolism and Excretion (ADME) studies and any development work such as process and formulation research that will be associated with producing an active substance to be tested in humans for the first time.

Pre-Clinical Development

Prior to the novel agent being administered in humans, research studies in animal models are required to assess the toxicity profile in order to minimize adverse events in the human population. The preclinical phase of drug development is relatively inexpensive compared to the clinical phases of drug development but can still last up to three years.

The key objective in this phase is to determine the key pharmacological characteristics (pharmacodynamics and pharmacokinetics) of a compound. In simple terms pharmacodynamics is the study of the drug with its target (i.e. the investigator tries to determine the relationship between dose of drug administered and its effect on some particular response (e.g. heart rate)) and pharmacokinetics is about the actions of the body on the drug. These characteristics are summarized by the acronym ADMET which stands for:

- Absorption: the principal factors which determine the absorption of drug into the blood stream are its physiochemical and pharmacological properties, the way it is formulated and the site to which it is applied.
- Distribution: the distribution of a drug throughout the body is governed by the affinities it has for various constituents of the tissues, including aqueous solubility, lipid solubility, binding to extracellular substances and intracellular uptake.
- Metabolism: the enzymatic changes undergone by a drug in the body usually result in the attenuation or loss of pharmacological activity. However, sometimes a pharmacologically active metabolite may be formed from an inactive precursor (pro-drug) or the metabolites of a drug may have a different type of action from the administered drug. The main organ concerned with drug metabolism is the liver but the kidney, lung, gut and plasma also contain important drug metabolizing enzymes.
- Excretion: the main route of excretion of drugs and their metabolites is in the urine; the next most important is in the faeces.
- Toxicology: the study of the adverse effects of chemicals and drugs on the human body. The most important aspect when evaluating toxicology is the dose. The therapeutic index is a comparison of the amount of a therapeutic agent that causes the therapeutic effect to the amount that causes toxic effects. It should be noted that a single drug can have many therapeutic indices, one for each of its undesirable effects relative to a desired drug action, and one for each of its desired effects if the drug has more than one action. A commonly used measure of therapeutic index is the lethal dose of a drug for 50 % of the population divided by the minimum effective dose for 50 % of the population. A narrow therapeutic index means that there is little difference between doses that produce a therapeutic effect and those that produce a toxic effect. For example the therapeutic index for ethanol is approximately 10.

Thus pharmacokinetics analyses what happens to the drug after it enters the body. Important terms that investors may come across in relation to this area are:

- Volume of distribution (V_d): the apparent volume of distribution is the volume of fluid that a drug would occupy if the total amount in the body were in solution at the same concentration as in plasma. In some cases the V_d of a drug corresponds to an anatomical compartment, but in others it is a purely mathematical concept (e.g. if a drug is selectively bound to constituents of tissues or is taken up selectively by tissue cells).
- Half life ($t_{1/2}$): the amount of time that it takes for the concentration of a drug to be reduced by half in the body. Some drugs stay in the body longer than others. A long half life indicates that a drug is present in the body for a longer amount of time compared to a drug with a short half life.

- Bioavailability: this is the term used to describe the fraction of an administered dose of unchanged drug that reaches the circulation. For example, if a drug is given by an intravenous injection, its bioavailability is 100 %. However when given orally or by other routes, the bioavailability decreases due to hurdles such as less than perfect absorption or first pass metabolism by the liver.

These determine the suitability of a new chemical to become a drug. An important goal of these preclinical animal studies is to characterize any relationship between increased drug doses and adverse events (side effects). Drug development will be halted if tests suggest that a significant risk may be posed in humans.

It is probably best for the individual investor to avoid stocks where companies only have drugs in the preclinical phase or in the discovery phase. The probability of a drug in pre-clinical development of reaching the market is very low (less than 10 %) and since there is so little data available, it is very hard to gauge the commercial potential. However even at this point, investors should be asking themselves if the drug appears to address a clearly recognized unmet medical need. Once that is ascertained, then the drug in development should offer the potential of significantly enhancing the current efficacy and outcome for the patient.

However since all drugs in the latter stages of drug development will have passed through the preclinical phase, there are questions which should be asked as part of the assessment of the pipeline potential. An important aspect of the interpretation of animal trials and a factor in determining commercial potential is the route of administration used. An example of this is how the management team envisages that the drug will be delivered to the patient. It is desirable to use the same route of administration in animal trials as with human use, where possible. This enables a more meaningful comparison of animal data and the potential risk–benefit profile in humans. The route of administration can be an important determinant of the commercial potential if the drug makes it to market. In general terms oral, once a day therapy is preferred rather than taking multiple pills over the course of the day. Oral therapies are preferred over injection or infusion routes, although in hospitals this issue becomes less relevant. So for example, if a company was developing a drug for hypertension but the formulation into an oral pill was proving difficult, the drug is unlikely to continue in development. The reason is that the use of injections would not be commercially viable in a marketplace dominated by oral pills.

Irrespective of the development phase of the compound, it is never too early for the manage-ment team (or indeed potential investors) to start thinking about the commercialization of the product, even though it may lie years in the future. For example, investors should determine early in the process if a drug will be for specialist (i.e. hospital) or general practitioner use. This seemingly simple question has a number of important points. First if the drug is for a general practitioner audience, it is unlikely that the biotechnology company will have the nec-essary resources to market it effectively. As an example a few hundred sales representatives should be enough to market one or two oncology therapeutics in the US to hospital-based specialists (one product may only need fewer than 100), with it being very rare to have more than 1000. In contrast, sales forces targeting general practitioners (also termed primary care physicians) tend to be organized into 500-strong sales forces with it being rare to have more than 2000 full-time equivalents on any one product at any one time. For broad-based primary care companies, this means few have more than 5000–6000 sales people in primary care in the US.

Routes of drug administration include:

- Oral: this is the most common way of drug administration and the drugs can be given as liquids or solid tablets. For a drug to be absorbed into the blood stream, it has to be soluble in the fluids of the gastrointestinal tract. Note that "biotechnology" drugs such as hormone replacements and monoclonal antibodies are not able to be given orally as their complex structure prevents absorption. A major disadvantage for oral administration is that drugs suffer "first pass" metabolism as they are absorbed from the gut and pass through the liver (where they are subsequently metabolized) before entering the general circulation. Metabolism not only decreases the bioavailability of a drug but may give rise to metabolites which may increase the side effect of a drug. Alternatively, some drugs are designed as pro-drugs and require metabolism to convert them to an active form. The key point is that the formulation must be aligned with the market need.
- Buccal: this means absorption from the oral cavity by placing the drug between the gums and the cheek. It has the advantage of avoiding first pass metabolism because the drug is absorbed before it reaches the gut.
- Sublingual: this means absorption from the oral cavity by placing the drug underneath the tongue. It has the advantage of avoiding first pass metabolism because the drug is absorbed before it reaches the gut.
- Rectal: this route may be chosen when the patient is unable to take the drug orally but absorption may be unreliable.
- Intravenous: direct injection into the bloodstream which offers rapid response and as such is useful in an emergency case. However the method is potentially the most dangerous. Intravenous injection can be of two types, bolus and infusion. A bolus injection takes the form of a single dose. An infusion is administered over time.
- Subcutaneous: an injection into the fat layer under the skin which can be used to deliver protein-based drugs. The absorption of the drug is faster than with the oral route.
- Intramuscular: injection into the muscle. Similar characteristics to subcutaneous but may be more painful for the patient. In both cases, the rate of absorption is determined by the blood flow pattern and diffusion of drug molecules in tissues.
- Transdermal: the drug is applied to the skin surface, typically using a transdermal patch. The site of action of the drug can be remote from the area of skin where the patch is located. The first pass metabolism effect is avoided.
- Topical: the drug is applied for local effects.
- Inhalation: aerosol particles of drug can be inhaled into the lungs. Absorption is rapid and effective and distribution of inhaled drugs is very quick.

Given the lengthy timescales of drug development, companies need to appropriately manage drug development to ensure that this study does not become a rate limiting factor for submission of an NDA. Careful design, conduct and interpretation of the results from these non-clinical research experiments normally determine which discovery leads have the necessary attributes to become marketed human therapeutic products. The toxicity studies (carcinogenicity and reproduction toxicity studies) are not needed ahead of the clinical studies in humans but must be completed before the regulatory submission.

In Case Study #1 at the end of the chapter, I briefly look at how important the formulation of a drug can be for gauging commercial potential, even many years from the assumed market launch.

Clinical Trials

Different countries have different requirements for clinical trials although there has been some convergence of standards under the guidance of the International Committee on Harmonization (ICH), and the process of preclinical and clinical testing is broadly similar throughout the developed world. Clinical trials are performed under Good Clinical Practice. This is a set of internationally recognized ethical and scientific quality requirements which must be used for designing, conducting, recording and reporting clinical trials that involve the participation of human subjects.

In the US, the sponsor company submits the information above to the Food and Drug Administration (FDA) in the form of an Investigational New Drug (IND) application. The data collected for the IND is reviewed and either the go-ahead is given for clinical trials to begin or the sponsor is notified that further data or changes are required. For other countries a notification has to be submitted to the respective regulatory authorities. For example Clinical Trial Exemption (CTX) applications are required for the UK and Clinical Trial Certificate (CTC) for the European Medicines Agency (EMEA) in Europe. Irrespective of the nationality, it is important to recognize that regulatory authorities play an important role to ensure compliance in the conduct of a clinical trial.

The key message is that for any developing biotechnology/pharmaceutical company, in which rational use of financial resources is critical, any study that is conducted should be done with a clear purpose as to how it fits into the overall drug development plan. Data generated from earlier studies should be used to guide the objectives of later studies. Potential investors should do a calculation estimating the cost of taking the drug asset to the next decision point (i.e. Phase 1 to 2, Phase 2 to 3 etc). It is also worth noting that orphan drugs have a reduced statistical burden placed upon them by the regulators as a reflection that the patient population is small. This results in the fact that many fewer patients may be required in clinical trials potentially offering a shorter and faster clinical development programme.

Major Considerations in the Design of Clinical Trials

There are five main considerations when designing clinical trials:

1. study objective,
2. study design,
3. study conduct,
4. study analysis and
5. study report.

A good resource to assess clinical trials is the web site http://clinicaltrials.gov/ which is provided as a service of the US National Institutes of Health. This site gives a current update on which trials are recruiting patients in a particular disease area and also allows one to gain insight into appropriate endpoints.

1. Study objective

The objective should be very clearly stated. A study is designed around its stated objective and, therefore, this should be clearly specified in the protocol. For each trial, the objective or purpose is clearly stated. The objective may read something like this: "The purpose of the study is to determine if reducing or eliminating a dopamine agonist causing one of the side effects of daytime sleepiness, swelling of the lower legs or feet, hallucinations or impulsive behaviors while adding orally disintegrating [specify drug] can eliminate the adverse effect and maintain control of Parkinson's disease symptoms".

2. Study design

The study design should be carefully chosen depending on the objective of the study and the stage of clinical development. The protocol should very clearly outline the various procedures that will take place in the study, what variables will be measured at which time points and how to follow up patients who discontinue from the trial. A study design could be summarized as follows: "Prevention, Randomized, Double-Blind, Placebo Control".

The selection of subjects is critical, especially during therapeutic confirmatory studies. As previously mentioned, patients in early-stage studies are usually very homogenous. However, later-stage larger clinical trials tend to have more heterogeneous patient populations that more closely reflect the real-world situation. All trials should have an adequate control group. The selection of the control group depends on the objective of the trial. It may be placebo, an active comparator, a different dose of the investigational drug or, in rare cases, an external (historical) control.

Control groups are necessary in order to distinguish the effect of the active treatment from effects due to other factors such as progression of disease, patient expectations or other treatments. In order to properly assess the efficacy of the active versus control groups in a study, it is important that patients are properly randomized to treatments and bias is minimized. Optimal randomization ensures that both test and control groups are similar at baseline, before receiving treatment, thus enabling a proper comparison between groups.

Blinding techniques are used to ensure that patients do not know whether they are receiving the active treatment or the control treatment. A trial may be single blind, meaning that the patient does not know what treatment is administered. A double blind trial means that neither the patient nor the investigator knows what treatment the patient is receiving.

How many subjects are required?   The number of subjects in a clinical trial needs to be large enough to provide a reliable answer to the study objective. The number of subjects included in a clinical trial is determined by the disease under investigation, the study objective and the primary variable. Statisticians estimate appropriate study sample sizes by examining the magnitude of the expected treatment effect, the variability and the chance of error (i.e. false positive or false negative results), as well as if there is a requirement for an interim analysis or a desire to collect large volumes of safety information. Investors should check what other companies have submitted to the regulators. For example, in July 2007 there was a lot of investor enthusiasm for the Swiss anti-infective company, Basilea Pharmaceutica. Its lead drug was partnered with Johnson and Johnson and pivotal efficacy data was anticipated. However, as a research note reported at the time,[11] "there do appear to be some concerns in the market regarding the size of the safety database required and the level achieved by Ceftobiprole. Recent regulatory submissions such as Zyvox (linezolid, from Pfizer) and Tygacil (tigecycline, from Wyeth) safety databases, comprised 2,046 and 1,415 patients respectively. J&J and Basilea have now completed both US and EU submissions, with a database of 1,600 patients, so these fears would appear to be unfounded."

All drugs are approved based on a balance of the benefits and risks of treatment (i.e. efficacy versus safety). Regulators expect that adverse events that occur with a cumulative three-month incidence of about 1 % will be well characterized. The safety evaluation of rare adverse events – i.e., less than 1 in 1000 patients – is not expected to be fully characterized during drug development.

The ICH guidelines make the following suggestions:

- Treatment of 300 to 600 patients for six months should be adequate to determine adverse events in the range of 0.5 % to 5 %.
- One hundred patients should be treated for at least one year, from a prospectively designed study, in order to assess if there are less common adverse events or adverse events that may occur only after treatment for more than six months.
- The total number of individuals treated with an investigational drug, at all stages of development, should be about 1500.

Study endpoints   It is vitally important to clearly specify primary and secondary endpoints in a clinical trial. The statistics are usually based on the primary variable. The methods used to evaluate the primary endpoint must be clearly stated and should be appropriately validated, whether historically by others, or for a novel endpoint, by a company prior to conducting therapeutic confirmatory trials (for example a new quality of life questionnaire needs to be appropriately validated before it will be accepted as an appropriate endpoint).

Finally, the study design should ensure there are appropriate methods to minimize bias, including proper randomization to treatment, suitable blinding techniques and an assessment of protocol compliance of both investigators and patients.

3. Study conduct

Third, the conduct of a study must be according to the principles of Good Clinical Practice. This can often be the downfall of a developing biotech/pharma company that either does not have in-house expertise or does not exercise suitable control over the use of contract research organizations. Inadequate adherence to the protocol has been the downfall of various companies seeking FDA marketing approval. It is too late to try to fix a study after it is finished. It is of paramount importance that a company carefully monitors the conduct of a trial during its progress to ensure that it meets the needs of the regulators and is conducted to the highest standards. It can be impossible to predict all questions and unusual circumstances that may arise during a trial, but it is vital that any unusual events are properly documented, thoroughly investigated and clearly accounted for in the clinical study report. Regulators do not like surprises, and all efforts that a company takes to ensure that it clearly documents how a trial was conducted will be worthwhile.

4. Study analysis

Fourth, all studies should include an appropriate analysis plan that meets the objectives of the study. Statistical methods should be clearly described, and the rationale and timing of any interim analyses should be included. When an interim analysis is performed, the statistical significance level should be appropriately adjusted. A company may perform an interim analysis and then continue with the study to its pre-planned ending. If this is the case, the required level of statistical significance for the final statistical analysis should be less than the usual confidence level ($p<0.05$) that might be used for a study with no interim analysis. The p value tells us the probability that an observed difference may have occurred by chance. Therefore it conveys information about the level of doubt. By not adjusting the significance level, the results are biased towards showing an improvement, since the more statistical tests that are performed, the greater the likelihood of finding a significant result.

Studies must then be analysed according to the plan, and any deviation justified. Any studies that are stopped prematurely, either based on formal stopping decisions from highly positive efficacy results or stopped early due to unforeseen safety side effects, must be duly analysed. All studies should have thorough safety reporting processes and results must be thoroughly documented.

5. Study report

Finally, all studies should have a detailed clinical study report outlining all findings. Every patient who has entered the study should be accounted for. Any discrepancies between how the trial was planned versus how it was actually conducted need to be explained.

When companies report study results, it is important to note whether the results are based on the full data set, i.e. "intent-to-treat" or a "per protocol" data set. The intent-to-treat analysis includes all randomized subjects regardless of how long they received treatment and how closely they followed the protocol. There are certain circumstances in which it may be justifiable to exclude a randomized patient, such as if no doses of study medication were taken or if there is a lack of any data post randomization. It can be difficult to account for patients who left the trial early, whether due to withdrawal of patient consent, protocol violations, etc. Statistical plans need to include how the study will account for incomplete patient data.

For example, one method is to carry forward the last value observed to the end of the trial. In all cases, the statistical plan should document exactly what analyses will be performed and how the data will be treated prior to starting any data management or analyses, and ideally prior to starting the study. The FDA typically requires a company to report study results based on the intent-to-treat analysis for superiority studies, as this is the most conservative. However, for equivalence trials, the intent-to-treat analysis may not be appropriate as it may not be sufficiently conservative.

The per protocol analysis only includes subjects who satisfy the major inclusion and exclusion criteria, who are more compliant with the protocol and who usually have completed a certain pre-specified minimal exposure to the treatment regimen. This analysis can introduce bias if adherence to the study protocol is related to the treatment and, thus, is a less conservative method of analysis for demonstrating superiority.

The Risk of Clinical Trials

Many new product development processes follow a sequence of distinct phases. The main assumption is that the process starts broad and follows several stages narrowing down to the focused fully defined new product. The drug development process is risky in that most compounds that undergo clinical testing are abandoned without obtaining market approval.

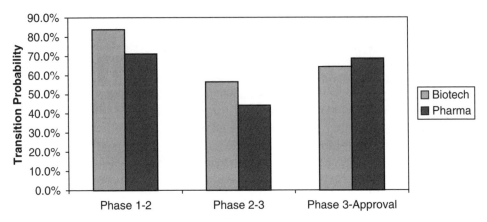

Figure 3.3   Summary of transition phase probabilities

An overall clinical approval success rate is the probability that a compound that enters the clinical phase of development will eventually be approved for marketing.

Attrition rates describe the rate at which investigational drugs fail testing in the various clinical phases. A phase success rate is the probability that a drug will attain marketing approval from the current phase. A phase transition probability is the likelihood that an investigational drug will proceed from one phase to the next.

As detailed previously, of 100 drugs which start a clinical trial development programme, about 70 will successfully complete Phase 1 trials and go on to Phase 2; about 33 % of the starting 100 will complete Phase 2 trials and go into pivotal Phase 3 trials and of these approximately 25 to 30 of the original 100 will clear this hurdle. On average about 20 % of the initial 100 will be approved for marketing. Looking at this attrition rate another way, a number of studies have shown a very low probability of drugs reaching the market.[12]

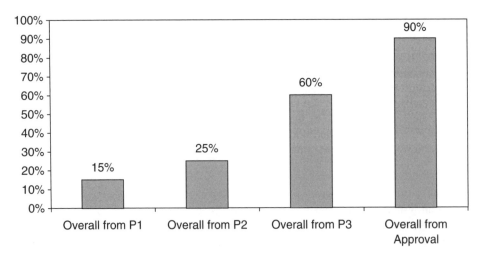

Figure 3.4   Summary of phase success probabilities

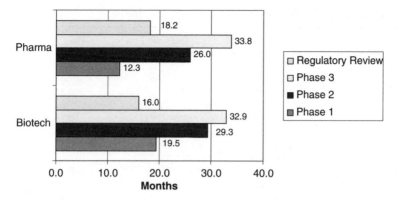

Figure 3.5 Clinical development and approval times
Source: Joseph A. DiMasi and Henry G. Grabowski, 2007, *Managerial and Decision Economics* 28: 469–479, reproduced with permission

Thus already we are seeing that the development process is an attrition course for drugs. We have also seen that the drug development process can be lengthy (industry estimates suggest that the time from discovery to approval is between 12 and 15 years with seven to nine years in human clinical trials) and capital intensive. The duration of developmental phases and their costs are important inputs to the valuation methods that are used in later chapters.

The previous data on success rates and trials duration is similar to data reported in another study[13] depicted in Table 3.2. It is obvious that in each of the drug phases, there are always more drugs successfully completing a given phase than failing it but the proportion of successes, in relation to failures, decreases as drugs move through the development process.

Investors should note that the probability of success depends on the type of disease; for example there are large numbers of drugs to treat high blood pressure but none to effectively treat head trauma. Therefore evaluating different drugs in the same phase but in different indications will result in different probabilities as shown in Table 3.3.

Clinical development

Clinical trials are broken down into four phases termed Phase 1, 2, 3, 4 (sometimes roman numerals are used, i.e. I, II, III and IV).

Table 3.2 Additional data on clinical development and approval times

	Phase 1		Phase 2		Phase 3	
	Cases #	Mean duration Months	Cases #	Mean duration months	Cases #	Mean duration months
Complete	999	22.1	881	34	448	44.9
Success	806	19.7	508	29.9	254	47
Failure	193	31.9	373	39.5	194	42.1
Probability of success		80.70%		57.70%		56.70%

Source: Rosa M. Abrantes-Metz, Christopher P. Adams & Albert D. Metz, 2005, *Journal of Pharmaceutical Finance, Economics & Policy*, 14(4) 19–37

Table 3.3 Clinical development and approval times according to disease indication

		Phase 1	Phase 2	Phase 3
All drugs	Prob. success	0.81	0.57	0.57
	Duration	*19.68*	*29.87*	*47*
Big Pharma	Prob. success	0.73	0.5	0.69
	Duration	*19.62*	*25.11*	*41.43*
Non Big Pharma	Prob. success	0.82	0.59	0.54
	Duration	*18.76*	*29.92*	*49.07*
Biologicals	Prob. success	0.9	0.67	0.7
	Duration	*17.87*	*31.87*	*45.63*
Alimentary	Prob. success	0.89	0.77	0.71
	Duration	*20.13*	*28.04*	*44.82*
Oral	Prob. success	0.88	0.77	0.71
	Duration	*20.49*	*28.31*	*44.88*
Intravenous	Prob. success	0.92	0.8	0.67
	Duration	*18.05*	*30.91*	*47.29*
Subcutaneous	Prob. success	0.97	0.81	0.88
	Duration	*19.5*	*34.16*	*49.86*
Intramuscular	Prob. success	0.91	0.79	0.85
	Duration	*21.4*	*31.73*	*53.18*
Respiratory	Prob. success	0.71	0.43	0.83
	Duration	*19.7*	*21.89*	*40.8*
Topical	Prob. success	0.89	0.79	0.71
	Duration	*15.32*	*23.22*	*56.16*
Transdermal	Prob. success	0.7	0.73	0.75
	Duration	*22.43*	*24.63*	*32.67*
Alzheimer's disease	Prob. success	0.83	0.6	0.33
	Duration	*19.37*	*46.11*	*39.5*
Arthritis	Prob. success	0.94	0.66	0.69
	Duration	*18.21*	*32.53*	*44.91*
Asthma	Prob. success	0.85	0.51	0.78
	Duration	*16.48*	*35.44*	*41*
Cancer	Prob. success	0.88	0.73	0.66
	Duration	*21.79*	*30.23*	*48*
Diabetes	Prob. success	0.86	0.65	0.89
	Duration	*18.58*	*23.15*	*47.75*
Hypertension	Prob. success	0.81	0.75	0.81
	Duration	*10.73*	*39.17*	*44.12*
HIV/AIDS	Prob. success	0.86	0.62	0.94
	Duration	*21.63*	*21.57*	*24.31*
Parkinson's disease	Prob. success	0.82	0.7	0.63
	Duration	*18.5*	*44.14*	*63.4*
Thrombosis	Prob. success	0.79	0.64	0.44
	Duration	*21.32*	*35*	*59.75*

Source: Rosa M. Abrantes-Metz, Christopher P. Adams and Albert D. Metz, 2005, *Journal of Pharmaceutical Finance, Economics & Policy*, 14(4) 19–37

Phase 1

Phase 1 is the first time a drug is tested within humans and the primary goal is to assess the safety of the drug. Testing is usually conducted in a small number of male volunteers (usually healthy) to obtain information on toxicity and safe dosing ranges in humans. Typically women of childbearing age are not included in early human clinical trials in order to minimize potential adverse effects to the woman's eggs or embryo/foetus if pregnant.

Data is also collected on the drug's absorption and distribution in the body, the drug's metabolic effects and the rate and manner in which the drug is eliminated from the body. Phase 1 development accounts for approximately 10 % of the overall R&D spend. Individual trials typically involve 20–80 patients and may last from several months to one year. The cost of such trials is approximately $ 5–6 million.

Phase 2

Phase 2 trials include the controlled clinical studies conducted to evaluate the appropriate dose range and effectiveness of the drug for a particular indication in patients with the disease under study and to determine common short-term side effects and risks associated with the drug. The drug is administered to a larger number of individuals selected from among patients for whom the drug is intended. It is common to conduct the trials with a control group in conjunction with the test group given the drug. Patients are randomized to the control or active arms of the trial. The data obtained when the trial finishes will provide comparative data about the safety and effectiveness of the drug versus placebo or standard of care treatment. These randomized trials are also usually blinded, i.e. the patients do not know whether they are receiving the investigational drug or the placebo. These protocols endeavour to remove bias from the studies.

Phase 2 is often split into two distinct phases. Phase 2a studies are called proof of concept studies and are designed to show that the drug has some clinical benefit in the target patient population. Phase 2b studies are designed to determine the most appropriate doses of the drug to use in the Phase 2 clinical trials – i.e. they are designed to help clinical trial designers choose the dose of the drug that can maximize the efficacy and minimize the adverse event profile. In addition to dosing information, the trials provide information on the optimum frequency of administration and duration of therapy. Phase 2 development may account for up to 25 % of the R&D spend.

Trials typically involve 100–200 patients and depending upon the number and availability of patients, these Phase 2 trials can last up to two years. The cost can range from $ 10– $ 15 million.

Phase 3

Phase 3 is the final clinical trial phase before the launch of the drug and typically involves large-scale trials on patients to obtain additional evidence of efficacy, which is statistically significant. These trials are often called pivotal trials because they are central to any drug filing. Larger sample sizes increase the likelihood that actual benefits will be found statistically significant and that any adverse reactions that may occur infrequently in patient populations will be observed. If for any reason the drug does not show significant advantage over current treatment, the result may be refined and certain subgroups analysed to determine if the effects are greater in one group than the other.

There are two main objectives for later-stage clinical trials:

1. to show efficacy and/or safety,
2. to assess relative efficacy and/or safety between two treatments.

Efficacy is best shown by comparison of an investigational drug to a control group, whether the control is a placebo or another active treatment. If a clinical trial is designed to show efficacy versus an active treatment, this is an "equivalence" trial, or a "non-inferiority" trial. The Phase 3 trials have the objective of showing that the investigational drug is more effective than the control by more than a defined amount.

If the purpose of the trial is to assess relative efficacy and/or safety, the objective of the trial is to show superiority to a control (either active or placebo). The trial must be designed to detect a difference between treatments in order to show useful comparative information.

For equivalence or non-inferiority trials, unless a placebo group is included in the study design, this type of study design will not usually satisfy the FDA as the sole measure of demonstrating equivalence for a new drug that is similar to an existing product from a different company, but potentially with a different dosing regimen. Historically the FDA has permitted non-inferiority trials for antibacterial trial protocols. However recent FDA updates have suggested that in some antibacterial indications non-inferiority designs would no longer be acceptable to the agency.

In both equivalence and non-inferiority trials, it is important that the appropriate dose of active control, as well as the appropriate patient population, is chosen, so as to ensure a lack of bias in favour of the investigational drug.

The actual number of patients involved will depend upon the disease for which the drug is intended (for example a cancer drug may only be investigated in a few hundred patients while a drug for a cardiovascular disease would be studied in several thousand). The key to determining the number of patients is the need to identify potentially rare side effects, as well as to perform statistical analyses on the results. The drug undergoing testing is often compared against placebo or compared to an existing gold standard of treatment.

Phase 3 trials are designed to approximate closely the manner in which the drug will be used after marketing approval. Patient numbers for Phase 3 can vary from several hundreds to thousands. Since these trials tend to be quite large and relatively complex, they are estimated to account for approximately 35 % of a company's R&D spend. Regulators usually require companies to conduct at least two Phase 3 studies. The duration of Phase 3 trials can last from two to five years. The costs of these trials are quite variable but typically fall within the range of $ 30–$ 65 million.

Phase 4

Phase 4 trials are increasingly being required at the time of marketing approval in order to provide more detailed information on some aspect of the drug. They are also known as "post marketing surveillance trials". As we have seen above, the FDA sometimes can approve a drug without this risk–benefit being either fully quantified or known explicitly at the time of approval. This usually applies to potentially life-saving therapies for severe diseases with significant unmet medical need.

What Investors Should Look For When Analysing Clinical Trials

The proper design and conduct of a therapeutic confirmatory clinical trial will have a critical impact on the approvability of a new drug. When examining a company's announcement of clinical trial results, it is important that clients are aware of what to look for. Often, what is not mentioned in a press release is more important than what is mentioned, so it is critical to look at what has been excluded as well as the quality of data that has been included.

A European biotechnology company published the following press release regarding the results of a Phase 3 trial on its lead drug candidate, which also comprised the vast majority of its market valuation: "Phase III trial in Europe demonstrates M6G's benefit compared to morphine in the treatment of post operative." At the time, my colleagues and I wrote a research note which stated:

> CeNeS has reported preliminary Phase 3 results for its lead drug, M6G for the treatment of post-op pain. M6G matches morphine for analgesic effect and also showed a significant reduction in the severity of post operative nausea and vomiting (PONV) compared to morphine. However M6G failed to show a significant difference in the primary endpoint of a reduction in the incidence and severity of nausea compared to morphine.[14]

We went on to state that whilst the top line results appeared positive and showed the benefits of the M6G profile over morphine, we did not believe that the results would be sufficient to allow CeNeS to submit the file to the regulator. Management agreed with this point on the conference call and three scenarios unfolded:

1. A partner can be brought on board quickly and this partner decides that there are enough positives in the data set to warrant European submission. This could lead to approval in 2008.
2. A partner is signed up but another Phase 3 trial is required for European submission, leading to European launch in 2011.
3. A partner does not sign up and CeNeS is required to go it alone, again leading to delayed launch but with additional costs and no deal-driven income.

The above is a good example demonstrating that investors need to read the entire press release carefully, and not just the headline. There is nothing untrue in the press release; it is just that the emphasis may be on different aspects compared to what the market may focus on. Furthermore, when biotechnology drugs are partnered with other parties, especially large pharmaceutical companies, it is imperative that investors read the press releases from both parties. As an example, see the headlines from the press releases below. Both have the same factual headline but the opening lines of the press releases are very different.

The biotech company Newron and its partner, Merck Serono, a division of Merck KGaA both announced 18-month safety and efficacy data of Phase 3 trial of Safinamide in Parkinson's disease. It is the third bullet point of the Newron press release[15] that informs us that the trial has not met its endpoint. The release states:

> For the primary efficacy endpoint (time to intervention), although a delay of 93 days in median time to intervention was observed, statistical significance was not reached, when data from all safinamide dose groups were pooled; the lack of a significant effect might be explained by the lack of response with the high dose group (150–200mg) as seen in the analysis of the first six months.

Merck Serono's press release[16] had the following opening bullet point:

> • The primary endpoint, time to intervention, did not reach statistical significance when data from both Safinamide dose groups (50–100mg, 150–200mg) were pooled.

Although investors may be initially confused by these different approaches, it merely reflects the relative importance of the compound to Newron and the relative unimportance of the compound to Merck. Newron's drug development pipeline at the time consisted of Safinamide in Phase 3 trials for two indications and another asset, Rafinamide in Phase 2 trials. Thus a significant component of the valuation of Newron can be reasonably associated with Safinamide.

In contrast, the Merck fact sheet highlighted that Merck Serono (the pharmaceuticals division of Merck KGAa) had sales in 2006 of €3.9bn and had over 30 clinical trial programmes on-going.

Potential investors should try and get answers to the following questions when examining a company's clinical results and should also keep in mind that bad news can sometimes be buried within a press release.

- What was the study objective?
- Do the primary endpoint and study design address the objective of the study?
- Is the design appropriate, i.e. blinded and appropriate choice of control group?
- Are the results presented on an intent-to-treat or per protocol basis?
- What variables are reported and what is not mentioned? In some cases, excluded information may be due to the need to preserve confidentiality for a future conference presentation or publication. But sometimes, the company may not want to disclose the data on non-primary variables if they are not fully supportive of the study objective.

Data that a company is not likely to disclose include the quality of the conduct of the study. This may be revealed during the regulatory review process, such as at an FDA panel meeting. Also, companies do not always provide detailed study information such as patient inclusion and exclusion criteria, which would be useful to know as it can dictate the patient population that is eligible to receive the drug once it receives marketing approval. However it is also worth remembering that even the best research can catch investors out. A good example is the fall-out surrounding GPC Biotech and the FDA's Oncologic Drugs Advisory Committee (ODAC) Advisory Panel on 24 July 2007. The committee recommended not to grant an accelerated approval for Orplatna (satraplatin) due to concerns about the design of the SPARC (Satraplatin and Prednisone Against Refractory Cancer) trial and the clinical endpoints. It also stated that an approvable decision should be deferred until survival data was available, therefore moving potential approval and launch from a widely anticipated last quarter 2007 to the first half of 2009. The crucial issue is that GPC sought accelerated approval based on a pre-specified endpoint. However what investors did not know ahead of the committee meeting was the high degree of scepticism that the FDA had about the prospects for accelerated approval. However, the FDA's communication to the Oncologic Drugs Advisory Committee on 24 July was unambiguous. The FDA made clear it had identified flaws in both the design and conduct of GPC's SPARC Phase 3 study of Orplatna to treat hormone-refractory prostate cancer (HRPC) that could preclude use of the trial to support accelerated approval. ODAC responded categorically, recommending unanimously that FDA defer action on the New Drug Application (NDA) pending receipt of overall survival data from SPARC.

The FDA and GPC have conflicting explanations about why prostate cancer patients, oncologists and investors who had expected accelerated approval of Orplatna by the 15 August Prescription Drug User Fee Act (PDUFA) deadline now will have to wait to see if the survival data are strong enough to support regular approval. The Prescription Drug User Fee Act is a programme under which the pharmaceutical/biotechnology industry pays certain "user fees" to the FDA. In exchange for these fees, the FDA agreed to a set of performance standards intended to reduce the approval time for NDAs. Hence drug approvals in the US usually have a timeline or PDUFA date associated with them.

Whilst I recognize that the current section may be hard going, I believe that having a basic understanding of what questions to ask offers investors a significant advantage when it comes to investing in therapeutic biotechnology companies.

Some companies announce positive data, particularly from Phase 2 or therapeutic exploratory trials, indicating clinical success, when the trial endpoints are based on inappropriate endpoints for the required indication or the endpoints are inadequately validated. This can lead to overly optimistic conclusions that may not be upheld in a therapeutic confirmatory trial with more appropriate endpoints.

A common criticism of clinical trials is that they are expensive and take a long time to complete. This has led to the suggestion that response variables (biomarkers or surrogate markers) that are continuous in nature may substitute for the clinical outcomes. Surrogate markers are used when the primary endpoint is undesirable or when it may be impracticable to conduct a trial of sufficient size to be statistically significant. In therapeutic exploratory trials, a surrogate marker may be used as an endpoint and, if results are positive, may indicate to a company whether it is worth spending the time and money to do a larger-scale therapeutic confirmatory trial. Surrogate markers that are validated might be considered as a better predictor of clinical success in a larger clinical trial than a non-validated marker. However, unless the regulatory authority has indicated that a surrogate marker is an appropriate endpoint for a therapeutic confirmatory trial (i.e. a reduction in cholesterol is considered an approvable surrogate marker for drugs designed to lower cholesterol and consequently reduce the incidence of heart disease – the endpoint is death from heart disease and the reduction in cholesterol is the surrogate marker), then inferring positive results from future trials with more meaningful endpoints should be done with great caution.

Conclusion

I have presented a summary of the amount of animal data required to commence clinical trials, the basic requirements for a clinical trial, various study designs and choices of control group. These factors form an important part of the drug development process.

The appropriate design and conduct of clinical trials form the basis of approval of an NDA by regulators. When a regulator fails to approve an NDA due to clinical data, it is usually because either the study was not designed to properly test the study objective or it was not conducted with sufficient quality such that the data is reliable and conclusions are valid. Thus, careful attention to these two issues can help avoid many problems that can arise later during the regulatory review and approval process.

THE REGULATORY PROCESS

To date, regulators globally have not created a single harmonized protocol for drug approval. As such, separate regulatory bodies and approval processes exist in each of the major markets of the US, Europe and Japan. While future harmonization is an objective, as things stand today a new drug will need to go through at least three separate approval processes if it is to be launched in the world's three largest markets. This is clearly both costly and time consuming. The requirements of the different regulators also mean that companies often have to undertake further clinical trials in order to meet the regulatory needs of the authorities in the different territories, a feature that further increases the already substantial costs of the regulatory process. Having said this, the actual filing requirements, across the three regulatory regimes discussed here, are gradually converging. However, one major difference between attaining marketing approval in the US and elsewhere is the need to agree pricing with the authorities in both Japan and Europe. Of itself, this often leads to significant delays between actual approval and product launch. After the clinical trial phases have been completed and the company believes it has sufficient evidence for approval, it submits a New Drug Application (NDA) to either the FDA (US) or EMEA (Europe) for review. In terms of the clinical data, this decision is based on weighing up the potential benefits of the therapy when compared to the risks.

Regulation in the US

As with drug development, the process of regulatory approval in the US falls under the supervision of the Food and Drug Administration (FDA). A new drug sponsor (invariably the drug manufacturer) will submit a file, called a New Drug Application (NDA), for a new chemical entity (NCE) to the FDA for approval to manufacture, distribute and market the drug in the US, based on the data collated through the clinical trial process. This file comprises a large amount of information, including written reports of each individual study, manufacturing data and a summary of all available information received from any source concerning the safety and efficacy of the drug. Included in this must be at least two pivotal trials, one of which must have been undertaken in the US (pivotal trials represent the key clinical trials confirming efficacy, and so on for any NCE submission). In addition, 120 days prior to a drug's anticipated approval, the sponsor must provide the FDA with a summary of all safety information surrounding the new drug, including any additional safety data obtained from trials undertaken during the review process.

Advisory Committees

Following NDA submission, the FDA has 60 days to inform the sponsor that the application is complete and worthy of review. At this stage, the FDA designates the review track for the product. A standard review process is 12 months. In the case of a therapeutic breakthrough, a drug may be granted an 'expedited' six-month review. Assuming FDA acceptance, the submitted NDA will be forwarded to a specialist therapeutic department, the bias of which depends on the drug. For example, a cancer treatment will be forwarded to the Division of Oncology, and so on. The FDA also frequently seeks advice from its 17 standing advisor committees on drugs particularly on NCEs. These comprise independent scientific experts, physician researchers and statisticians who will make a recommendation to the FDA as to whether an NDA should be approved or not. The FDA is not, however, obliged to heed their advice, though usually it does follow their advice.

From an investment perspective, advisory committees can be volatile periods for a stock, as investors take positions as to whether the drug will get a positive opinion. The briefing documents are usually available a few days ahead of the meeting and while the decision is not known until after the meeting, sometimes the documents have a clear positive or negative tone from which investors try to draw conclusions. However as the example below shows, predicting panels can be very difficult.

On 19 July 2007, the European CHMP recommended against approving Tysabri to treat Crohn's disease. In a statement following the decision, EMEA said the benefits of Tysabri in Crohn's were only modest and did not outweigh its risks. The FDA panel was looking at exactly the same data set and while a vocal minority of the FDA's panel members was unconvinced by the data, the committee was clearly swayed by arguments from attending patients, care-givers and physicians that Crohn's is a serious and disabling condition that is not well controlled using existing therapies and that almost always results in surgery. Although the 12–3 vote in favour, with two abstentions, looked like a fairly solid recommendation, it masked an apprehensive undercurrent among panel members. Thus panels pose a difficult dilemma for investors.

Approvable and Approved

Assuming that the NDA meets the efficacy and safety requirements of the FDA, and if there are no outstanding issues, a drug may be granted an immediate approval at the end of the formal review process, which is usually one year. However, often if there are outstanding labelling issues or if the FDA has requested additional clinical trial data, a drug will be deemed "approvable", with formal approval following some months later once the outstanding issues are resolved. Formal approval by the FDA typically follows within three months, following discussions on the prescribing label (see below) and, once received, the drug may be launched.

Investors should note that receipt of an approval letter has a tendency to drive stock prices down. Yet it should not always be the case. Investors should check historical precedent to see if approvable letters are the norm for the particular indication and also to check the actual wording of the press release very carefully. All of the previously mentioned caveats regarding company press releases apply but it is very rare for the actual letter from the FDA to be made available to the public.

On 21 December 2006, Shire Pharmaceuticals issued a press release informing the market that it had received another approvable letter for VYVANSE (lisdexamfetamine dimesylate, formerly known as NRP104) for the treatment of Attention Deficit Hyperactivity Disorder (ADHD). Indeed this was the second letter the company had received from the FDA.

However, an informed investor would have known that drugs for ADHD commonly receive approvable letters as the company and the regulator discuss the claims that the company wants to add to the drugs label (more on this below). Furthermore the press release also stated that no additional studies have been requested by the FDA as a condition for approval of VYVANSE, thereby removing the fear (in the investor's mind) that the possibility of additional costly and time consuming clinical trials would be required. The release also stated that the data requested was routine, and was not expected to delay a launch of VYVANSE in the second quarter of 2007. This also allays any doubts regarding the commercial launch – remember it's the cash flows that are important and any delay to launch would impact negatively. In addition, if analysts were factoring in VYVANSE as a key drug for Shire (and in my models it was very significant), any commercial delay would probably result in a lowering of the target price for Shire, potentially resulting in a fall in the share price. Thus investors need to be aware of the general regulatory responses for drugs in a given therapeutic area.

It is also worth remembering that not all approvable letters are so benign. On 15 June 2007 Encysive Pharmaceuticals Inc. announced that the Company had received its third approvable letter from the FDA for Thelin(tm) (sitaxsentan sodium), which was under review for the treatment of pulmonary arterial hypertension (PAH).

In this third approvable letter, the FDA stated that Encysive's development programme for Thelin did not demonstrate the evidence of effectiveness needed for approval. The FDA did note, however, that the Thelin development programme provides some evidence that Thelin improves exercise tolerance in PAH. The FDA encouraged the Company to conduct an additional study to demonstrate the drug's effectiveness in exercise capacity as measured by the change in distance travelled during a six-minute walk.

This is what could be termed a very bad approvable letter. The stock fell over 50 % and ten days later the company announced that a new chief executive officer had been appointed and that the company would be restructured. Encysive continued to question the FDA regarding the approvable letter and on 5 September 2007, Encysive announced that the FDA's reviewer agreed with the decision of the Division of Cardiovascular and Renal Products that, while the data provided in the NDA are suggestive of the effectiveness of Thelin, it did not provide the substantial evidence of effectiveness needed for approval.

The Drug Label and Black Boxes

The period between receipt of an approvable letter and FDA approval itself can, however, take considerably longer. This may be because the FDA believes that further information is required, confirming safety or efficacy before launch. Alternatively, the delay may surround debate between the drug sponsor and the FDA on what should or should not be incorporated on the drug's label. A drug label represents the information that must be made available to consumers whenever that drug is dispensed (that is, that sheet of paper inside every drug packet that we throw away as soon as we've torn open the packaging). Importantly, the label details all the safety data, together with any specific marketing or superiority claims permitted by the FDA (in other words, claims made following clinical trials that demonstrate the drug's superior efficacy relative to other products). In certain instances, the FDA may require that the label emphasize potential drug side effects, i.e. a health warning is required. This might be by way of bold text or, in extreme cases (and typically if the drug can result in fatalities), the addition of a warning in a clearly visible black box. This is excitingly entitled a "black box" warning and clearly is not conducive to sales.

Some companies believe they can obtain a broad label claim based on the results of a study that did not show convincing efficacy and/or safety results for all aspects of the label claim. The drug label provides basic information about the drug ingredients, instructions for use and any important cautions and interactions. The term broad refers to the uses for the drug – the label is broad means that a large number of patients can take the drug for a given indication. It is narrow if there are a lot of restrictions defining particular subgroups of patients that can take the drug. For instance, the overall results of a study may be positive, but if the patients have been stratified by disease severity or age group, and only certain strata are responsible for the overall positive results, then regulators are unlikely to approve a broad label claim. Regulators are not prone to generalize results beyond the specific patient population tested and for which positive data have been obtained.

Some companies state that their drug is "different" and they can seek marketing approval based on a limited drug development programme, i.e. usually simply demonstrating equivalence to an existing marketed drug. Based on my experience, this is only true in a minority of cases. The number of companies that I hear of claiming this far exceeds the number of companies that, based on my experience, will actually be able to accomplish it.

Other Drug Submissions

Outside new drug applications (and the Investigational New Drugs discussed in the Research and Development section of this chapter) the FDA also frequently deals with two other types of drug application – supplemental new drug applications (sNDAs) and abbreviated new drug applications (ANDAs).

- ANDAs: an ANDA is the submission required for launch of a generic version of an exis approved drug. They are called abbreviated because they are not required to include data animal and human clinical studies. Rather, they must demonstrate that the generic drug is bioequivalent to the innovator drug. This means that the generic drug is chemically identical to the branded product and is absorbed by the patient in the same way, such that the blood concentrations of the two are identical.
- sNDAs: supplemental NDAs are those filed for drugs that are already approved, but for which a new/additional indication is being sought (for example, the use of the anti-depressant, Prozac, for treatment of pre-menstrual tension). Depending on the indication, the drug company may or may not be required to submit clinical data demonstrating efficacy in this additional indication, together with additional safety data. The time frame for approval is six months if clinical data is not required, or twelve if a review of clinical data is necessary.

Regulation in Europe

Until the mid-1990s, the medical committees of the different national European states determined regulatory approvals in European markets. Limited harmonization existed and approval of a single medicine across Europe was often time consuming and costly. However, in 1995 a new European system for the authorization of medicinal products came into operation with the foundation of the European Medicines Agency (EMEA). EMEA's main role is to coordinate and manage the drug approval system within Europe. The system evaluates any new product marketing application through either a Centralized Procedure, Mutual Recognition Procedure or National Authorisation Procedure. Biotechnology products have to be evaluated through the centralized procedure whereas new chemical entities (NCEs) can be evaluated through any of the routes although normally the centralised procedure is used. Approvals for generics and line extensions (additional indications) must go through the national regulatory bodies using an abridged procedure.

The EMEA comprises four bodies, one of which, the Committee for Proprietary Medicinal Products (CPMP), is responsible for formulating the EMEA's scientific opinion on marketing applications for human medicines. This regulatory committee is comprised of scientific experts in medicinal product evaluation who are invariably employees of national regulatory authorities and are given responsibility for issuing an opinion on whether a new drug may be marketed to the Board of the EMEA. The Board then reports to the European Commission which issues marketing authorization.

The Centralized Procedure

Under the centralized procedure a new drug sponsor submits its application direct to the EMEA. The application is presented at the next monthly meeting of the CPMP and two committee members (entitled Rapporteurs) are appointed to coordinate evaluation of the application. The national regulatory authorities of the appointed committee members then normally undertake evaluation. Once evaluation has been completed and reported to the CPMP, the CPMP will issue a scientific opinion regarding the product. This opinion is then conveyed to the European Commission, which is authorized to convert the opinion into marketing authorization valid through the entire European Union.

EMEA guidelines are that the entire process should take no longer than 300 days. The CPMP is obliged to issue an opinion within 210 days of receipt of an acceptable dossier. However, if questions are raised during evaluation that require additional information the clock stops until the questions are resolved. Post the CPMP issuing its opinion, the EC has an additional 90 days to convert the opinion into a final decision.

Overall, the CPMP has proven very efficient in evaluating new products. Between 1995 and 1998 the average time taken before issuing an opinion on all the biotechnology products reviewed was 174 days. However, the total timeframe can prove disappointingly long. As much as anything this is because the EMEA take an average of 40 days to transmit the CPMP opinion to the EC at which time EU member states are allowed to raise further questions. Thus for the 1995–98 period, while the time taken for the CPMP to issue an opinion was only 174 days, time to approval was actually 305 days. This timeframe also excludes "stop-clock" periods, which can be considerable.

Mutual Recognition Procedure (MRP)

Under the MRP system, an NDA is initially forwarded to one member state. If national authorization is granted in that state it allows for extension to one or more other member states. Under the MRP, the holder of the national authorization for which mutual recognition is sought may then submit an application to other member states certifying that the dossier is identical to the one for which first approval was granted (or explaining any differences). Within 90 days of receiving the application and assessment report, each member state must then decide whether to recognize approval. When such mutual recognition between member states is not possible, the EMEA will arbitrate and the EC issues a binding decision.

National Authorisation Procedure

The applicant submits an application to the competent authority in that country. In many ways the National Authorisation route is superseded by the Centralised and Mutual Recognition routes.

Pricing, Efficacy and Formularies

Subsequent to approval the sponsor must then enter negotiations with the relevant bodies over price and formulary inclusion. Time taken for this process can again be considerable. In addition, if the member state believes that the medicine does not offer value for money or a significant medicinal advantage, it need not approve its inclusion on formularies and may even recommend that physicians do not prescribe it. Thus for example, the UK's National Institute for Clinical Excellence (or NICE) recommended that Glaxo's flu treatment Relenza was neither included on formularies nor prescribed by physicians.

A drug is not permitted for sale until the marketing application for the new drug has been reviewed and approved by regulatory authorities such as

- Food and Drug Administration (FDA/US)
- European Agency for the Evaluation of Medicinal Products (EMEA/EU)
- Ministry of Health, Labour and Welfare (MHLW/Japan)

The Label

The label is important to the drug company as it determines which claims for the product can be made in marketing. Promotional claims cannot be made, unless they are included in the drug's label. The FDA controls the prescribing information of drugs, also known as the label. A drug's label contains a variety of information, summarizing its properties. This includes the results of clinical trials, usually the Phase 3 studies used in the approval. The label will detail the rates of adverse reactions in patients taking the product. It will also state the formal indications that the drug is approved for – hence the term "off-label use" to describe prescribing a drug in an indication where it lacks formal approval.

A drug's label is crucial to its success. The label represents the FDA's current thinking on the drug. A company can only legally advertise and promote what is on the label (or what data appears in peer reviewed trials). If the label contains a "black box" warning (highlighting that serious adverse events may be associated with use of drug and that the prescriber should use caution), drug sales people must highlight it every time they try and sell the product to a doctor. The advertising of drugs is also scrutinized by regulatory authorities to ensure that there are no false representations or claims for the drug.

Timelines for Approval

Various mechanisms exist to allow promising drugs to be prescribed prior to approval to those with serious or life-threatening diseases where no other therapy exists. Special regulations may also apply to drugs designed to treat HIV, which can be supplied for compassionate use. Products may also qualify for any of the first three procedures individually or may go through the fast track programme, which was established in the FDA Modernization Act, 1997 to streamline the entire process. Some samples of these are explained below:

- An expedited review allows drugs to be considered for approval at the end of Phase 2 and is intended for drugs treating life-threatening and severely debilitating illnesses, especially when no satisfactory alternatives exist.
- An accelerated review is used in similar situations to those above. It allows the use of surrogate markers as endpoints rather than having to show clinical benefit i.e. evidence that a drug improves a laboratory finding that is "considered likely to predict clinical benefit for the patient". The sponsor must continue to do post approval studies in order to demonstrate that clinical benefit does exist but the drug can be marketed in the meantime.
- A priority review is granted if the product would be a significant improvement compared to marketed products including non-drug products/therapies in the treatment, diagnosis or prevention of a disease. This procedure speeds up the time taken to review the NDA, from the 12-month target to six months.
- The fast track development programme consolidates all of the above schemes for any drug intended for the treatment of a serious or life-threatening condition and demonstrates the potential to address unmet medical needs for such a condition. It allows access to the three programmes above, and allows companies to submit individual portions of their NDA to the FDA in advance of the whole application (hence the term, rolling review) to enable any problems to be highlighted and addressed early.

Post Approval

After the drug has been approved and marketed, there is continuous monitoring of the safety and performance of the drug to ensure that it is prescribed correctly and adverse events are investigated. The FDA uses a system of post marketing surveillance (PMS) in order to monitor the risk–benefit ratio of drugs as used in the clinical setting. If significant side effects are discovered after a drug has been approved, the FDA is at liberty to alter a drugs label or take measures such as the inclusion of a "black box" warning for serious side effects in the label (prescribing information) or a letter warning doctors of potential side effects (known as a Dear Doctor letter).

INVESTMENT LESSONS

Investors tend to value the biotech company on their pipeline, so what can one take from the drug development process in order to help form an investment view?

- The overall portfolio of drug assets should be taken into account as firms inevitably have failures and thus a company with two drug assets is less risky than a company with one.
- Companies with products in the late stage of development are less risky (i.e. the drug has completed Phase 2).
- If investors are valuing the company on the basis of the pipeline assets, one must remember that commercialization (i.e. realization of cash flows) can be a very long way off. Refer to the data in this chapter regarding average phase timelines.
- Clinical trials can be very expensive to run as the data suggests. Use the average costs provided in this chapter to total up expected cash burn of the company and compare with its cash balance. If the trial for one drug asset is expected to cost $ 25 million and the company has $ 15 million on its balance sheet, how will the shortfall be managed?
- Is the compound likely to be partnered with another company and at what phase is this ideally planned for? Although partnering can be beneficial especially in terms of providing an endorsement of the drug and providing the opportunity to target large primary care markets, remember that the partner is taking a slice of the economics so that the NPV associated with the compound and available to the investor will decrease.
- Only in exceptional circumstances, will a Phase 1 compound be licensed so keep this in mind if out-licensing to an external partner is an integral part of the business model.

Case Study #1

Crohn's disease is a chronic inflammatory bowel disease that occurs in approximately 0.05 % of the US population. It usually occurs in the lower part of the small intestine, with an inflammation that extends deep into the lining of the affected organ. The diagnosis can be difficult because its symptoms are similar to other intestinal disorders such as irritable bowel syndrome. The disease results in continuous hyperstimulation and chronic inflammation of the bowel, which can be attributed in part to the increased production of pro-inflammatory cytokines (soluble mediators that aid in communication between cells, many of which are released during phases of host defence).

Advances in the knowledge of the biology of chronic inflammation has led to the development of specific biological therapies that mechanistically target individual inflammatory pathways. In July 2002, the US FDA granted marketing approval to remicade (infliximab) to provide long-term remission control. It was the first biologic approved to reduce the signs and symptoms and induce and maintain clinical remission in patients with moderate to severely active Crohn's disease who have had inadequate response to conventional therapy.

The importance of formulation in terms of assessing commercial potential can be seen from a research note written in 2005[17] on UCB, the Belgian biopharmaceutical company which bought Celltech, the UK biotechnology company which had developed Cimzia.

The research note stated that "Cimzia is dosed 400 mg monthly, given as two large bore injections simultaneously, each of 200 mg, subcutaneously. While the once-a-month dosing may offer an advantage over Humira (weekly or fortnightly dosing) and Remicade (bi-monthly iv infusions), Cimzia is not yet available in a pre-filled syringe (as is Humira). On the webcast, management were reticent to talk about support activities but stated that patients did not have problems with the administration. Although the number of injection site reactions was lower in the drug treated group compared to placebo we think that the rate will increase as the drug is used in the wider population." In 2006, the FDA also approved Humira[18] a biologic drug that works in a similar way to Cimzia. This increased the competitive landscape significantly.

In this paragraph one can see that at the time my colleagues and I were trying to assess the utility value of the less frequent dosing versus the additional effort involved with a lyophilized (in lay terms, freeze-dried) solution which could potentially offer administration benefits by making the solution less viscous. The analyst's preoccupation with formulation was also being driven by the market entry position in the indications. At the time it was thought that Cimzia might be the first non-infused (i.e. acute injection rather than infusion) biological therapy in Crohn's disease but was coming rather late to the rheumatoid arthritis market. Once first mover advantage is lost, additional differential attributes increase in importance in terms of the commercial potential.

It is not advisable to assume that one formulation injection will automatically be preferred by the patient. Literature studies suggest that in general, treatment by means of assisted IV infusions had higher compliance rates than self-administered subcutaneous injections.[19] In a survey that asked which route of administration for anti-TNF therapy was preferred by Canadian patients with RA[20], results indicated a preference for intravenous administration over a subcutaneous injection regimen. In this survey, factors for this preference included patients' general dislike of subcutaneous injections, pain and irritation at the injection site, more frequent administration of the subcutaneous injection administered drug, difficulty in handling secure medication containers, and the clinical assistance attendant on intravenous administration.

4

Biotechnology Company Valuation

We are now ready to start putting together our biotechnology company valuation. In previous chapters we have covered the drug development process to help us understand what technical hurdles biotechnology companies face as they develop their pipeline of drug assets and to facilitate our analysis we have collated historical statistics regarding the success rates of drugs in the various stages of development.

This clinical development process is crucial to overcoming these hurdles, and so in Chapter 3, I have provided an overview of the key issues that potential investors should address in trying to assess the quality or robustness of the clinical trial design. The previous chapter reviewed some of the more normal valuation metrics that can be used for estimating the value of a company. In this chapter, I will go through methods for evaluating biotechnology compounds and also discuss the use of conventional valuation metrics and when to use them and highlight some of the pitfalls.

I should make it clear that there is no obvious or accepted way of applying valuation in the biotechnology industry. The onerous regulatory hurdles and the inherent complexity of trying to understand how drugs will react within the physiology of the human body to address underlying pathology add further hurdles for the person trying to ascertain value. The diverse nature of biotech business models, the relative newness of the company, the lack of many tangible assets, the limited financial histories available and the spectacular growth forecasts make any such attempt demanding. These challenges make valuation a balance between quantitative and qualitative metrics but this in itself poses additional difficulties.

This level of uncertainty and the long development times have resulted in the use of some very spurious metrics such as the area of the laboratory space or the number of scientists employed. In this chapter, I will develop the financial concepts discussed in previous chapters and apply them to value a biotechnology company. In the first instance I will work up a valuation using the probability weighted NPV of the development pipeline, a tool that I recommend for initial assessments of valuation. Whilst this method lacks some of the financial rigour of the DCF approach, it is a useful tool for first assessments and variations on this method are used by many analysts. The calculations involved in this method essentially assume that the biotechnology company will mature and become similar to a pharmaceutical stock, which can then be valued using conventional metrics.

The next step will be a DCF of the whole company, highlighting some of the pitfalls when using this technique for loss-making companies, followed by a variation of this technique which looks at the individual cash flows arising from individual drug assets. Finally we will assess the use of relative valuation metrics in the case of biotechnology companies. In the next chapter we will build on our DCF framework and introduce decision trees and real options analysis.

As stated previously in this book, valuation is a combination of art and science and it is up to the investor or analyst to get the mix right! As I have stated in another chapter, the decision whether to invest in a company has a large component of subjective analysis (one should assess the quality of the management – and their ability to do deals – the potential of the company and the quality of the science and technology underpinning its business). Various valuation tools can be used to assess the potential, products and/or technology of a biotechnology company. There is no one correct way to value the sector, given the diversity of the companies under examination and the markets in which they operate.

Thus the subjective assessment of a company, especially an early-stage one, is just as important (if not more so) as the hard data points. The management team is a crucial component of a successful biotechnology company. Opportunities to meet a management team should not be rejected lightly as even if you have not got much to say, you can learn a lot by how well the management copes with various types of questions ranging in scope from the scientific to the commercial. Furthermore the credibility of the answers should be an important factor in your investment decision.

I believe that it was Warren Buffet who once stated that he did not invest in anything he did not understand. This is a very good point and one that should not be overlooked. Sure the science underpinning biotechnology companies may be complex and the disease processes that drugs seek to cure are not simple, but a company should be able to provide the average investor with an understanding of what the problem is and how they are trying to design a drug to address the failings of the body. More importantly they should be able to provide an assessment of the market opportunity, backed up by data on patient numbers, how they are treated currently and the cost of such treatment. Finally the management team should be able to highlight competitive threats, whether they are specific, such as other drugs in development, or vague, such as changes in re-imbursement that may negatively (or positively) impact the commercial decision.

Biotechnology by its very nature is technical but not overwhelmingly so. A common danger for both investors and analysts is to become overly fixated on the technology or drug in question. It is important that investors are able to step back and look at the company in terms of a sustainable model. Inevitably, there are issues and instances where a certain level of expertise will be required but in the main, biotechnology can be assessed by using common sense, i.e. does the business model make sense and can management deliver on its promises?

From the heady post genomic boom of early 2000, the biotechnology industry is facing up to the fact that it is just that, an industry, and must behave as such. The days of the irrational exuberance driven by exceptional expectations for the utility both practical and commercial of the genome project are over. The biotechnology industry must make money, for itself and for investors. In my opinion investors may be willing to pay for potential cash flows from companies with a history of delivery, on development and financial milestones. However the rose-tinted spectacles that were used to view the potential of biotechnology have been largely replaced by a set of reading glasses used to view the fine print of the risks instead.

In the broadest sense, therefore, the valuation of biotechnology companies should therefore be no different from the valuation of any other industry. In my view, the overriding principle should be that companies are worth the money that they are expected to make. Since most biotechnology companies are not profitable this poses a problem in terms of estimating the value. The figure below shows that only 23 biotechnology companies in the US were profitable in 2006, representing a mere 7 % of an estimated 329 public companies.

The problem with biotechnology firms in general, and new biotechnology firms in particular, is not that they lose money, have no history or have substantial intangible assets. It is that they make their initial public offerings far earlier in their life cycles than firms have in the past, and often have to be valued before they have an established market for their product. In fact, in some cases, the firms being valued have an interesting idea that could be commercial but has

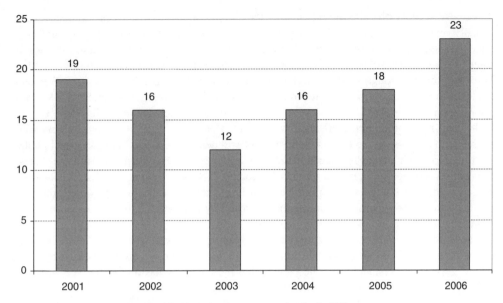

Figure 4.1   Number of profitable biotechnology companies in the US

not yet been tested. The problem is not a conceptual problem but one of estimation. Thus the true value lies in the potential of the company's science and technology base. The value of a firm is still the present value of the expected cash flows from its assets, but those cash flows are likely to be much more difficult to estimate.

No matter what a company's estimated fair value may be, the cycles of the past few years have shown that investors are prepared to apply significant discounts to stock prices as they (over) react to negative market sentiment and news flow from other, similar stocks. Just as in biotech boom time, when investors have been prepared to (over) pay for stocks, in bearish markets, stocks tend to get oversold.

Accordingly it is important to benchmark stocks against peer groups and against broader market indices. Benchmarking can yield not only interesting analyses of what stocks appear cheap and what stocks appear expensive, but also what level of discount or risk premium is being applied to similar companies, and similar business models on a global basis.

DATA COLLATION

However, before one dives off and opens the spreadsheet, there is important data collection to be completed. Most of the information can be obtained from the company web site and from regulatory filings (especially in North America where the data contained in the Securities and Exchange Commission (SEC) filings is very comprehensive).

The first task, in my view, is to learn the company history. In the biotechnology area, this means finding out when the company was started and by whom. It is very important to know if the current management contains the scientific founder and what their current role is. A stellar scientist may not be the best person to be CEO of a biotech company about to initiate a complex clinical development programme.

It is also very worthwhile to find out who the early financial backers of the company were (usually venture capital groups (VCs)) and to determine if they are locked in (not able to freely trade their shares). It can be informative to check the early-stage investors and to ask oneself some questions such as: are they experienced in the field and have they raised funds recently? This can provide a rough guide as to the "quality" of due diligence that was undertaken and the latter may indicate if additional funds are available if required. For example if a VC has not raised money in five years and is not experienced in life science investing, the VC may be looking for a quick exit from their investment. Remember VCs also have backers who also require a return on their investment. The lock-in defines the period post an initial public offering during which management and the early investors in the company may not sell shares. This period is typically six months but may be longer. It is also worth noting that if the market perceives that a VC may want to exit such an investment post the lock-in period, this can overhang the stock performance in the market resulting in relative underperformance of the shares.

Check information on issues that may positively or negatively impact upon the future value of the company. This can be hugely important for biotechnology companies as it requires one to have an understanding of the patents that the company has and at the very least an informed view as to whether the company has the freedom to operate in its chosen space. We view the intellectual property protection for a drug as a key priority. Composition of matter patents protect the drug "ingredients". These patents are generally regarded as the strongest protection for drug therapies. Despite the lack of composition of matter patents, formulation and method of use patents, while not as solid as composition of matter, could provide firm protection against competition.

Details of ongoing or pending lawsuits should be noted for further investigation. When valuing a firm, you draw on information from three sources.

1. *Current financial statements for the firm.* You use these to determine how profitable a firm's investments are or have been, how much it reinvests to generate future growth and for the inputs that are required in any valuation model. Or, in the case of the majority biotechnology companies, you are getting an estimate of how much money the company has raised in the past and how it has spent it.

2. *Past history of the firm*, both in terms of earnings and market prices. A firm's earnings and revenue history over time lets you make judgements on how cyclical a firm's business has been and how much growth it has shown, while a firm's price history can help you measure its risk. It can also be useful to check whether management met the milestones they set out (usually found in the full year results). Most companies produce a checklist of historic accomplishments as well as anticipated future milestones. The impact of achieving or missing these milestones can also be interpreted in terms of the stock price reaction.

3. *The firm's competitors or peer group* to get a measure of how much better or worse a firm is than its competition, and also to estimate key inputs on risk, growth and cash flows (or cash burn).

What makes technology firms, and especially new biotechnology firms, different? First, they usually have not been in existence for more than a year or two, leading to a very limited history. Second, their current financial statements reveal very little about the component of their assets – expected growth – which contributes the most to their value. Third, these firms often represent the first of their kind of business. In many cases, there are no competitors or peer group against which they can be measured. When valuing these firms, therefore, you may

Table 4.1   Useful web resources

www.BIO.org	Biotechnology Industry Organisation	US trade association promotes
		UK
www.BioIndustry.org	BioIndustry Association	biotechnology
www.phrma.org	Pharmaceutical Research and	US trade association
	Manufacturers of America	
www.Biospace.com	Biospace	news and features
www.signalsmag.com	Recombinant Capital	online magazine
www.sec.gov	Securities and Exchange Commission	public company filings
www.fda.gov	US Food and Drug Administration	regulatory news and updates
www.emea.europa.eu	European Medicines Agency	regulatory news and updates
www.uspto.gov	US Patent and Trademark Office	patent information

find yourself constrained on all three counts, when it comes to information. In the table below I have compiled a selection of web sites and resources that may be useful for garnering further information.

How have investors responded to this absence of information? Some have decided that these stocks cannot be valued and should not therefore be held in a portfolio. Their conservatism has cost them dearly as technology stocks have powered the overall markets to increasing highs. Others have argued that while these stocks cannot be valued with traditional models, the fault lies in the models. They have come up with new and inventive ways, based upon the limited information available, of justifying the prices paid for them.

Now is the time to start putting your new found knowledge to work. Many sell side analysts value the drug pipeline as a means of ascribing a value to the overall company. Whilst many aspects of this are factual there is an overwhelming sense of art used in performing this exercise. We will go into this in much more detail in the following chapters but here we will start to collate the basic data that is available to us as investors.

Let me introduce you to a typical biotech company, Blue Sky Therapeutics. It is a public company having listed in 2000. It has two compounds in Phase 3 trials ongoing, two Phase 2, two Phase 1 and four compounds in various stages of preclinical development.

As one prepares to take the first steps in biotech investing, a good place to start is the company's web site. Here one will find the corporate address, the management team, press releases, financial information and most importantly, the drug portfolio. In my experience most

Table 4.2   NPV valuation summary table

Drug name	Indication	Status
Asset 1	Indication 1	Phase 3
Asset 2	Indication 2	Phase 3
Asset 3	Indication 3	Phase 2
Asset 3	Indication 3	Phase 2
Asset 4	Indication 4	Phase 1
Asset 5	Indication 5	Phase 1
Asset 6	Indication 6	Pre-
Asset 7	Indication 7	Preclinical
Asset 8	Indication 8	Research
Asset 9	Indication 9	Research

companies have a page devoted to their drug development projects providing an overview of the name of the drug, the disease indication that it aims to treat and the current phase of development. This is when all the hard slog of the last chapter bears fruit!

Note that this is a stylized example although one should bear in mind that as one progresses through the development process, the number of assets drops off. I refer to the projects as drug assets because in the absence of cash flows (which is very typical of biotech investing and a topic we will discuss later) the majority of a company's current and prospective value comes from its drug pipeline.

The first step is to remove the research stage and preclinical assets. As I have discussed above, the development timelines are so long and the probabilities of success so low that it is not material to the valuation to include these assets at this stage. Most analysts will not evaluate the research and preclinical projects, irrespective of how much emphasis the company puts on them.

It is very difficult to get a sense of the drug's profile (termed the target product profile or TPP) until post the Phase 2 data. For example, a drug asset in preclinical studies today could reasonably be expected to launch in 2014, following seven years of clinical development. Assuming that it successful and sells at $ 1 billion dollars, and is commercialized through a royalty agreement (20 % of sales) then this asset's NPV would add to the company's NPV by $ 635 million today. However, that is assuming the drug is successful. By factoring in a standard attrition rate of 1 %, this NPV contribution drops to $ 6 million.

An additional $ 6 million might be significant, but we have also assumed sales of $ 1 billion, when 66 % of marketed drugs generate peak sales of less than $ 100 million,[1] suggesting optimism regarding the commercial potential. Since we do not know the drug's profile, it is prudent to assume average drug sales rather than "blockbuster" potential. Using this average figure for sales potential ($ 100 million), drops the NPV contribution to $ 1.6 million. To summarize, leave the preclinical compounds out of the analysis.

The next step is to add in additional columns to the NPV table. These additional headings are:

- Estimated launch date
- Partnering

The launch date will be used later to drive a monetary value for the drug assets. It may be disclosed in company web sites or press releases. Sometimes, a request to the investor relations person at the company will suffice. However one can use the typical drug timelines provided in the previous chapter to estimate the launch date based on the current phase of the drug. It is worth doing this exercise anyway, and if the company's estimate is different from your own calculation try and gauge why that is the case. It may be that the drug is in a niche indication and requires a smaller number of patients or it may be that the company lacks the finances to start a large trial ahead of some partnering discussions.

Alliances are very important for biotech companies and their investors. In the best alliances, the biotech company gains from the cash received (usually an upfront payment and additional milestone payments) as well as being a major contributor to the credibility of the programme. Thus partnerships and alliances give a strong endorsement of both the technology or drug asset as well as the commercial and business development potential of the management team. It may be worth adding in a column to the NPV table and noting details of the partner.

The table now looks like this:

Table 4.3   NPV valuation summary table 2

Drug name	Indication	Status	Launch	Partner
Asset 1	Indication 1	Phase 3	2009	Pharma X
Asset 2	Indication 2	Phase 3	2009	None
Asset 3	Indication 3	Phase 2	2011	None
Asset 3	Indication 3	Phase 2	2012	None
Asset 4	Indication 4	Phase 1	2015	None
Asset 5	Indication 5	Phase 1	2015	None

NPV OF THE PIPELINE

The majority of companies' financial projections will not lend themselves to conventional valuation methodologies until some distant date in the future, for the most part, because such companies are not forecast to make profits or positive cash flow in the near to medium term. In order to gauge the value of such stocks we calculate an NPV of the component parts of the business and sum these to yield a valuation. For the majority of companies, these component parts are therapeutic candidates, but for others it might be, or include, a royalty stream or valuation of intellectual property. This method assumes that over time biotechnology companies become more like pharmaceutical companies. I believe that this is a reasonable assumption, especially as forecast growth rates decline and drugs derived from biotechnology methods are not immune from patent erosion and biosimilar drugs[2] (see Appendix 2).

In summary, to calculate the probability weighted NPV of a compound, take a peak sales estimate (usually one can assume that this takes place five years after assumed launch, although one can choose any number) and then estimate how much net profit the biotech company obtains. The cash flow could be in the form of a royalty payment or direct sales.

Once the peak cash flow has been forecast, this number is probability weighted according to the likelihood of the compound reaching the target market. The probabilities that I have used are in the table below but they are not set in stone. Factors such as the compound history, target product profile, indication and development partner all influence the analysis. As one gets more experienced one can alter these probabilities slightly to reflect additional elements such as if a credible partner has signed up or the indication is notoriously difficult to treat (e.g. stroke). In the previous chapter I gave an overview of the different probabilities of success associated with the different clinical phases. In the table below I highlight the probabilities that I use in my own analysis. In my view it is not worth getting hung up about the variation in the probabilities of success associated with each phase but better to understand that clinical trials represent an objective measure of the progress of a drug from a research lead to a marketable product.

The probability weighted estimated peak earnings is then further discounted to the present year and then a multiple applied to yield the NPV. The P/E multiple is used because the net profit has been estimated on each compound. Summing these NPVs across drug assets yields the probability weighted NPV of the product portfolio (pNPV), and hence for a drug development-oriented organization, the company itself.

At first this may appear to you as random number generation. However let me assure you it is not. As one becomes experienced one can assess the potential market very quickly. A

Table 4.4   Summary of probabilities of success

Overall from P1							15 %
Overall from P2							25 %
Overall from P3							60 %
Overall from Approval							90 %

	MBC	DiMasi	CMR Self-originated	CMR In-licensed	Tang	Abrantes-Metz	Keegan
Phase 1		100 %				81 %	
Phase 2	60–82 %	71 %			80 %	58 %	
Phase 3	42–61 %	31 %			30 %	57 %	
Registration	65–88 %				80 %		
Approval	90–92 %						
Overall from P1	15–40 %	22 %	7 %	14 %		26 %	15 %
Overall from P2	25–49 %	22 %	12 %	20 %		33 %	25 %
Overall from P3	59–81 %	31 %	63 %	63 %		57 %	60 %
Overall from Approval	90–92 %		94 %	94 %			90 %

Sources: www.massbio.org
DiMasi, J.A., and Grabowski, H.G. (2007) The cost of biopharmaceutical R&D: is biotech different, *Managerial and Decision Economics* 28: 469–479.
Center for Medicines Research International 2006/2007 *Pharmaceutical Factbook*.
Tang, C.M. (2002) The essential biotech investment guide: how to invest in the healthcare biotechnology and life sciences sector. Mainland Press (Singapore).
Abrantes-Metz, R.M., Adams, C.P. and Metz, A.D. (2005) Pharmaceutical Development Phases: A Duration Analysis, *Journal of Pharmaceutical Finance, Economics & Policy* 14 (4): 19–37.

common misconception is that drugs make lots of money and indeed the media is full of examples regarding blockbuster drugs (drugs can sell >$ 1billion in a given year). However, the reality is rather different. According to an article,[3] of the 200 best selling prescription drugs in 2006, only 103 generated over a billion dollars (the hurdle most commonly used for a blockbuster). Furthermore although the top selling drug (Pfizers Lipitor) had enormous sales ($ 12 986 million in 2006), the next best seller (Plavix/Isocover) sold $ 6 345 million. An impressive number but it is significantly behind the number one drug. The 200th best selling drug in 2006 merely sells $ 384 million (GSK's Fraxiparine).

This leads to a cautionary fact: most drugs make less than $ 100 million in annual sales. In general, the management of biotechnology companies put a huge emphasis on the ability of their scientists to create value and too little thought goes into the ability of the company to capture the value created. The consequence of this is that the firms' ability to target an attractive market position is overestimated and the potential level of competition is underestimated.

Thus one should be very cautious about plugging in a large sales number. It is worth noting that the projections of new drug sales have almost always been too high. As a case in point, it is interesting to compare the actual sales of what were highlighted as future blockbusters in 2004.[4] Of the ten potential blockbusters, three are not on the market in early 2008 and of the remainder, only Avastin, Cymbalta, Spiriva and Zocor/Zetia are on track to meet or exceed expectations. The latter case is confounded by the fact that Zocor is off patent and the forecast was for both Zocor and Zetia.

Furthermore, as I have stated previously, it is almost impossible to assess a potential drug's profile (in order to do a competitive analysis) ahead of obtaining the Phase 2 data and thus rough estimates of commercial potential work fine.

Table 4.5 Future blockbusters fail to deliver

Product	Indication	Projected Peak Sales (US$m)	2006	2007	Launched
Avastin	Cancer	3000	1746	2296	2004
Exanta	Thrombosis	1300	Withdrawn 2006	n/a	2004
Alvesco	Asthma	1200	n/a	18	2004
Arcoxia	Osteoarthritis	2500	Not Approved	n/a	n/a
Caduet	Hypertension	1090	370	560	2004
Cymbalta	Depression	2200	1316	2102	2004
Zocor/Zetia	Cholesterol	3000	3203	3286	1992
Genasense	Malignant melanoma	900	Regulatory delay	n/a	n/a
Lyrica	Neuropathic pain	2000	353	564	2005

Source: Humphreys, A. (2004) Future Blockbusters, *MedAdNews*, January, 1–12 and company annual reports

The estimation of peak sales is difficult especially if the pipeline of drug assets is early. In my view one needs Phase 2 clinical development to have been completed before one can derive a target product profile and begin to assess the potential competitive profile of the drug. Most companies in their presentations will provide an estimate of market size, usually in US dollars. This is your first data point in estimating the sales potential.

However, many companies present the overall size of the market and do not give specific estimates of drug sales. In this case one has to estimate the penetration of the drug into that market. A neat way of overcoming these difficulties is to look at what sales are being achieved by drugs treating the indication today. It is a reasonable assumption that the drug asset one is evaluating could achieve the average peak sales of similar drugs on the market. Obviously it is more difficult if the drug is targeted at an indication where there is currently no therapy. As more data becomes available, then it becomes easier to assess the future commercial potential. Obviously subsequent entrants to a market tend to capture less market share so the drug in question needs to be better than current drugs on the market. However at this stage, a more detailed analysis is unwarranted.

One can build up a quick market model. The two ways that such estimates are obtained are bottom up (treatable population × estimated market penetration × annual cost per patient) or top down (total current market multiplied by estimated market penetration). There are a number of errors that can be easily avoided when trying to estimate the commercial potential of a yet to be developed pharmaceutical. I have tried to highlight some of these with respect to the various forecast inputs.[5] The bottom up approach is detailed below:

1. Determine the disease incidence/prevalence. This can be easily achieved for clearly defined diseases in markets where good epidemiological data exists but incidence is often under-estimated in less developed markets where measurement is less accurate or not performed at all. Generally try and use data from a wide variety of sources including the companies' own estimates in addition to published scientific papers. I suggest using PubMed to obtain estimates of epidemiology numbers.[6] One should be cautious when using patient numbers from disease advocacy groups as the likelihood is that they are inflated in order to draw the maximum attention possible to the disease.
2. Calculate the potential market size. The further down the drug development process, the easier it is to estimate the likely cost of the drug by comparing it with similar drugs, or drugs treating the same disease. Naturally pricing is more difficult to estimate when a company

is entering a new market with a new product, at least until the pharmacoeconomic benefits of the new drug become known. A further complication is that pricing will differ between markets (especially between the US and the rest of the world) but in this initial estimate, an average price will suffice. This treatment cost is usually given as an all in cost for a course of a drug or may refer to a price per day. Price estimates in the US can be obtained from the Medicare Part B Drug and Biological Average Sales Price Quarterly Payment files[7] or commercial suppliers such as the Red Book.[8] For European prices, I tend to use the US price and apply a discount of between 10 and 20 %.

3. The multiplication of patients taking the drug by the theoretical number of doses per treatment period (usually referred to as "days of therapy") yields the theoretical volume. For example, an antibiotic may be given for a short period, say ten days, but a chronic disease might require the patient to take the drug every day. However the major assumption underlying this is that patients always take the drug according to the labelling instructions. Compliance refers to a patient's behaviour in taking the prescribed dose per day. For chronic therapy regimens, the long duration also becomes an issue (i.e. patients continue on therapy and obtain timely refills). Data on these issues is hard to come by but my suggestion is that if one is using a "days of therapy" approach, be aware of these issues and make an allowance. In my experience there is never going to be 100 % compliance across a patient population but assuming a 60–80 % compliance ratio seems reasonable, especially for chronic medications. Thus if trying to forecast an expected 365 days per year, it may be better to forecast a lower number (e.g. 270) to take non-compliance into account.

4. The top down approach can be facilitated by using the sales figures in the tables below.

Table 4.6   Global sales forecast for brand name pharmaceuticals

Therapeutics class	2005a	2006	2007	2008	2009	2010	Annual Growth (%) 2000– 2005	Annual Growth (%) 2005– 2010
Diabetes	15 947	18 808	22 399	26 105	29 633	33 173	13	16
Vaccines	9575	11 994	13 718	15 756	18 001	19 564	19	15
Cancer	36 217	43 928	52 497	60 330	68 607	73 824	22	15
Inflammation	13 688	15 337	16 951	18 845	20 750	22 514	8	10
Dermatology	2651	2851	3357	3630	3938	4272	3	10
Metabolism/ endocrinology	6793	7242	7848	8427	9048	9456	14	7
Genitourinary	3892	3889	3927	4424	4908	5339	17	7
Hematology	11 177	11 549	12 515	12 976	13 577	14 506	12	5
Sexual Dysfunction	2876	3026	3302	3502	3634	3697	15	5
Immune System	4617	4927	5167	5516	5660	5690	14	4
Ophthalmic	3360	3618	3846	4028	4188	4059	17	4
CNS	59 874	65 275	68 460	70 279	68 032	70 134	12	3
Hormone Control	16 890	17 793	18 933	18 189	18 221	19 403	8	3
Cardiovascular	74 680	76 850	76 403	78 378	82 209	85 416	10	3
Respiratory	26 440	26 875	28 017	27 886	28 929	30 187	11	3
Gastrointestinal	19 142	19 481	20 694	21 279	21 279	20 994	4	2
Anti-infectives	40 927	39 910	40 294	41 293	40 712	41 707	6	0
TOTAL	**394 767**	**419 799**	**444 255**	**466 753**	**488 020**	**508 792**	**9.5**	**5.2**
Annual Growth (%)	**7**	**6**	**6**	**5**	**5**	**4**		

Source: ADIS information, 2006

Table 4.7 US sales forecast for brand name pharmaceuticals

Therapeutics class	2005a	2006	2007	2008	2009	2010	Annual growth (%) 2000–2005	Annual growth (%) 2005–2010
Diabetes	7372	9307	11 475	13 892	16 083	18 164	9	20
Vaccines	4047	5175	6090	7145	8380	9174	16	18
Cancer	17 797	21 908	25 978	29 699	33 893	35 984	18	15
Dermatology	1267	1316	1699	1907	2157	2428	−1	14
Inflammation	7961	8707	9417	10 761	12 196	13 462	6	11
Genitourinary	1497	1671	1597	1935	2203	2437	18	10
Immune System	1256	1304	1465	1652	1838	1965	6	9
Ophthalmic	1118	1347	1420	1510	1551	1630	10	8
Metabolism/ endocrinology	3076	3203	3475	3781	4116	4306	15	7
Sexual dysfunction	1392	1419	1584	1711	1778	1783	10	5
Hematology	6908	7006	7503	7930	8258	8797	9	5
Gastrointestinal	9575	10 073	10 686	11 237	11 320	11 386	2	4
CNS	35 604	39 864	41 697	42 210	39 370	40 724	10	3
Cardiovascular	34 420	35 472	33 944	35 317	37 733	40 005	9	3
Respiratory	14 397	14 213	14 896	14 327	14 893	15 563	12	2
Anti-infectives	16 690	15 695	16 245	16 549	15 905	16 846	3	0
Hormone control	8196	8768	9275	8230	8169	8861	4	2
TOTAL	**190 020**	**204 248**	**215 462**	**227 102**	**237 423**	**250 468**	**7.9**	**5.7**
Annual growth (%)	**5**	**7**	**5**	**5**	**5**	**5**		

Source: ADIS information, 2006

One can use these sales numbers to reality check with your own or the company's estimate of sales. Importantly, I do not include the cash per share in this analysis. Cash is irrelevant in valuing an ongoing biotechnology business because the likelihood of management giving it back to you is very remote. I believe that the net cash on the balance sheet should and will be used to drive the products through development. There is no guarantee that additional cash will be available from the equity markets. The fact that many biotech and internet companies trade at or below the value of their cash reserves reflects the fact that as they develop their businesses they burn cash, and there is an appreciable risk of them running out of cash before revenues flow. Cash can give an investor comfort as to how much life there is in a company ahead of the next financing, but it should be viewed as a tool that the company is expected to use by transforming it into value added technologies or pipeline advancements.

In addition, the companies that this method is most useful for tend to be loss-making. Thus I leave out the tax effect as most are many years from making sustainable profits and also have a level of tax loss write-offs to use. As a reminder this approach values the pipeline of drugs, not the company. Nonetheless if you want to include tax, it is easy to do and I would use the marginal rate of tax of the country in which the company is based. Putting the analysis together, it is best to start to estimate some sales for the drugs in the various indications and to estimate the NPV of the each drug asset before summing the NPVs to get a value of the firm.

However my approach to cash is one that has been developed for use as a sell side equity analyst where I have to provide a forecast price target for the stock 12 months hence. Not everyone needs to do this! The topic of whether to include the cash in the valuation is always contentious. In DCFs cash is included but (as I am valuing the firm) the pNPV only values the pipeline assets and does not take into account the cash burn explicitly required to develop the pipeline. However the market sometimes reflects my view and there are many examples of companies that trade below their level of cash per share. However the important point is not whether you include cash but that you are aware of its contribution to your estimate valuation.

Calculations

In order to complete the NPV analysis, some additional columns need to be included.

A full schematic layout is detailed in Table 4.8.

Working through the table, start with the assumptions which will be used to drive the calculations.

Assumptions

- NPV (in terms of local currency: GBp refers to UK stock listed in pence per share): estimated NPV per share in local currency obtained from the pNPV table;
- Current price as stated, although the convention is to use the mid price close from the previous day's trading
- Upside/downside as stated calculated using the formula "NPV per share/ current price – 1". For example, if the NPV is estimated to be 125p per share and the stock is trading at 100p per share,

$$125/100 - 1 = 25\,\%\,\text{upside}$$

- NoSH – number of shares outstanding. I have consistently used the weighted average number of shares outstanding. The amount of shares outstanding will often change in a company over the course of the year as the company may issue new shares or retire shares. The weighted average of outstanding shares is an important number as it is used to calculate key financial measures such as earnings per share for the time period.
- For example, if a company has 100 000 shares outstanding at the start of the year and issues an additional 100 000 midway through the year, this results in 200 000 outstanding at year end. The weighted average number of shares is calculated by taking the number of outstanding shares and multiplying the portion of the reporting period those shares covered. If at the end of the year the company reports earnings of £ 200 000, which amount of shares should be used to calculate EPS: 100 000 or 200 000? If the 200 000 shares were used, the EPS would be £ 1, and if 100 000 shares were used, the EPS would be £ 2. This potentially large range is the reason why a weighted average is used, as it ensures that financial calculations will be as accurate as possible in the event the amount of a company's shares changes over time. The earnings per share calculation for the year would then be calculated as earnings divided by the weighted average number of shares (£ 200 000/150 000), which is equal to £ 1.33 per share.
- Current market capitalization is the price per share multiplied by the number of shares outstanding.
- Implied market capitalization is the market capitalization implied if the price per share equalled the NPV per share.

Table 4.8 NPV summary table

Assumptions/Results

NPV (GBp)	**125**
Current price (GBp)	125
Upside (Downside)	(0 %)
NoSH	55.6
Current market	69.5
Implied market	69.5
Pharma PE	17.0x
Discount rate	15.0 %
Current year	2006

Cash per share

Cash (GBPm)	20.00
per share (p)	36

FX

US$ – GBP	1.80
C$ – GBP	2.10
US$ – C$	0.83

Notes:
1) Pharma PE – current year PE for global pharma
2) Discount rate is level of risk associated with entire portfolio

Drug name	Indication	Status	Estimated launch	Years to Launch	Years to Launch plus 5	Success?	Peak Sales (US$m)	Probability weighted Peak Sales (US$m)	Royalty Rate	Profitability	Probability weighted Peak Profit (US$m)	Discount Factor	NPV (GBp)
xxxxxxxxxxxxx	vvvvvvvvvvvvv	Phase ?	2009	3	8	25 %	150	37.5	15 %	100 %	5.63	3.06	31.2
xxxxxxxxxxxxx	vvvvvvvvvvvvv	Phase ?	2009	3	8	25 %	150	37.5	15 %	100 %	5.63	3.06	31.2
xxxxxxxxxxxxx	vvvvvvvvvvvvv	Phase ?	2009	3	8	25 %	150	37.5	15 %	100 %	5.63	3.06	31.2
xxxxxxxxxxxxx	vvvvvvvvvvvvv	Phase ?	2009	3	8	25 %	150	37.5	15 %	100 %	5.63	3.06	31.2
												Total	**125**

		Chance of success					
		20 %	25 %	30 %	35 %	40 %	45 %
Royalty rate	5.0 %	102	104	106	108	110	112
	7.5 %	106	109	112	116	119	122
	10.0 %	110	115	119	123	127	131
	12.5 %	115	120	125	130	135	141
	15.0 %	119	125	131	137	144	150
	17.5 %	123	130	137	145	152	159
	20.0 %	127	135	144	152	160	169
	22.5 %	131	141	150	159	169	178
	25.0 %	135	146	156	167	177	187

Source: Company data and CanaccordAdams estimates

- The Pharmaceutical P/E ratio. The multiple used is the typical P/E multiple applied to pharmaceutical companies. The use of this multiple is based on the assumption that the company will ultimately mature and resemble a pharmaceutical company. Furthermore, given that many biotechnology companies partner their drug assets, it seems reasonable to me to reflect the rating of the partner rather than the biotechnology company. The P/E is the ratio of the market value of a single share of stock divided by the total earnings for that share. So a P/E of 10 means that every $ 10 of stock returns a dollar of profit per year. According to Charles Schwab Company, the historic average P/E ratio for all the Fortune 500 companies is around 16 and, of course, varies with the economy. Blue chip stocks, the shares of those industries like car manufacturers or utilities companies, tend to have smaller P/E ratios – under 10. The low number reflects the fact that these industries are established as long-term, secure earners but offer limited growth potential. The P/E of growth industries, like those in the health sector, tends to be larger. The market average for major pharmaceutical companies is around 16.5, according to BioCentury[9] and the average pharmaceutical P/E has hovered at 16–17 over the last two years. Profitable biotech companies tend to be even higher, reaching 27.7 at the end of Q2, 2007. This multiple is considerably lower than what profitable biotechnology companies were trading on a few years ago. In 2001, the P/E average for the largest biotechnology companies reached nearly 50×. Small publicly traded biotechnology companies can be higher still. The high P/E ratio of pharmaceutical companies and biotechnology companies means that the earnings per share are low with respect to the cost of the stock, but, more importantly, that investors have high expectations for the companies to show significant growth and yield large profits in the future.
- Discount rate. Insert the discount rate you feel comfortable with. I use 15 % consistently as a standard and provide a sensitivity analysis to reflect other views. If one looks at analyst's reports a wide range of discount rates can be observed ranging from 10 to 40 %! Sometimes the estimated cost of capital for the company is used as the discount rate. I prefer to keep the cost of capital for valuation of the whole company and use a discount rate suitable for projects. Several surveys have been performed of the hurdle rates used by US pharmaceutical companies. A general finding is that hurdle rates for US companies are typically greater than the weighted average cost of capital computed by CAPM analysis.[10] An informal study of six pharmaceutical companies in mid 2001 was undertaken with respect to the hurdle rates that drug firms utilize in their R&D investment decisions. The survey yielded nominal hurdle rates from 13.5 % to over 20 %. If one takes 3 % as the long run expected rate of inflation then a 12 % real rate of return corresponds to a nominal rate of 15 %. This rate is within the range of hurdle rates utilized by the pharmaceutical firms but is at the lower end of the range. This is consistent with the view that a CAPM analysis provides conservative estimates on the industry's cost of capital.[11]
- Current year as stated

In the NPV table we have already filled in the details of the drug asset, the proposed indication, the stage of development and an estimated launch year. One should also have assigned a probability of success to the drug based on its clinical phase and incorporating other factors such as partnerships etc.

To facilitate the calculations it is worth inserting two columns in between "estimated launch" and "success?" in the excel spreadsheet.

1. Years to launch. The cells of this column calculate the number of years to launch by subtracting "current year" in the assumptions box from "estimated launch" in the table.

2. Years to launch plus five. One can choose any year to estimate peak sales. However looking at data from the expected life cycle sales profiles of new drugs in the 1988–1992 period shows that the five-year estimate is close for the second decile, the median and the mean drug compounds.[12]
3. For drugs in the first decile, the peak occurs around year 10.

The worked example in Table 4.9 and Table 4.10 shows which formulas are in which cells.

Royalty Rates

A frequent feature of early-stage biotech companies is that they partner with pharmaceutical companies (and indeed larger biotech companies). In my view, biotech companies enter into alliances for many reasons, including accessing another firms' technology, external signalling, generating cash and risk sharing. In terms of valuing early-stage biotech companies, it has been demonstrated that third parties (companies and investors) rely on the prominence of the affiliates of those companies to judge the quality. The evidence suggests that privately held biotech firms with prominent strategic alliance partners and equity investors benefit from the transfer of status from those entities by going public faster and at higher valuations than do firms that lack such partnerships.[13] The existence of a partnership can be reflected in the probability of success that one attaches to a drug asset, depending of course upon who the partner is and the level of expertise associated with the partner. For example, a global partnership with a large pharmaceutical company that has extensive marketing experience in a particular indication or disease area is viewed more positively than a deal with a small regional marketing player who is relatively unknown. There are of course exceptions when the regional player is an expert in a therapeutic specialty but in general the bigger and more well-known the partner, the better for the biotech company. Table 4.11 details some typical biotechnology deals for a given stage of drug development.

One should note that there is a tendency for biotech companies to highlight the largest deal value possible when announcing a licensing deal. "Bioworld dollars" is a term often used to describe these sums. It is not that the value alluded to is untrue, it is just that the agreement needs to work absolutely perfectly (meeting and possibly exceeding all technical and commercial expectations) and possibly including indications that are merely options at the current time. It is almost impossible to get management to disclose details of these deals. In such an imperfect world, analysts' reports are probably the best source for gauging the scope of the deal terms.

I have been asked what is the appropriate discount rate to use when attempting to find the NPV of an anticipated royalty stream? In my view, a discount rate equal to the licensor's own cost of capital is appropriate if the riskiness of that income stream is comparable to the risk the company encounters in its normal business.

Some biotechnology companies also have significant patent estates which provide them with a significant revenue stream. For example Serono (acquired by Merck KGaA in 2006): historically Serono had a significant royalty stream which accounted for 9–13 % of revenues as shown in Table 4.12.

Serono also had to pay out royalties to third parties although this cash outflow was accounted for in a different manner. This is called royalty stacking. The concept of royalty stacking arises from the risk that multiple patents may affect a single product. Royalty stacking arises when, in order to take a product to market, the developer of the product takes licences from all the

Table 4.9 Screenshot of pNPV table in Excel

Company Name

Assumptions / Results

NPV (US$)	**16.38**
Current price (US	10.00
Upside (Down	**64%**
NoSH	50.0
Current market ca	500.0
Implied market cap	818.3
Pharma PE	17.0x
Discount rate	15.0%
Current year	2008

Drug name	States	Estimated launch	Years to Launch	Years to Launch plus 5	Success?	Peak Sales (US$m)	Probability weighted Peak Sales (US$m)	Royalty Rate	Profitability	Probability weighted Peak Profit (US$m)	Discount Factor	NPV (US$)
Drug 1	Phase 3	2010	2	7	60%	500	300.0	15%	100%	45.00	2.66	5.75
Drug 1	Phase 3	2010	2	7	40%	750	300.0	100%	20%	60.00	2.66	7.67
Drug 1	Phase 2	2012	4	9	25%	500	125.0	15%	100%	18.75	3.52	1.81
Drug 1	Phase 2	2013	5	10	25%	250	62.5	15%	100%	9.38	4.05	0.79
Drug 1	Phase 1	2015	7	12	15%	250	37.5	15%	100%	5.63	5.35	0.36
											Total	**16.38**

Source: Company data and Canaccord Capital estimates

Inputs are in blue
Calculations are in black

Table 4.10   Screenshot of pNPV table in Excel with underlying formula

| | | L7 | | f_x | | | | | | | | | | |
| A | B | C | D | E | F | G | H | I | J | K | L | M | N | O |

Company Name

Assumptions / Results

NPV (US$)	**16.38**
Current price (US	10.00
Upside (Down	64%
NoSH	50.0
Current market ca	500.0
Implied market ca	818.3
Pharma PE	17.0x
Discount rate	15.0%
Current year	2008

=D20-$C$15

=E20+5

=H20*G20

=(($C$13/M20*L20))

I20*J20*K20

=EXP((LN(1+$C$14)*F20))

Drug name	Status	Estimated launch	Years to launch	Years to launch plus 5	Success?	Peak Sales (US$m)	Probability weighted Peak Sales (US$m)	Royalty Rate	Profitability	Probability weighted Peak Profit (US$m)	Discount Factor	NPV (US$)
Drug 1	Phase 3	2010	2	7	60%	500	300.0	15%	100%	45.00	2.66	5.75
Drug 1	Phase 3	2010	2	7	40%	750	300.0	100%	20%	60.00	2.66	7.67
Drug 1	Phase 2	2012	4	9	25%	500	125.0	15%	100%	18.75	3.52	1.81
Drug 1	Phase 2	2013	5	10	25%	250	62.5	15%	100%	3.38	4.05	0.79
Drug 1	Phase 1	2015	7	12	15%	250	37.5	15%	100%	5.63	5.35	0.36
											Total	**16.38**

Source: Company data and Canaccord Capital estimates

Table 4.11   Typical biotechnology deal terms according to phase of compound

Biotech Deals	Upfront ($m)	Milestones ($m)	Royalty (%)
Preclinical	2	15	7
Phase 1	5	25	10
Phase 2	10	35	20
Phase 3	15	50	25

owners of patents that affect the final product. When the royalty payments are combined, the licensee may find itself with an unprofitable product.

Thus the royalty received should be the net royalty, i.e. after any third parties have been paid. This simplifies the analysis because one can assume that the individual royalty stream has 100 % margin and hits the bottom line.

Profitability

As of 31 December 2006, the two largest biotech companies, Amgen and Genentech, had operating margins of 27 % and 34 % respectively and net margins of 21 % and 23 %. Note that these are the margins for the entire company and thus the margins associated with individual drugs should be higher. In practice I generally use a margin of between 20 % and 60 % depending on what I can learn about other factors such as:

• Pricing power in the market
• Cost of goods (especially important for biological drugs)

Sensitivity Analyses

Predicting the future is difficult so it is important to perform sensitivity analyses on the key variables. Sensitivity analysis allows one to anticipate how changing assumptions underlying one parameter can affect the overall valuation. Thus one can drive a reasonable range of valuations rather than one specific number.

When using the above probability weighted NPV approach, it is very useful to use data tables to sensitize around key variables. The following pNPV table is one that I used for the valuation of Cambridge Antibody Technology, prior to its acquisition by AstraZeneca in June 2006 (Table 4.13). Performing such analyses can seem daunting given the number of inputs but valuations typically have 2–4 key variables that significantly drive (or destroy) value. Using

Table 4.12   Serono's royalties contributed significantly to revenues

	2003	2004	2005
Sales	1858	2178	2339
Royalty income	161	280	248
Total revenues	2019	2458	2587
Royalty %	9 %	13 %	11 %
Royalty expense	−29	−38	−43

Source: Company accounts and Annual Reports

Table 4.13 Probability NPV table for Cambridge Antibody Technology

CAT

Assumptions/Results

Total NPV (p)	**130**
Number of shares (m)	52.7
Pharma PE	17.0x
Discount rate	15 %
Current year	2006

Product Development

Drug name	Generic Name	Indication	Status	Estimated launch	Years to Launch	Years to Launch plus 5	Success?	Peak Sales (GBPm)	Royalty Rate	Profitability	NPV (GBp)
ABT-874 (Abbott)	anti-IL-12	Crohn's	Phase 3	2009	3	8	50 %	200.0	2.84 %	100 %	29.9
ABT-874 (Abbott)	anti-IL-12	Multiple sclerosis	Phase 2	2010	4	9	30 %	285.7	2.84 %	100 %	22.3
ABT-874 (Abbott)	anti-IL-12	Psoriasis	–	2011	5	10	10 %	142.9	2.84 %	100 %	3.2
LymphoStat-B (HGSI)	anti-BLyS	SLE	Phase 2	2009	3	8	20 %	85.7	3.08 %	100 %	5.6
LymphoStat-B (HGSI)	anti-BLyS	RA	Phase 2	2008	2	7	40 %	285.7	3.08 %	100 %	42.7
HGS-ETR1 (HGSI)	anti-TRAIL-1	solid tumours	Phase 2	2009	3	8	25 %	285.7	3.08 %	100 %	23.2
MYO-029	anti-GDF-8	Muscular dystrophy	Phase 1/2	2010	4	9	10 %	85.7	3.08 %	100 %	2.4
CAT-3888	anti-CD22	Refractory HCL	Phase 2	2010	4	9	10 %	1.7	25.0 %	90 %	0.4
CAT-8015	anti-CD22	NHL & CLL	PC	2012	6	11	0 %	285.7	15.0 %	90 %	0.0
											129.7

Source: Company data

Figure 4.2 Building a sensitivity table (1)

the sensitivity analysis can highlight what these variables are and their associated impact. One can then decide if the uncertainty on one variable is so important that additional work on this topic may be required.

It is worth noting that the sales are in pounds sterling and that the NPV of the drug assets are converted to a per share value. At first the pipeline looks full and one may be wondering how does one sensitize around such a huge array of variables? The first step is to look at the obvious key drivers of the valuation, the discount rate and the multiple. We have already seen that choosing the appropriate discount rate can be fraught with problems. So it is worth doing a sensitivity analysis.

Start by typing the valuation into a new cell (= B5) and this new cell should now read 130. Select this cell and highlight a number of cells across and down. The number of rows and columns chosen does not really matter but five or six is usually fine (Figure 4.2). The number chosen only reflects the number of discrete values one wants to use in the sensitivity.

Keeping the cells highlighted as above, use the DATA, TABLE command from the menu in Excel. A dialogue box similar to the one below should appear (Figure 4.3).

Choose then which variables one wants to run a sensitivity analysis on. In this case it is the discount rate and the multiple. Therefore in the dialogue box, input the cells which contain those variables and click OK (Figure 4.4).

Going across from the cell containing "130", add in the value that you think is a viable range for the value of the Pharma PE and likewise, in the cells beneath the "130" add in a range of discount rates. The table should look like the one in Table 4.14.

Tidying the table up, one can obtain an easily understandable sense of the valuation sensitivity to both P/E and discount rate used. The range of valuations provided goes from a low of 66p per share to a high of 192p per share (Table 4.15).

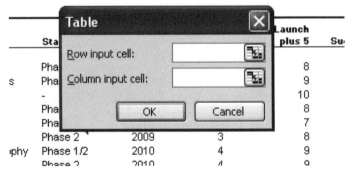

Figure 4.3 Building a sensitivity table (2)

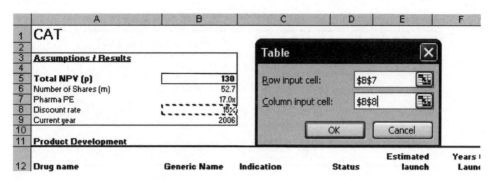

Figure 4.4 Building a sensitivity table (3)

Experience can help narrow these potential ranges. The data provided on P/E suggest that it is unlikely that the Pharma P/E will significantly appreciate and is also unlikely in the near term to fall to as low as 10×. Thus a narrower band of 15–17× seems appropriate. In terms of the discount rate, it is more difficult to determine for a loss-making company, Cambridge Antibody Technology was unlikely to have a cost of capital in the 10–11 % range. Thus 13 % would be the lowest discount rate I would use. The cap at the high end of the discount rate is harder to assess as it depends upon the individual's appetite for risk. However, given that the individual drug programmes are probability weighted, the use of 19 %+ discount rates seems harsh. Even so, using these simple assumptions, the broad range of valuations has been curtailed dramatically to a more narrow range of 87–149p (Table 4.16).

This analysis also tells us that our current valuation of 130p per share has more potential downside than upside when viewed as a function of these parameters. The next step is to look at the pipeline. In the table in Table 4.17 I have detailed the projects but also calculated their percentage contribution to the valuation.

Table 4.14 Building a sensitivity table (4)

130	13	15	17	19
11 %	131	152	172	192
13 %	114	132	149	167
15 %	99	114	130	145
17 %	87	100	113	126
19 %	76	87	99	111
21 %	66	77	87	97

Table 4.15 Sensitivity analysis flexing the discount rate and the multiple

		Pharmaceutical multiple			
		13	15	17	19
	11 %	131	152	172	192
	13 %	114	132	149	167
Discount rate	15 %	99	114	**130**	145
	17 %	87	100	113	126
	19 %	76	87	99	111
	21 %	66	77	87	97

Table 4.16   Sensitivity analysis can help narrow the probable range of valuation

		Pharmaceutical multiple			
		13	15	17	19
	11 %	131	152	172	192
	13 %	114	132	149	167
Discount rate	15 %	99	114	**130**	145
	17 %	87	100	113	126
	19 %	76	87	99	111
	21 %	66	77	87	97

Although there are a number of different indications, the value appears to be driven by three drug assets, namely:

1. ABT-874, comprising 43 % of the valuation
2. LymphoStat B comprising 37 % of the valuation
3. HGS-ETR1 comprising 18 % of the valuation.

Given their significant contribution, it is worthwhile assessing these drug assets in more detail. It should be obvious that one can sensitize these tables ad infinitum and that some judgement needs to be exercised. As an example I shall highlight a number of analyses concerning the lead drug in the pipeline, ABT-874 and the leading indication, Crohn's disease.

In Table 4.18 I have assessed the impact of launch year and level of peak sales of ABT-874 in Crohn's disease on the current valuation of 130p per share. As one moves the launch year forward or back, the impact appears to be about 4p per share. In this manner, all other parameters are maintained constant. One can extend the analysis across multiple parameters using another Excel tool function called pivot tables but since this pNPV analysis is supposed to be a relatively quick and easy way to assess a company's pipeline, I think that the risk of doing so confuses the issue rather than simplifying it. As one might have guessed beforehand, changing the peak sales estimate by £ 100m changes our valuation by 15p/share.

As the peak sales input is obviously a key driver, I have flexed the years to peak sales and the probability of success of the drug reaching the market (Table 4.19). Both have an impact

Table 4.17   Percentage contributions of pipeline assets to overall valuation

Drug asset	pNPV	%
ABT-874 (Abbott)	29.9	23 %
ABT-874 (Abbott)	22.3	17 %
ABT-874 (Abbott)	3.2	2 %
LymphoStat-B (HGSI)	5.6	4 %
LymphoStat-B (HGSI)	42.7	33 %
HGS-ETR1 (HGSI)	23.2	18 %
MYO-029	2.4	2 %
CAT-3888	0.4	0 %
CAT-8015	0.0	0 %
	129.7	100 %

Table 4.18   Sensitivity analysis flexing the launch year and peak sales of ABT-874

		Launch Year		
		2008	2009	2010
	100	117	115	113
	200	134	130	126
Peak sales	300	151	145	139
	400	169	160	152
	500	186	175	165
	600	203	190	178

Table 4.19   Sensitivity analysis flexing the peak sales and years to peak sales of ABT-874

		Years to Peak		
		6	8	10
	100	120	115	111
	200	139	130	122
Peak sales	300	159	145	134
	400	179	160	145
	500	199	175	156
	600	219	190	168

Table 4.20   Sensitivity analysis flexing the peak sales and probability of success of ABT-874

		Probability of Success		
		50 %	60 %	70 %
	100	115	118	121
	200	130	136	142
Peak sales	300	145	154	163
	400	160	172	184
	500	175	190	205
	600	190	208	226

but in my view, it is the years to peak sales that may need additional attention in the valuation. Note that if one decides to lengthen the time to peak sales (say to 10 years as a reflection of Grabowski's work referenced earlier), the peak sales need to almost double before the valuation estimate exceeds our original estimate by 10 %.

Likewise with the probability of success (Table 4.20). One may decide that the 50 % chance is too low and that the compound in question is typical of a drug for gastro-intestinal indications and thus move its chance of success to 60 %.

I hope that I have demonstrated a relatively easy way of getting a valuation range for a company which is depending upon its developmental drug assets for its valuation. Of course there are shortcuts in the method and some may argue that it is not quite robust in terms of financial theory. I agree with this view but I also contend that it is useful to do the equivalent of a "back of the envelope" calculation before expending a lot of time and resources working on a comprehensive model. The pNPV approach also has the advantage of highlighting areas that you, as the one trying to ascribe value, may want to focus on. Over the past 11 years I have found the method to be very useful, especially when I make notes of the assumptions underlying my inputs. The method is also reasonably useful at guiding one's assessment of how a change (positive or negative) will impact a stock. For example, if the company announces that one of its assets has successfully finished Phase 2 clinical trials and that Phase 3 will start before the year end. What potential valuation impact could its announcement have on the stock? This approach can let one make those changes and flex them very rapidly. In the Appendix at the end of this chapter I have included some real examples to highlight this (see Example 1).

DCF OF WHOLE COMPANY

The market-based valuation of a company can be divided into two parts, value from existing business and value of growth opportunities. The purpose of DCF valuation is to determine the value of a company in terms of its future cash flows. However it can be difficult to put a value on a biotechnology company that offers little more than an escalating cash burn and the promise of success in the future. So, despite the robustness of the DCF concept, it can prove difficult to implement in high uncertainty environments. As with the pNPV approach, it is best to ignore drugs that are in the preclinical stages of development.

In essence the DCF calculation for biotech companies is the summation of an expected positive future cash flow from drug sales and a negative cash flow from drug development and is discounted using a weighted cost of capital (WACC). If one is valuing an asset, a discount rate consistent with the level of risk associated with the asset should be used. As the amount of data has increased and the key risk drivers become more estimable, discount rates can now be chosen more reasonably but they are still arbitrary; thus traditional DCF remains an unreliable measure of biotech value.

Realizing that this is too simple and a very unrealistic approach, some investors and biotech companies adjust the NPV with the accumulated expected success rates of the stages in the R&D phase. The resulting expected NPV (ENPV) or risk adjusted net present value (rNPV) is a more realistic valuation,[14] although it is still merely a downwards adjustment of the calculated NPV, albeit a nonlinear one. The probability adjusted DCF allows one to calculate the value of the assets that underpin biotechnology companies.[15] The flexibility that was incorporated into the pipeline NPV table is also easily incorporated into this approach, allowing one to determine the potential effect that a significant event may have on a stock. Although the valuation derived from DCF valuations may be full of simplifications, the mere fact that one can model the cash flows can achieve important insights into the value drivers of the company.

Thus the steps involved are similar to constructing a DCF for any company. However as with the pNPV model forecasting the revenues (or drug sales across the life cycle) can be a very difficult process. Depending upon the available information and the time needed for a steady revenue flow, a forecast period of 5 to 10 years is most commonly used.

According to Ekelund,[16] the DCF approach would be appropriate if there were no uncertainties and a minimum of risk. However in the realm of biotechnology a high level of technical (success rates), regulatory and commercial hurdles contribute to a high degree of uncertainty. Indeed the biggest complaint about DCF is that it does not capture the uncertainty and flexibility inherent in R&D programmes.

In order to perform a DCF analysis, the key data inputs concern the cash flows, terminal value and applicable discount rate. For companies that are still pre-revenue generating, a lot of the near term cash flows will be outflows associated with the cost of running the company, especially the clinical trials. As I have highlighted previously there is a relatively large amount of data on the success rates of drugs in clinical trials. Biologic drugs have a slightly higher chance (a few percentage points) of reaching the market than have traditional small molecules,[17] although the cost of manufacturing biologics is significantly higher. Biologics require extremely sophisticated manufacturing techniques. Biologics manufacturers must programme a living source to mass-produce a specific biological material. In contrast, traditional pharmaceutical drugs are "small molecule" compounds that are chemically synthesized, and usually consist of pure chemical substances. They are easier to manufacture, and they are also easier to analyse after they are manufactured. Cell culture facilities require sizeable capital and labour investment, taking, on average, three to five years to construct and costing $ 250–$ 450 million. Investment in manufacturing plants must often be made before drugs enter clinical testing. Cost of materials is also high; in 2002 these materials cost twenty to one hundred times more than those used for small molecule drugs.[18]

However as in the pNPV table, one can choose a probability of success. Note that one should use the probability of moving into the next phase. Thus only the current cash flows, notably the expenditure on the current clinical trials, are certain. Using the data on clinical trial costs, one can estimate the costs of each trial. Note that all cash flows both inflows and outflows are adjusted by the likelihood of their occurrence.

The discount rate is, as ever, difficult to derive. However as for conventional companies, one can use the Capital Asset Pricing Model (CAPM[19]) to derive a discount rate.[20,21] According to CAPM, and as discussed previously, the firm's cost of capital is a weighted average of its cost of capital on its debt and equity capital. Given the low debt values of large pharmaceutical firms, the equity cost of capital becomes the key factor driving the weighted cost of capital. In the case of biotech firms the debt component is negligible, given that the long-term debt after 1990 is less than 1 % of the market capitalization. Thus for biotech companies the equity cost of capital is equivalent to their weighted cost of capital. The difficulty that this poses in terms of valuation is that the cost of debt is relatively transparent whereas estimating the cost of equity can be more challenging.

The cost of equity (k_E) can then be calculated as follows using the CAPM. For other methods aside from the CAPM (for example APV) see general finance books:[22]

$$k_E = r_f + \beta(r_m - r_f)$$

r_f = risk-free rate
β = measure of the relative riskiness of a specific stock. In general financial theory associates a higher beta with higher risk and reward
r_m = long-term rate of return for a market basket of stock

One needs to be aware of the challenge posed by the use of the CAPM and in particular the components that yield the cost of equity. For example, the beta used should ideally be forward looking but it is not possible to reliably estimate this. The most important caveat regarding the use of beta, in my view, is that judgement needs to be exercised. For example a common mistake is to look at the values of beta (obtained from Bloomberg and shown in Table 4.21) and assume that one company is riskier than another.

Table 4.21   Betas for a selection of pharmaceutical and biotechnology stocks

	NBI	FTSE100	MSCI World
GSK	0.471	0.631	0.532
Astra Zeneca	0.599	0.92	0.834
Sanofi	0.628	0.754	0.751
Roche	0.515	0.627	0.568
Novartis	0.522	0.658	0.596
Actelion	0.66	0.87	0.993
Arpida	0.826	0.898	1.048
Basilea	0.783	0.949	1.059
Plethora	0.491	0.371	0.517
UCB	0.469	0.548	0.551
YM Biosciences	0.978	1.23	1.062
Ondine Biopharma	0.526	0.67	0.674
Genmab	0.732	1.165	1.191
Vectura	0.487	0.719	0.853
Merck KGaA	0.711	0.79	0.796
Shire	0.722	0.84	0.78
MMI	0.883	0.902	0.916

Source: Bloomberg

Three values of beta are given, one relative to the NBI (Nasdaq Biotechnology Index), another relative to the FTSE100 and the third relative to the MSCI world index.[23] It is hard to imagine that investors view these stocks as differing significantly in their risk profile. GlaxoSmithKline and AstraZeneca are so different based purely on their betas (GSK 8.7 %; AZN 10.5 % assuming a risk free rate of 5 % and a market premium of 5 %). This also highlights that the beta measures the relative risk of an asset and thus values of beta are standardized around one. In financial theory the beta is defined as measuring the risk added on to a diversified portfolio (or market portfolio) but it is difficult to obtain a global financial index that reflects the market portfolio. Thus in the example above, the beta derived from comparing the stock relative to the NBI is probably less robust than comparing relative to the FTSE100, a more diversified index. The choice of which can significantly alter the value of the beta. My suggestion is to use the index as determined by who the marginal investor in the firm is. If you would like to compute the beta yourself, you can estimate it by regressing the stock returns against the returns on an index representing the market portfolio over a reasonable time period, at least two years. A high level of judgement is required!

A sensible check is to find publicly traded comparable companies and estimate their expected return on equity as if they were 100 % equity financed. For biotechnology companies this should be straightforward as the majority are debt-free. However if the comparable companies chosen have debt, one can unlever the equity beta of each comparable using the formula to get the all equity or asset beta (β_A):

$$\beta_A = \beta_E E/E + D + \beta_D D/E + D$$

Note that market values should be used but if a market value of debt is not readily available, use the book value in the balance sheet. Debt beta is typically low for healthy, low debt firms

Table 4.22   Cost of capital for biotech companies in the period 1989–2004

	1989	1994	2000	2004
Nominal cost of capital	19.0 %	17.0 %	15.0 %	13.0 %
Inflation	5.0 %	4.5 %	3.0 %	3.0 %
Real cost of capital	14.0 %	12.5 %	12.0 %	10.0 %

Source: Dimasi, J.A., and Grabowski, H.G. (2007), The cost of biopharmaceutical R&D: is biotech different, *Managerial and Decision Economics* 28: 469–479

but rises with increasing leverage. The debt beta can be calculated from the formula

$$k_D = r_f + \beta_d(r_m - r_f)$$

k_D = cost of debt
r_f = risk-free rate
β_d = debt beta: a measure of the risk of a firm defaulting on its debt
r_m = long-term rate of return for a market basket of stock

Once the unlevered beta (asset beta) of the comparable company is obtained, one can use this to calculate the all equity cost of capital. Thus while the imperfections of the use of beta are apparent, currently it is the best we have.

The market risk premium is another parameter where judgement is required. Historically this value has been around 6 % but it is worth noting that the equity risk premium is constantly changing. My view is to pick a premium that seems reasonable: 4–6 %.

In a previous study[24] published in 1995 and using data from 1989, the cost of capital for seven biotechnology and specialty pharmaceutical firms was calculated to be 19 % in nominal terms and 14 % in real terms. These firms had higher betas than the major pharmaceutical firms, presumably reflecting the fact that the smaller biotech firms had fewer commercialized products and proportionately more projects in early R&D. Dimasi and Grabowski (2007) use the same methodology and assess the cost of capital for biotech companies at five-year intervals (Table 4.22).

The declining value for the cost of capital reflects the decline in the risk-free rate and the equity premium in recent years compared to the earlier periods. The data suggests that a cost of capital in the region of 11 to 12 % would be appropriate for biotechnology companies.

In the valuation section for conventional stocks, the NPV is calculated using the following formula:

$$NPV = \Sigma(1 + r)_i^{-t} CF$$

For the biotechnology DCF, we adjust each cash flow by its probability to occur:

$$NPV = \Sigma(1 + r)_i^{-t} P_{CFti} CF$$

A common approach to discounted cash flow valuation is to divide the cash flow forecast into two periods. During the explicit value period, cash flow projections are valued directly. During the continuing value period, cash flow projections are implicit in a capitalized value that is measured as of the time of the last explicit forecast. After the explicit value period, instead of projecting cash flows forever, it is common to estimate a continuing value. However, it does not rely on explicit forecasts of the cash flows that are to be received during the continuing value period. Instead, the forecast of cash flows is implicit in the assumptions that are used to estimate the terminal value.

Table 4.23 Three-stage DCF model

		1. Explicit forecast			2. Medium term growth			3. Terminal growth

(US$ '000)	FY05A	FY06A	FY07A	FY08E	FY09E	FY10E	FY11E	FY12E	FY13E	FY14E	Terminal Growth Rate
Compounding factor	0.0	0.0	0.5	1.5	2.5	3.5	4.5	5.5	6.5	7.5	
Revenue	97 389	81 989	84 180	86 917	89 525	92 211	94 977	97 826	100 761	103 784	
Growth rate (%)		−15.8%	2.7%	3.3%	3.0%	3.0%	3.0%	3.0%	3.0%	3.0%	2.5%
EBIT	42 031	27 699	29 996	31 083	31 334	27 663	26 594	25 435	25 190	23 870	
Operating margin (%)	43.2%	33.8%	35.6%	35.8%	35.0%	30.0%	28.0%	26.0%	25.0%	23.0%	
Taxes	−10	−9	−10	−10	−10	−9	−9	−8	−8	−8	

The two most common ways to compute the terminal value are

• Perpetuity calculation
• Multiple calculation.

The terminal value is calculated using the perpetuity method as follows:

$$TV = FCF_T(1 + g)/r_A - g$$

FCF_T = terminal free cash flow in the last explicit forecast year
   g = terminal growth rate
  r_A = discount rate

The calculation of terminal value is often a key limitation when one is applying DCF techniques to a biotechnology company as often the explicit forecast period fails to capture a significant portion of the anticipated high growth phase because of the limited time horizon. Furthermore the terminal value is derived from the final year explicit forecast cash flow and as such is a poor approximation of the expectations of the business. For many biotechnology companies, approximately 90 to 95 % of the value can reside in the terminal value, as often the cash flows in the explicit forecast period are negative. This again reflects the long time frames associated with drug development and the high capital intensity required to run the clinical trials.

One way to overcome this limitation is to use a three-stage DCF model (Table 4.23). In addition to the explicit forecast period and the terminal value, a medium-term growth rate period is inserted. This can be explicitly modelled but is more usually based over a period in which premium growth rate can be maintained.

Another issue with DCF is that it does not capture the ability of management to change strategy in response to continuing changes in the level of data available. An options approach to valuation captures the flexibility of management to only invest capital when things look promising and to avoid investment when the outlook is poor. The value of many drug development programmes depends upon both existence of real options (typically the right to structure the project in stages and then expand or abandon them depending upon future developments) and the assumption that management will exercise these options at the right time. Real options will be discussed in the next chapter.

EBIT DCF OF PRODUCTS

A refinement of the above DCF approach which I think is useful is to break out the product sales and associated costs to give an EBIT or operating margin for each drug asset. A study[25] in 2002 reported that the top 10 pharmaceutical companies in the US by sales had a median profit as a percentage of revenues of 17 %. Assuming a marginal tax rate this would imply an operating margin in the region of 25 %. Recently Elan and Biogen-Idec gave guidance on their drug Tysabri, which targeted a gross margin of 70–80 % of revenues and implied an operating margin in the 30–40 % range.

Breaking out the drug asset allows one to associate the various costs as much as one can to each drug, especially those that are still in development and thus need probabilities of success assigned to their cash flows. The following example is from a model on Shire Pharmaceuticals in 2004 (Table 4.24). Note that the modelled EBIT is checked with the forecast EBIT according to the model.

Table 4.24   DCF using drug margin assumptions

Revenues	2007A	2008E	2009E	2010E	2011E	2012E
Adderall	0.0	0.0	0.0	0.0	0.0	0.0
Adderall XR	0.0	829.9	414.9	124.5	99.6	79.7
Daytrana	0.0	120.0	140.0	150.0	150.0	150.0
Fosrenol	0.0	162.6	230.1	283.4	321.2	342.9
Vyvanse	0.0	367.4	624.6	811.9	1014.9	1167.1
Dynepo	0.0	50.0	100.0	175.0	200.0	200.0
Elaprase	0.0	198.0	229.5	276.4	316.9	341.2
Lialda (US)/Mezavant (EU)	0.0	100.0	150.0	175.0	200.0	200.0
Agrylin (US)/Xagrid (EU)	0.0	76.8	84.5	88.7	84.3	80.1
Pentasa	0.0	202.9	213.0	202.4	192.2	182.6
Proamatine	0.0	6.6	5.9	5.3	4.8	4.3
Carbatrol	0.0	75.9	75.9	72.1	68.5	61.7
Equetro	0.0	25.0	29.0	29.0	30.0	30.0
Replagal	0.0	170.0	170.0	170.0	170.0	170.0
Other products	**2170.2**	**151.8**	**209.0**	**244.6**	**303.8**	**411.3**
Royalties & Licensing and Development	266.1	272.4	273.6	208.6	204.0	200.2
Total	2436.3	2809.3	2950.0	3017.0	3360.2	3621.1

EBIT Margins						
Adderall	0.0 %	0.0 %	0.0 %	0.0 %	0.0 %	0.0 %
Adderall XR	0.0 %	49.9 %	49.5 %	49.5 %	50.2 %	50.6 %
Daytrana	0.0 %	27.4 %	26.5 %	26.0 %	26.7 %	27.1 %
Fosrenol	0.0 %	1.9 %	5.2 %	4.9 %	5.1 %	5.4 %
Vyvanse	0.0 %	13.9 %	18.5 %	24.5 %	31.2 %	37.6 %
Dynepo	0.0 %	27.4 %	26.5 %	26.0 %	26.7 %	27.1 %
Elaprase	0.0 %	39.9 %	51.5 %	56.5 %	62.2 %	64.6 %
Lialda (US)/Mezavant (EU)	0.0 %	27.4 %	26.5 %	26.0 %	26.7 %	27.1 %
Agrylin (US)/Xagrid (EU)	0.0 %	27.4 %	26.5 %	26.0 %	26.7 %	27.1 %
Pentasa	0.0 %	(0.1 %)	11.5 %	16.5 %	22.2 %	22.6 %
Proamatine	0.0 %	27.4 %	26.5 %	26.0 %	26.7 %	27.1 %
Carbatrol	0.0 %	27.4 %	26.5 %	26.0 %	26.7 %	27.1 %
Equetro	0.0 %	27.4 %	26.5 %	26.0 %	26.7 %	27.1 %
Replagal	0.0 %	(0.1 %)	16.5 %	21.5 %	27.2 %	32.6 %
Other products	0.0 %	27.4 %	26.5 %	26.0 %	26.7 %	27.1 %
Royalties & Licensing and Development	100.0 %	100.0 %	100.0 %	100.0 %	100.0 %	100.0 %

	2008E	2009E	2010E	2011E	2012E
Sub-total EBIT	986.1	987.9	952.4	1152.2	1323.5
Shared costs	367.5	385.9	405.2	425.4	446.7
EBIT	618.6	602.0	547.2	726.7	876.8
Tax rate	23.0 %	23.5 %	24.0 %	24.5 %	25.0 %
EBIT*(1-t)	476.3	460.5	415.9	548.7	657.6
Add D&A	234.5	246.3	258.6	271.5	285.1
Add FAS-123	90.2	108.3	129.9	155.9	187.1
Remove Capex	(397.9)	(406.8)	(196.1)	(205.9)	(216.2)
Change in working capital	91.8	(11.5)	(1.0)	45.8	41.0
FCF	311.5	419.8	609.3	724.5	872.6
Terminal value					14 626.8
Total FCF	311.5	419.8	609.3	724.5	15 499.4
Discounted Cash Flows	285.4	352.4	468.6	510.5	10 006.8

On the estimates used in the model, the company faces a significant issue in 2007 as Adderall XR goes generic and significant sales revenue is lost in that year. Accordingly, a near-term DCF model for Shire was built but, in addition, the EBIT contributions of the major franchises were modelled explicitly (in an attempt to model in the cost of goods and the selling and marketing expenses for the Adderall franchise and Fosrenol) and used to guide P&L assumptions.

It was not attempted to value each franchise on a stand alone basis, and R&D and other operating expenses such as depreciation and amortization were apportioned across the franchises as an equal percentage of sales.

COMPARABLES VALUATION

A comparable valuation uses the market value of comparable companies or transactions that have been completed within a reasonable period of the valuation date as reference points, hence this method is also called the market approach or secondary valuation. The general approach when using this technique is to assign the market value of the firm as the numerator and a particular aspect of the firm as the denominator. There are four main types of multiples:

1. Value multiples which use cash flow-based metrics such as earnings or EBITDA as the denominator
2. Price multiples which are also cash flow-based but use price as the numerator (price/ earnings)
3. Asset-based value multiples which use firm value as the numerator and metrics, such as book value of assets, as the denominator
4. Industry-specific value multiples.

A key issue with comparable valuation is that one has to assume that the market has properly valued the comparable companies. In addition most early-stage companies tend to be loss-making and thus data points for the comparison become more spurious. In cases where one requires a valuation, metrics such as the amount spent on R&D, the number of people working for a company and the level of revenues can be viewed as indicators. For public companies information on financial and personnel metrics is available from the stock exchange. For private companies, information of the last financing rounds can be utilized. It is worth noting that one needs to get a balance with regard to the number of companies that one chooses as comparators. Selecting too many firms may result in a selection that is not truly comparable, whilst too few firms may result in the average reflecting idiosyncrasies of specific firms.

A variation of this method involves the use of market-derived pricing multiples based on the projected earnings of comparable companies. The selected pricing multiples are applied to the subject company's projected earnings. Unfortunately, many early-stage companies do not project positive profitability for several years.

Another difficulty in valuing early-stage companies using the market approach is finding appropriate guideline companies for comparison. Most of the companies that are publicly traded have an existing track record, are substantially larger than an early-stage company in terms of revenue and asset size and are more diversified. For public companies value information is available from the stock exchange. For private companies, information of the last financing rounds can be utilized.

Table 4.25   Range of multiples that could be used to derive a valuation range

EV/Revenues	Market Cap (US$m)	2008	2009	2010	
Novo Nordisk A/S	39 642	4.17×	3.85×	3.54×	
H. Lundbeck A/S	6 017	2.55×	2.39×	2.26×	
Shire plc	11 791	4.51×	4.11×	3.85×	
Actelion Ltd.	4 982	3.58×	3.34×	3.16×	
AstraZeneca plc	62 909	2.42×	2.33×	2.32×	
GlaxoSmithKline plc	130 427	2.90×	2.82×	2.74×	
Novartis AG	120 674	2.82×	2.62×	2.43×	
Sanofi-Aventis	118 478	2.72×	2.63×	2.42×	
	Average	3.21×	3.01×	2.84×	
	Stripped mean	3.12×	2.94×	2.77×	
	Median	2.86×	2.72×	2.58×	
2	6	19	20	21	
EV/EBITDA	**Market Cap (US$m)**	**2008**	**2009**	**2010**	
Novo Nordisk A/S	39 642	14.2×	12.7×	11.3×	
H. Lundbeck A/S	6 017	8.3×	7.6×	7.0×	
Shire plc	11 791	14.0×	12.2×	11.7×	
Actelion Ltd.	4 982	11.9×	11.0×	11.4×	
AstraZeneca plc	62 909	6.7×	6.2×	6.0×	
GlaxoSmithKline plc	130 427	7.6×	7.2×	7.1×	
Novartis AG	120 674	10.0×	9.1×	8.3×	
Sanofi-Aventis	118 478	7.0×	6.7×	6.4×	
	Average	10.0×	9.1×	8.6×	
	Stripped mean	9.8×	9.0×	8.6×	
	Median	9.1×	8.3×	7.7×	
2	6	24	25	26	
EV/EBIT	**Market Cap (US$m)**	**2008**	**2009**	**2010**	
Novo Nordisk A/S	39 642	17.2×	15.3×	13.5×	
H. Lundbeck A/S	6 017	10.0×	9.1×	8.4×	
Shire plc	11 791	17.5×	14.8×	13.4×	
Actelion Ltd.	4 982	14.1×	13.1×	12.5×	
AstraZeneca plc	62 909	8.0×	7.4×	6.8×	
GlaxoSmithKline plc	130 427	8.7×	8.4×	8.0×	
Novartis AG	120 674	12.4×	11.2×	10.3×	
Sanofi-Aventis	118 478	7.8×	7.4×	7.3×	
	Average	12.0×	10.8×	10.0×	
	Stripped mean	11.7×	10.7×	10.0×	
	Median	11.2×	10.1×	9.4×	
2	6	29	30	31	
PE	**Market Cap (US$m)**	**2008**	**2009**	**2010**	**PEG**
Novo Nordisk A/S	39 642	22.5×	19.8×	16.9×	1.11×
H. Lundbeck A/S	6 017	13.7×	12.2×	11.6×	1.33×
Shire plc	11 791	22.2×	18.3×	16.7×	1.09×
Actelion Ltd.	4 982	17.2×	16.1×	15.0×	2.18×
AstraZeneca plc	62 909	10.7×	9.4×	8.7×	0.77×
GlaxoSmithKline plc	130 427	11.4×	10.5×	9.8×	1.22×
Novartis AG	120 674	14.3×	12.8×	11.3×	0.89×
Sanofi-Aventis	118 478	10.6×	9.8×	9.0×	1.01×
	Average	15.4×	13.6×	12.4×	1.20×
	Stripped mean	14.9×	13.3×	12.2×	1.11×
	Median	14.0×	12.5×	11.5×	1.10×

Thus multiples incorporate a lot of information and correlate your valuation with other valuations set by the market. Despite the shortcoming of the approach, it is worth noting that sometimes what the investor carrying out the valuation cares about is what the market will pay and concerns of fundamental value are not important. Nonetheless my view is that it is best to use a range of metrics when using multiples and it is probably best to use them only as a reality check on DCF-based valuation.

Although international GAAP is becoming the international standard of choice, using multiples across geographies requires a level of caution. Furthermore when choosing a multiple metric, the higher the metric occurs in the income statement (for example, sales), the less open it is to accounting subjectivity. However by choosing such a multiple, the less it reflects differences in operating efficiencies across firms. As ever sound judgement is the key. Table 4.25 details a range of multiples from comparable companies that could be used to derive a valuation range.

NPVS ARE ADDITIVE

Sometimes valuing companies is not straightforward, especially when their business models include widely differing business units. Furthermore it may be become clear in the course of a valuation that a certain drug asset has a significant proportion of the valuation, triggering a more in-depth analysis. In both of these cases, the simple answer is to remember that NPVs are additive. Thus it is possible to use different techniques to value different parts of the firm and then to sum the individual NPVs to obtain a value for the whole. Table 4.26 shows this technique can be used to value a relatively complex mid-sized biopharmaceutical company, Merck KGaA, which has four business divisions with different drivers and dynamics.

USING ALL THE TOOLS AVAILABLE TO REACH A VALUATION CONCLUSION

Merck KGaA is a global pharmaceutical and chemical company that was founded in 1668.[26] Its pharmaceutical division includes generic and prescription products, the latter being mainly focused on oncology, cardiology and more recently reproductive health following the acquisition of Serono in 2007. The chemical division includes the liquid crystal division and a wide range of chemicals. Merck enjoys a natural hedging in the healthcare sector with its balance of ethical/generic and a sector hedging of healthcare-chemical/technology.

Merck thus has a number of business units. In the note there is a comparable analysis on each business line (except the Liquid Crystal line which does not have any obvious publicly-quoted comparables) on an EV/EBIT and EV/EBITDA basis, in addition to a DCF. Table 4.26 summarizes the three ways of valuing Merck.

In order to compare and contrast the DCF valuation with other companies, a comparable analysis for each line of the business was also performed, with the exception of the Liquid Crystal division, due to a lack of identifiable stand alone publicly traded comparators. The analyses from that research note are detailed below and highlight the importance of coming at the valuation from a variety of different angles and balancing the results that each valuation approach provides. The note was published on 12 June 2007 when the stock was at € 102.5 per share. The target price was € 117 per share.

Table 4.26 Valuing a company using different multiples

		DCF Valuation	Comps EV/EBIT	Comps EV/EBITDA
Liquid Crystals**				
	Enterprise value	8743.1		
	Debt as proportion of revenues	191.4		
	Equity value	8551.7		
	NoSH	204.3		
	Price per share	41.9		
Perf. & LSC				
	Enterprise value	2249.6	2005.0	1780.1
	Debt as proportion of revenues	230.8	230.8	230.8
	Equity value	2018.8	1774.3	1549.4
	NoSH	204.3	204.3	204.3
	Price per share	9.9	8.7	7.6
Merck Serono				
	Enterprise value	13 601.5	11 366.8	12 201.8
	Debt as proportion of revenues	789.2	789.2	789.2
	Equity value	12 812.3	10 577.6	11 412.6
	NoSH	204.3	204.3	204.3
	Price per share	62.7	51.8	55.9
Consumer Health Care*				
	Enterprise value	672.1	860.7	820.0
	Debt as proportion of revenues	77.0	77.0	77.0
	Equity value	595.1	783.6	743.0
	NoSH	204.3	204.3	204.3
	Price per share	2.9	3.8	3.6
Total		**117.4**	**106.2**	**109.0**

* computed on KKR/Alliance Boots deal
** computed using DCF only

The following extract is from the actual research note.

Performance & Life Sciences Chemicals
We have compared the Performance & Life Sciences Chemicals on an EV/EBIT and EV/EBITDA basis to chemical players. We have retained the stripped mean value as the most appropriate. Our DCF valuation yields an enterprise value of € 2.2 billion, which represents a 10 % premium over the EV/EBIT valuation obtained on a comparable basis. We believe such a premium has no justification and believe the comparable valuation on EV/EBIT basis is more appropriate for Merck.

Merck Serono
We have compared Merck Serono to biotech companies as we believe biologics are increasingly becoming the main drivers of the business. The average EV/EBIT valuation is € 11.4 billion and the

Table 4.27 Performance & Life Science Chemicals comparables

EV/EBIT	2007E	2008E	2009E
Sigma Aldrich Corp.	13.3×	12.3×	11.1×
Bayer AG	14.5×	13.5×	11.9×
Solvay	10.2×	10.0×	10.2×
BASF AG	7.1×	7.4×	9.0×
Dow Chemicals Company	8.7×	9.8×	NM
Stripped mean	10.7×	10.7×	10.6×
Perf. & LSC Valuation			
Stripped mean	1917	2005	2093
EV/EBITDA	**2007E**	**2008E**	**2009E**
Sigma Aldrich Corp.	11.0×	10.3×	9.5×
Bayer AG	9.0×	8.1×	7.3×
Solvay	7.1×	7.1×	6.8×
BASF AG	5.2×	5.2×	5.3×
Dow Chemicals Company	6.8×	7.0×	NM
Stripped mean	7.6×	7.4×	7.1×
Perf. & LSC Valuation			
Stripped mean	1684	1808	1848

Table 4.28 Merck Serono comparables

EV/EBIT	2007E	2008E	2009E
Amgen Inc	12.4×	11.4×	10.5×
Novo Nordisk A/S	14.6×	12.9×	11.4×
Genentech Inc	18.1×	15.0×	13.1×
Genzyme Corp.	14.7×	12.9×	11.1×
Biogen Idec Inc	13.1×	11.4×	10.4×
Lundbeck A/S	10.3×	9.2×	8.5×
Shire PLC	24.8×	18.3×	14.5×
Stripped mean	15.1×	13.1×	11.5×
Merck Serono Valuation			
Stripped mean	12 252	11 164	10 725
EV/EBITDA	**2007E**	**2008E**	**2009E**
Amgen Inc	10.3×	9.8×	9.8×
Novo Nordisk A/S	11.9×	10.7×	9.7×
Genentech Inc	18.3×	15.8×	13.3×
Genzyme Corp.	NA	NA	NA
Biogen Idec Inc	10.4×	10.0×	NA
Lundbeck A/S	8.5×	7.8×	7.2×
Shire PLC	21.0×	15.9×	12.4×
Stripped mean	12.7×	11.6×	10.6×
Merck Serono Valuation			
Stripped mean	12 130	12 193	12 321

Table 4.29   Consumer Health Care comparables

	2007E	2008E	2009E
EBIT (GBPm)	703	766	766
EBITDA (GBPm)	933	1009	1194
EV/EBIT	15.8×	14.5×	14.5×
EV/EBITDA	11.9×	11.0×	9.3×
EV (EBIT)	839.4	848.6	894.0
EV (EBITDA)	858.5	840.3	761.0

average EV/EBITDA valuation is € 12.2 billion. This is a 16 % and 10 % premium, respectively, over our DCF valuation of € 13.8 billion. While this premium appears important, we believe the expected strong growth of the business justifies this premium, and retain our DCF valuation as the fairest way of valuing Merck Serono.

Consumer Health Care (CHC)
Given the limited number of pure CHC players, we have compared the CHC business to the multiples of the recent acquisition of Alliance-Boots by KKR for GBP 11.1 billion.
   We obtain an average valuation of € 861 million and € 820 million for the EV/EBIT and EV/EBITDA comparables, respectively. This represents a 21–27 % premium to our DCF valuation. Given our stance that the Consumer Health Care will be the next business likely to be disposed, we believe the comparable valuation is the best way of valuing this business. We however consider that an EV/EBITDA valuation presenting a 21 % premium is more appropriate.

Summary
While we believe that using comparables is a sensible way of valuing the Perf. & Life Science divisions and the Consumer Health Care division, the Merck Serono division and the Liquid Crystal division should be valued on a DCF basis. Indeed, we believe that the Merck Serono division and the Liquid Crystal division offer both a higher than average growth prospect and a natural hedging that cannot be captured by comparable analysis.

The importance of each different parameter can be determined through sensitivity analysis and the results can be depicted in the form of a tornado diagram shown below which makes the sensitivities more visually clear. The potential positive and negative effects of each parameter on the NPV can be read directly.

MARKET MODELS

As discussed earlier, estimating peak sales can be a key driver of the NPV. As the drug asset continues to move through clinical development more and more data becomes available to allow one to build up a picture of the target product profile (TPP). This is what the drug should be like if and when it reaches the market. The parameters that are usually assessed are

- Efficacy
- Side effects
- Dosage form
- Administration frequency

This is a good practice to develop but in addition to the clinical and commercial hurdles a drug must face, there is also the small matter of competition. It is very rare for a drug to have no competition from other assets under development. These potential competitors may be ahead

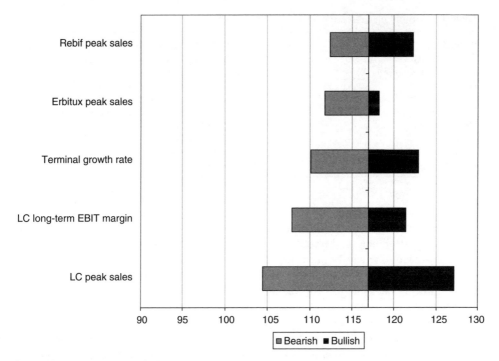

Figure 4.5 Sensitivity analysis

or behind in development terms, may have different mechanism of action or may even herald such a breakthrough that they have the potential to totally transform the current clinical and therapeutic paradigm.

This is why it may be worth building a market model to determine the potential market size for new models and it also allows one to flex the assumptions underlying the model to account for different future competitive scenarios. In companies and investment banks, these market models are developed in two ways, either using a patient-based algorithm or a prescription-based algorithm. The latter requires a subscription to a prescription monitoring service and is outside the realm of private investors. The former are easier to put together and can be a great tool to assess the market potential and dynamics.

The patient-based algorithm starts with the theoretical maximum of patients with a particular condition and then this set of patients is gradually reduced through a number of steps to an estimate of patients on a particular drug.

In Appendix 1 I have provided two examples of disease models. Example 2 provides a worked example of a relatively straightforward disease model, whilst Example 3 offers some increasing complexity as the model tries to assess the market dynamics including patients dropping out and switching between therapies.

Conclusion

Hopefully this chapter has highlighted how the conventional valuation approaches can be adapted to use for biotechnology technology valuation. Yet this is not a plug and play approach and each individual valuation will come with its own challenges and issues. That

Table 4.30 Building a disease model

Population	From government sources including growth rate
Epidemiology	Incidence or prevalence data from literature
Total Population Pool	Population × Epidemiology
Diagnosed	% of patients that are diagnosed correctly
Total Patient Pool	Total Population Pool × % Diagnosed
Patients treated	% of diagnosed patients that receive intervention
Drug treated	% of patients that receive a drug
Drug 1	estimated drug share
Drug 2	estimated drug share
Drug 3	estimated drug share

is why I advocate the use of multiple techniques which allows one to triangulate a probable valuation range. Building on the contents of previous chapters, I have shown that even with a little knowledge, one can begin to build up a realistic picture of what the drug pipeline is about. In cases where management is not forthcoming, the use of industry standard timelines and attrition rates can provide valuable clues as to valuation inputs. The examples in the appendix to this chapter show how the probability weighted NPV table can be used to reflect changes in the stock prices of companies as they react to various new releases. When the valuation is highly dependant upon one drug or a company has a number of drug assets under development targeting one disease area, it may be worthwhile to build up a disease model. Although these models are never a true reflection of reality they can provide insight as to how a market may develop and can also highlight areas that need further investigation. For example, if management believes their drug will be a blockbuster yet the model suggests that the patient pool would need to double, one can begin to check this assumption out.

In Appendix 2, I briefly review the state of play regarding biosimilar compounds. Whilst there is a lot of information regarding the generic erosion of small molecules, the future regarding genericization of biological molecules is uncertain. However if one is developing a forecast over the next five years, I believe that one should be aware of the issues and adapt the model accordingly.

APPENDIX 1

Example 1

Using the NPV Analysis to Evaluate Impact of News Events

On 20 February 2007, CeNeS announced that CeNeS has reported preliminary Phase 3 results for its lead drug, M6G, for the treatment of post-op pain. M6G matches morphine for analgesic effect and showed a significant reduction in the severity of post operative nausea and vomiting (PONV) compared to morphine. But M6G failed to show a significant difference in the primary endpoint of a reduction in the incidence and severity of nausea compared to morphine.

The stock reacted badly over the course of the week falling from 8.4p to 7.12p, a decline of 15 %. The table below shows how the valuation was derived prior to this announcement.

Table 4.31 CeNeS pipeline valuation

Product Development

Drug name	MoA	Indication	Status	Launch	Success	Sales	Royalty	Profit	NPV(GBp)
M6G(Europe)	Opioid metabolite	Post-operative pain	Phases 3	2008	60%	66.1	15%	90%	8.3
M6G(US)	Opioid metabolite	Post-operative pain	–	2010	30%	94.0	15%	90%	4.5
CNS-5161	NMDA antagonist	Neuropathic pain	Phase 2	2010	15%	200.0	15%	100%	5.3
CNS-7056X	GABAa agonist	IV sedative	PC	2012	0%	0.0	15%	100%	0.0
COMT inhibitor	–	Parkinson's	PC	2012	0%	0.0	15%	100%	0.0
								Total	**18.1**

Source: Company data and CanaccordAdams estimates

The announcement, in our view, signalled that there was probably going to be a delay in the anticipated launch of M6G, moving from 2008 into 2011. Inputting this new launch date alters the valuation to 15.3p from 18.1p, a change of 15 %.

On 6 September 2007, Plethora Solutions released top-line data of a Phase 2 study investigating PSD597 in interstitial cystitis and painful bladder syndrome. The study met its primary endpoint as PSD597 showed a statistically significant improvement of the Global Response Assessment score (GRA) (p<0.01). The study also showed that the product was safe and well tolerated with a drop rate of only 7 %. A follow-on open label study was also conducted and data are currently being analysed. Full data of the Phase 2 study should be available by the end of the year. The valuation change implied by the pNPV was approximately 4 %. The stock increased 13 over two days but rapidly settled down, with a gain of +7 %.

These examples demonstrate the utility of the NPV table to identify mispricing and in addition, the percentage change is usually a good guide as to the potential impact of a piece of news. Of course, the change will not match the market's reaction exactly but it gives a useful guide to the scale of any anticipated share price move.

Example 2

Building Disease Models

This example works through a spreadsheet to estimate the sales potential of a new therapeutic to treat Crohn's disease. Most models such as these start with estimates for the US because data is usually easier to get and it is the world's largest pharmaceutical market. Once this is complete, Europe can be modelled explicitly or the US sales potential can be factored according to population estimates.

Most models start with the population statistics and also incorporate the census office estimates of growth. The next step is to estimate the number of people with the disease using epidemiology data. Epidemiology data comprises two broad categories, prevalence and incidence. Prevalence refers to the total number of cases in a given year, whilst incidence is a measure of the risk of developing a disease within a specified period of time. Thus incidence conveys information about the risk of contracting a disease whereas prevalence indicates how widespread it is.

Example 3

Building Disease Models

In this example, I used the prevalence because I want to estimate how many patients have been diagnosed with multiple sclerosis (MS) and then segment them into the four types of MS.[27] Taking current forecasts for US population growth, and a search of available data sources on the prevalence and incidence of multiple sclerosis in the US, suggests that there are approximately 370 000 MS sufferers in the US, of which approximately 80 % are diagnosed.

The level of diagnosis is not likely to improve dramatically in the coming years, but rather there will be a gradual improvement in the techniques and technologies. Indeed, diagnosis currently takes a number of years of observation, so any improvements are likely to be later rather than sooner. At a diagnosis rate of 80 %, there are approximately 300 000 diagnosed MS patients in the US.

Table 4.32 Patient-based model for Crohn's disease

Crohn's Disease		2005	2006	2007	2008	2009	2010	2011
US adult population (m)		216.1	218.3	220.6	223.0	225.4	227.8	230.0
Growth		1.0%	1.0%	1.0%	1.1%	1.1%	1.0%	1.0%
Crohn's prevalence		0.24%	0.24%	0.24%	0.24%	0.24%	0.24%	0.24%
Crohn's sufferers (m)		0.52	0.53	0.53	0.54	0.54	0.55	0.56
Diagnosed (m)	60%	0.31	0.32	0.32	0.32	0.33	0.33	0.33
Treated (m)	95%	0.30	0.30	0.30	0.31	0.31	0.31	0.32
Mild (m)	30%	0.09	0.09	0.09	0.09	0.09	0.09	0.09
Moderate (m)	45%	0.13	0.14	0.14	0.14	0.14	0.14	0.14
Severe (m)	25%	0.07	0.08	0.08	0.08	0.08	0.08	0.08
Treated with anti-inflam, immunomods (m)	Mod & Severe	0.21	0.21	0.21	0.21	0.22	0.22	0.22
Treatment failures (m)	50%	0.10	0.11	0.11	0.11	0.11	0.11	0.11
Penetration into treatment failures		50%	65%	70%	75%	75%	75%	75%
Potential pool of biologic patients		52 018	68 325	74 352	80 530	81 397	82 238	83 060
Average Cost (US$ per treatment year)		15 000	15 000	15 000	15 000	15 000	15 000	15 000
Increase/(Decrease)		0%	0%	0%	0%	0%	0%	0%
Total $ market size (US$m)		780	1 025	1 115	1 208	1 221	1 234	1 246

DRUG		2005	2006	2007	2008	2009	2010	2011
US patient pool	2	52 018	68 325	74 352	80 530	81 397	82 238	83 060
Global pool		104 035	136 651	148 704	161 059	162 794	164 475	166 120
Penetration		0%	0%	5%	10%	15%	20%	22%
Patients	15 000	0	0	7 435	16 106	24 419	32 895	36 546
Global revenues (US$m)		0.0	0.0	111.5	241.6	366.3	493.4	548.2
Global revenues (EURm)	1.2	0.0	0.0	92.9	201.3	305.2	411.2	456.8

This refinement is carried out because the target product of the drug in question is seeking to treat MS patients with the relapsing remitting and secondary progressive forms of the disease. This split has been obtained from the national Multiple Sclerosis Society. Such patient organizations are usually sources of background data and may even have a web forum to discuss therapies that are undergoing clinical trials. The two patient segments comprise the majority of the patients – an important point for assessing the commercial potential.

It is also important to consider the number of patients treated – not just the number of patients diagnosed with MS. A survey in the US suggests that around 40 % of diagnosed patients are not being treated with medications.[28] In a survey of 562 patients with RRMS and SPMS, and of 251 neurologists who treat MS, the results suggest that 42 % of patients diagnosed with MS were not receiving an FDA approved treatment.

Of those patients not receiving treatment, the most common reason given (by 43 % of patients) was that they had not had a relapse. As a check on patient numbers, incidence data suggest that approximately 200 new patients come on to therapy every week in the US, and that would translate into 10 000 new patients per year. The prevalence-derived patient estimates match this figure. If possible it is very worthwhile to include such checks in market models.

The next step in the model to translate the patient dynamics into commercial terms, so a financial picture of the disease area can be compiled. This particular model was built in 2005. The current dugs on the market are listed alongside the last full year of sales. Using the total revenue for the last full reported year divided by the estimate of the total number of patients treated gives an estimate of the average price per therapy (in this case $ 15 119). Using the reported revenues and implied prices, an estimate of market share for each of the four current drugs can be obtained. The therapy prices (which drive the model) are set by dividing the total US revenues of the four main MS treatments into our treated population estimate. This gives our average cost per therapy per year. Finally, to set the prices for the individual therapies, use the average price as the price for Biogen's Avonex and set premiums and discounts to it according to the Red Book[29] pricing for the other therapies.

Patients

The hypothesis underlying the market model is that there are two patient pools to consider:

- New patients coming on to therapy for the first time
- Switching patients who decide to change therapy.

New patients   As discussed, the model assumes approximately 10 000 new patients per year going forward, and we assign the majority of these to Antegren (Tysabri). Given the emerging profile of the drug (at the time, the preliminary efficacy data suggested an effectiveness significantly higher than the therapies currently on the market), as compared to currently available therapies, it seems reasonable that more patients would be put on Antegren than on any other therapy. The base assumption is that 75 % of new patients are put on to Antegren, and the rest are split across the other four therapies.

Switching patients   MS is a lifelong disease so any therapy, other than one that would reverse the disease totally, would probably be required indefinitely. However if patients are unable to adhere to treatment for a reasonable length of time, then even modest benefits will not be gained. A study has recorded the amount of (and the reasons for) switching (either off

Table 4.33 Patient-based model for multiple sclerosis

Disease epidemiology	2004	2005	2006	2007	2008	2009	2010
US population data – US census bureau							
http://www.census.gov/							
US population (m)	**285.3**	**287.7**	**290.2**	**292.6**	**295.0**	**297.4**	**299.9**
growth		0.9 %	0.8 %	0.8 %	0.8 %	0.8 %	0.8 %
MS epidemiology							
Source: http://www.nationalmssociety.org/Brochures-Just%20the.asp							
Source: http://www.mayoclinic.com/invoke.cfm?id=DS00188							
Theoretical patient population	**370 846**	**374 031**	**377 199**	**380 357**	**383 512**	**386 667**	**389 821**
Prevalence	0.13 %	0.13 %	0.13 %	0.13 %	0.13 %	0.13 %	0.13 %
Diagnosis rate	80.0 %	80.5 %	81.0 %	81.5 %	82.0 %	82.5 %	83.0 %
Diagnosed US MS sufferers	**296 677**	**301 095**	**305 531**	**309 991**	**314 480**	**319 001**	**323 551**
Diagnosed prevalence	0.10 %	0.10 %	0.11 %	0.11 %	0.11 %	0.11 %	0.11 %
Split by type of MS							
Source: http://www.nationalmssociety.org/What%20is%20MS.asp							
Relapsing-Remitting 50 %	148 338	150 547	152 765	154 996	157 240	159 500	161 776
Primary progressive 5 %	14 834	15 055	15 277	15 500	15 724	15 950	16 178
Secondary progressive 35 %	103 837	105 383	106 936	108 497	110 068	111 650	113 243
Progressive relapsing 10 %	29 668	30 109	30 553	30 999	31 448	31 900	32 355
Target population (RRMS & SPMS)	**252 175**	**255 931**	**259 701**	**263 493**	**267 308**	**271 150**	**275 018**
40% of diagnosed patients are not on treatment							
Source: Taylor & Leitman (Harris Interactive) Vol1, issue 15 (2001)							
Total MS market penetration	57.0 %	60.0 %	63.0 %	66.0 %	69.0 %	72.0 %	75.0 %
Total MS patients treated	**143 740**	**153 558**	**163 612**	**173 905**	**184 443**	**195 228**	**206 264**
200 new patients per week equals 10,000 per year							
Source: http://www.nationalmssociety.org/Brochures-Just%20the.asp							
New patients		**9818**	**10 054**	**10 293**	**10 537**	**10 786**	**11 036**

Table 4.34   Patient pricing calculations

Pricing and patient calculation	2004	
Total MS patients treated	143 740	Taken from the Epidemiology calculations

2004 revenues from products in the US		
Rebif sales	295.6	
Avonex sales	922.6	
Betaseron sales	330.0	Revenues as reported for FY/04 in US$m
Copaxone sales	625.0	
New treatment sales	0.0	
Total top 4 sales	2173.2	

Using top 4 products as proxy for whole market		
		Use 2004 total revenue; divided by Total MS patients treated (our estimate)
Total market (US$m) assumption	2173	
Gives an implied ave. price per therapy	15 119	To give implied average price per therapy per year

Use implied price as price for Avonex	April Red Book AWP		Implied Price	Premium	
Rebif (Premium to Avonex)	1 517.75	19%	15 293	19%	
Avonex	1 277.50	0%	12 851	0%	Avonex is used as the base, less discount of 15%
Betaseron (Discount to Avonex)	1 261.07	(1%)	12 723	(1%)	With premium/discounts for the other therapies
Copaxone	1 402.80	10%	14 136	10%	
New treatment (Premium to Rebif)			17 587	15%	

Derived 2004 patient data from reported revenues and implied prices		
Rebif patients	19 329	Rebif revenues divided by Rebif implied price
Avonex patients	71 791	Avonex revenues divided by Avonex implied price
Betaseron patients	25 938	Betaseron revenues divided by Betaseron implied price
Copaxone patients	44 213	Copaxone revenues divided by Copaxone implied price
New treatment patients	0	
Derived patients	161 271	Does not quite match total MS patients treated, because of pricing differentials

Derived 2004 patient market share from derived patients		
Rebif patient-market share	12%	
Avonex patient-market share	45%	
Betaseron patient-market share	16%	These figures are used to drive the model forward in the **Patients sheet**
Copaxone patient-market share	27%	
New treatment patient-market share	0%	

therapy altogether or on to another agent).[30] This was a relatively small study (of 844 patients, in British Columbia only) but is illustrative of the fact that patients can and do switch MS therapy – whether it be seeking fewer side effects or greater efficacy. The reasons for interruption of therapy given by patients receiving interferon therapy are detailed in Table 4.36.

It is clear, therefore, that once on therapy, patients can and do switch between medications, and we have attempted to model this switching into our estimates. To do so we include the previous year's new patients in the current year's switching pool. In a similar way to the new patients, we assume that Antegren has "first call" on patients switching from other therapies, and that other therapies gain a share of the "switchers" that are not taken by Antegren. Hence, the assumption that Antegren takes 40% of all patients who switch from other therapies.

Table 4.35   Estimated split of new patients

		2004	2005	2006	2007	2008	2009	2010
Antegren patients	75%	0	4182	6631	6818	7009	7204	7400
Rebif patients	30%	2492	2091	663	682	701	720	740
Avonex patients	20%	1661	1394	442	455	467	480	493
Betaseron patients	20%	1661	1394	442	455	467	480	493
Copaxone patients	30%	2492	2091	663	682	701	720	740
Total new patients		8307	11 152	8842	9091	9345	9605	9867

Table 4.36   Top 7 reasons given for switching off IFN therapy

	Betaseron	Rebif	Avonex
	n = 185	n = 75	n = 21
Lack of efficacy	29 %	24 %	57 %
Injection site reaction	17 %	4 %	0 %
Flu-like symptoms	10 %	9 %	10 %
Depression	7 %	11 %	14 %
Headache	8 %	8 %	10 %
Liver test abnormalities	4 %	16 %	0 %
Fatigue	6 %	5 %	5 %

Source: Tremlett & Oger (2003)[30]

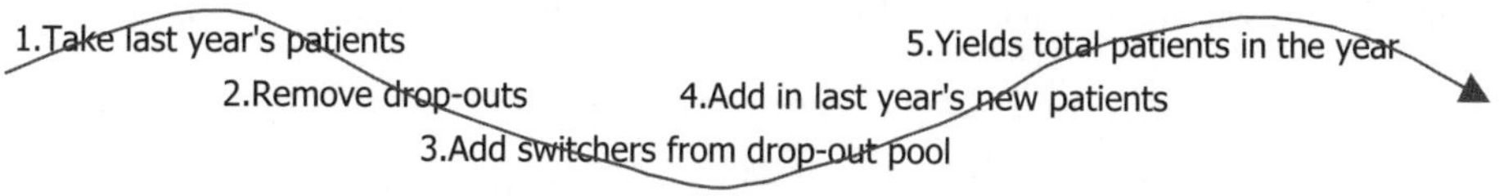

Figure 4.6   Corkscrew schematic of patient calculations

To calculate the number of switching (or "not new") patients on Antegren and on other therapies, the model incorporates a corkscrew calculation as illustrated in the Figure above and those calculations for Antegren are detailed below. This assumes a 10 % 12-month drop-out rate from Antegren.

For the other products, the following 12-month drop-out rates were assumed:

- Rebif – 10 %
- Avonex – 15 %
- Betaseron – 20 %
- Copaxone – 10 %

Furthermore switchers from Antegren are assumed to be taken up by other treatments and, for simplicity, that there is no overall drop-out from the model. In other words the hypothesis is that all patients dropping off therapy re-emerge on another therapy, i.e. that Rebif takes 40 % of switching patients that are not taken by Antegren (and also 40 % of those patents that drop off Antegren), and for the other products proportions of 25 % opting for Avonex, 5 % for Betaseron and 20 % of patients opting for Copaxone.

Table 4.37   Antegren's portion of the switching patients

		2004	2005	2006	2007	2008	2009	2010
Antegren patients treated		0	4112	16 106	29 137	40 684	51 011	60 338
Calculations								
Previous year's patients		0	0	4112	16 106	29 137	40 684	51 011
12-month drop-out rate	10 %	0	0	411	1611	2914	4068	5101
New patients from drop-out pool	40 %		4112	8224	8010	7643	7387	7224
New patients from last year		0	0	4182	6631	6818	7009	7204

Table 4.38 Model output – patient forecasts

	2004	2005	2006	2007	2008	2009	2010
Rebif patients	23 699	30 249	33 195	36 074	38 987	41 938	44 931
Avonex patients	63 261	59 527	54 436	50 198	46 798	44 116	42 048
Betaseron patients	26 473	23 727	20 340	17 496	15 274	13 550	12 227
Copaxone patients	44 870	47 657	47 588	47 665	47 981	48 518	49 259
Antegren patients	0	8294	22 738	35 955	47 693	58 215	67 739
Total patients	**158 303**	**169 455**	**178 296**	**187 387**	**196 732**	**206 337**	**216 204**

Outputs
These patient calculations, with the pricing calculations detailed above, lead to the revenue forecasts for the five main brands of MS treatment available in the US.

Antegren outputs   Using the assumptions detailed herein, the most important of which are:

Price: 30 % premium to Rebif or US$ 18 111 per patient per year
75 % of new patients go on to Antegren
40 % of switching patients opt for Antegren

yields a 2010 revenue for Antegren of approximately US$ 1.2 billion.

Antegren sensitivities   Finally, the sensitivity analyses that assess the results of flexing the major model assumptions on the level of sales Antegren may make in the US market. As discussed, the model assumes no significant near-term changes in either the rate of diagnosis or of treatment rate, but rather models moderate increases in both over the medium term. Rather, the significant drivers are cost, penetration into new patients and penetration into switching patients.

The model assumes a 30 % premium to Rebif, or a price of US$ 18 111 per year. This gives our 2010 revenue estimate of US$ 1.2 billion. However, with a 50 % premium or US$ 20 897 price, Antegren revenues would approach US$ 1.4 billion in 2010.

Flexing the patient assumptions, but keeping the pricing fixed at US$ 18 111 gives the following table of sensitivities:

Table 4.39 Model output – revenue forecasts (US$M)

	2004	2005	2006	2007	2008	2009	2010
Rebif	330.2	421.4	462.4	502.6	543.1	584.2	626.0
Avonex	740.6	696.9	637.3	587.7	547.9	516.5	492.3
Betaseron	306.8	275.0	235.7	202.8	177.0	157.0	141.7
Copaxone	577.8	613.7	612.8	613.8	617.9	624.8	634.3
Antegren	**0.0**	**150.2**	**411.8**	**651.2**	**863.7**	**1054.3**	**1226.8**
Total	**1955.4**	**2157.2**	**2360.1**	**2558.0**	**2749.6**	**2936.9**	**3121.1**

Table 4.40 Increasing Antegren pricing and effect on 2010 revenues

Premium to Rebif	0 %	10 %	20 %	**30 %**	40 %	50 %	60 %	70 %
2010 sales	944	1038	1132	**1227**	1321	1416	1510	1604
Price (US$)	13 931	15 324	16 718	**18 111**	19 504	20 897	22 290	23 683

Table 4.41 Proportion of new and switching patients – effect on revenues (2010)

		% of new patients							
		25 %	35 %	45 %	55 %	65 %	75 %	85 %	95 %
% of	**10 %**	377	458	539	620	700	781	862	942
switchers	**20 %**	541	620	700	779	858	937	1017	1096
	30 %	697	774	852	930	1008	1086	1164	1242
	40 %	844	921	997	1074	1150	**1227**	1303	1380
	50 %	985	1060	1135	1210	1285	1360	1436	1511
	60 %	1118	1192	1265	1339	1413	1487	1561	1635
	70 %	1244	1317	1389	1462	1534	1607	1680	1752
	80 %	1364	1435	1506	1578	1649	1721	1792	1863

Table 4.42 Model summary

Summary outputs

New treatment pricing assumptions	
Premium to Rebif	15%
Implied price of New treatment (US$)	17 587

New treatment patient assumptions	
Percentage of new patients	50%
Percentage of switching patients	30%

	2005	2006	2007	2008	2009	2010
Current Canaccord forecasts for Rebif in the US						
Current Rebif forecasts (US$m)	382.5	477.7	563.7	625.7	669.5	703.0
variance	0.4%	(2.8%)	(5.4%)	(2.0%)	(1.3%)	(2.2 %)
Model driven revenue forecasts						
Rebif sales (US$m)	380.9	491.3	596.0	638.5	678.2	718.8
Avonex sales (US$m)	794.4	774.9	762.0	717.4	680.0	651.6
Betaseron sales (US$m)	285.7	281.1	279.4	261.2	247.1	237.7
Copaxone sales (US$m)	627.3	694.0	758.9	772.9	787.2	804.4
New treatment sales (US$m)	0.0	0.0	0.0	205.0	401.9	579.9
Total sales (US$m)	**2088.4**	**2241.3**	**2396.2**	**2595.1**	**2794.5**	**2992.4**
Summary market data						
Rebif $-market share	18%	22%	25%	25%	24%	24%
Avonex $-market share	38%	35%	32%	28%	24%	22%
Betaseron $-market share	14%	13%	12%	10%	9%	8%
Copaxone $-market share	30%	31%	32%	30%	28%	27%
New treatment $-market share	0%	0%	0%	8%	14%	19%
Rebif patients	24 907	32 126	38 974	41 752	44 350	47 004
Avonex patients	61 815	60 297	59 291	55 826	52 916	50 701
Betaseron patients	22 459	22 093	21 958	20 534	19 423	18 682
Copaxone patients	44 377	49 097	53 683	54 675	55 685	56 902
New treatment patients	0	0	0	11 656	22 853	32 974
Total patients	**153 558**	**163 612**	**173 905**	**184 443**	**195 228**	**206 264**
Rebif patient-market share	16%	20%	22%	23%	23%	23%
Avonex patient-market share	40%	37%	34%	30%	27%	25%
Betaseron patient-market share	15%	14%	13%	11%	10%	9%
Copaxone patient-market share	29 %	30%	31%	30%	29%	28%
New treatment patient-market share	0%	0%	0%	6%	12%	16%
Total	100%	100%	100%	100%	100%	100%

Table 4.43   Sensitivity outputs

New treatment sensitivity outputs

Peak sales by proportion of patients			% of new patients							
			0%	10%	20%	30%	40%	50%	60%	70%
% of	**0%**		0	55	110	165	220	275	330	385
switchers	10%		105	160	215	270	325	379	434	489
	20%		208	263	317	372	426	481	536	590
	30%		308	362	417	471	526	580	634	689
	40%		405	460	514	568	622	676	730	785
	50%		500	554	608	662	716	770	824	878
	60%		593	646	700	754	807	861	915	969
	70%		683	736	789	843	896	950	1,003	1,057

Peak sales by pricing assumption	Premium to Rebif	0%	5%	10%	15%	20%	25%	30%	35%
	2010 sales	504	529	555	580	605	630	656	681
	Price (US$)	15,293	16,057	16,822	17,587	18,351	19,116	19,881	20,645

New treatment active-switching outputs

If new treatment data is good enough, patients will be told to switch by the physician, rather than passively drop-off therapy	
Patients on therapy in 2010	206,264
Of which are new patients	11,036
Switchable patients (who have been on therapy for more than one year)	195,228
Percentage on new treatment	50%
New treatment patients	97,614
Add in new patients in 2010	5,518
Total new treatment patients in 2010	103,132
Price (US$)	17,587
New treatment sales in 2010 (US$m)	**1,813.8**

Finally, another assumption might be that patients are actively switched from other therapies, and Antegren might be used by 50 % of all patients other than the new category (of which 75 % are already assumed to be put on Antegren). Using this assumption, Antegren peak sales would reach US$ 2 billion in the US alone.

APPENDIX 2

In the following section I highlight some of the issues that biotechnology companies may face in terms of potential generic erosion. The processes and commercial impact are well known for small molecule drugs but the regulatory and potential commercial impact is much less clear to biological drugs.[2]

Biosimilar Update

Although generic formulations of off-patent small molecule drugs are commonplace, the idea of generic biological products (protein therapeutics) or biogenerics is a relatively new concept. Despite recent patent expirations for biological drugs and the increasing attention on the extremely high cost of these products, several barriers continue to stall their progress to the market. We believe that the key obstacles for the genericization of biologics include:

- the lack of a clear regulatory approval process (more so in the US than in Europe);
- the need to approve and implement a clear legislative framework; and
- the debate over differences related to manufacturing processes and the impact on safety for the patient.

However, given the potential size of the market (in 2006 the top 11 biologics generated US$ 18.2 billion in revenue), we believe it will continue to attract companies seeking to overcome these obstacles.

The primary driver for the global biogeneric push is the expectation of cost controls for the increasing number of these approved drugs that can cost up to 100 times more than the average pharmaceutical. Many of today's cutting-edge and most efficacious therapies are biologicals that often cost more than US$ 20 000 per year (with some costing hundreds of thousands of dollars per year), well beyond the means of most patients. The recent implementation of Medicare Part D was designed to contain the cost of the majority of prescription medication in the US; however, there was no mechanism in place to reduce the burden of the cost of biological products.

Some studies have suggested that biological therapeutics represent a significant portion of the overall healthcare expenditures in the US. Europeans have taken the initial steps to introduce biosimilar products, but this path is by no means well-trodden or risk-free. Recent proposed legislation (BPCIA) in the US by Senator Edward Kennedy (D-MA) is focused on bringing biosimilars to market in a timely manner to increase healthcare savings; however, this Act (and the relatively high barriers for biosimilars) is strongly opposed by the generics industry, which could face long periods of exclusivity for innovator products.

Contradicting this view that biologic drugs are a significant burden on US healthcare, the Biotechnology Industry Organization (BIO) has suggested that this is not the case. BIO estimates that biologics represent approximately 2 % of total healthcare spending in the US. Key to the BIO argument is that there will remain significant barriers for generic manufacturers even if legislation is passed and a regulatory path is established. These barriers include high manufacturing costs, intellectual property protection of innovator products and the unlikely event that many biosimilar drugs will be AB rated and will thus not be interchangeable with the branded drug.

Potential Impact of Biosimilars

The introduction of complex protein biotherapeutics more than 20 years ago led to an unprecedented level of innovation in patient therapy. Many of these biologic drugs targeted rare indications with no prior therapeutic options (for example, Fabry's disease and Gaucher disease) and therefore the need for new treatments was great. However, as previously mentioned these novel protein drugs have been associated with higher development and manufacturing costs that are often pushed down to the patient. The process for approval of biosimilars in the US has been evaluated by the Generic Pharmaceutical Association (GPhA), the BIO and the FDA. Of primary importance is the need to provide patients with drugs that are safe and efficacious, but debate lingers with respect to manufacturing consistency and ultimately product similarity and comparability. An important outcome of this debate will be the decision on the interchangeability of biosimilars for branded drugs, which will have a direct impact on penetration and pricing of "generic" proteins.

In a recent submission to the FDA, BIO outlined its position on biosimilars. This was highlighted by the expectation that follow-on products should require extensive clinical testing to gain approval, similar to that indicated in the EMEA guidelines. BIO believes that clinical studies are "fundamental" to demonstrating safety and efficacy of biosimilars. In particular, BIO stated that testing for immunogenicity is of utmost importance. The position paper also proposed increased intellectual property protection and mechanisms for non-patent data

Table 4.44   Selected biotherapeutic patent expiration dates

Drug name	Biotherapeutic class	Earliest patent expiry	2006 sales (US$ (bn))
Saizen	Growth hormone	2003	0.3
Avonex	Interferon	2003	1.5
Procrit	Erythrpoietin	2004	3.3
Epogen	Erythrpoietin	2004	2.5
Protropin	Growth hormone	2005	0.5
Neupogen	Growth factor	2006	1.2
Cerezyme	Enzyme replacement	2013	0.9
Neulasta	Growth factor	2013	2.3
Humalog	Insulin	2014	1.2
Lantus	Insulin	2015	1.2
Aranesp	Erythrpoietin	2016	3.3

exclusivity; we believe this latter proposal could be a key impediment for the biosimilars' path to FDA approval.

The opportunity is large and the stakes are high for both sides of the debate. At present, there are a number of marketed biologics with expired patents, including blockbusters such as Procrit and Epogen. These drugs represent current and future opportunities for generics manufacturers, but a tougher regulatory pathway can increase barriers to entry to help protect the biotech innovators.

Until now, the lack of a suitable abbreviated approval pathway for biosimilars has allowed the branded biologics to maintain their market dominance. It is estimated that the eventual introduction of biosimilars could result in greater distribution of these life-saving products along with a significant negative impact on pricing in the branded EPO, human insulin, interferon (IFN) and granulocyte colony stimulating factor (G-CSF) markets. However, if, as some of our panel experts predict, near-term biosimilars are not AB rated, we believe that much of the market share erosion and price impact on branded drugs could be muted.

Decision Trees and Real Options

In the previous chapter, we looked at methods that can be used to value biotechnology companies and some of the shortcomings of the methods used were highlighted, the most important of which is that the DCF approach to valuation offers no flexibility. The conventional view is that the NPV of a project is the measure of value it is expected to add to the firm, i.e. investing in a positive NPV value project is expected to increase the value of a company and taking on a negative NPV project is expected to reduce it. An increasing amount of studies agree that traditional valuation approaches struggle to capture the prospective growth opportunities and shareholder value creation potential of technology intensive companies. In the biotechnology industry, many companies have significant valuations long before they earn any profits from selling their products. In essence the use of the DCF model to evaluate a drug development project is requiring us to commit to the expected future decision, even if the NPV is negative. However as I have already described, the development process for a drug is a long and tortuous path with a set number of developmental stages. Management has the flexibility to continue or stop the programme at each stage as long as the drug successfully achieves the endpoints required at each stage.

In this chapter, I want to develop the method of DCF but incorporate the use of decision trees and extend into real option analysis. Decision tree analysis is a method of modelling decision situations that are characterized by a sequence of subsequent decisions and uncertainties. This is typical for long-term R&D projects that consist of multiple stages with certain probabilities of success and which require decisions to be made throughout the life of the project. The decision tree allows alternative decision paths to be described including data on their costs and possible outcomes. Probabilities are used to weight different outcomes. It is very important to note that these probabilities are subjective and are one of the most important inputs for decision tree analysis. Again this highlights the level of art required in valuation.

The concepts used in the decision tree will then be incorporated into developing a framework for real options analysis. Neither are a replacement for DCF methodologies but rather add a layer of sophistication which tries to objectively ascribe a value to the optionality that managers often feel exists within their projects. If one tries to evaluate an early-stage investment in pharmaceutical or biotechnology R&D using DCF, one will almost certainly conclude that the project displays negative static NPV and therefore the investment should not be made. The DCF valuation technique and the static NPV rule assume that managers must make a single "now or never" decision at the point of the valuation, either commit to the entire project or walk away forever. This traditional static analysis, which compresses all future decisions to one "go or no-go" decision before the process has begun, misses the high level of flexibility in management decisions throughout the pharmaceutical R&D process.

Real options analysis develops the concepts used in decision tree analysis. In this book I focus on two approaches to real options analysis, the use of the Black-Scholes Equation and the use of binomial lattices. The binomial tree is very similar to the decision tree methodology. The fundamental difference between the two approaches is that the DCF tree weights cash flows by using actual probabilities and uses a risk-adjusted rate for discounting, while the binomial lattice applies risk-neutral probabilities, which allows the use of the risk-free interest rate in discounting.

An options approach to valuation captures the flexibility of management to only invest the large sums of capital when things look promising and to avoid investment when the outlook is poor. The value of the development projects depends upon both the existence of real options (typically the right to structure the projects in stages, and then abandon or expand them depending upon future developments), and the assumption that management will exercise those options at the right time.

DECISION TREES

The decision tree approach is effectively the use of DCF in conjunction with probabilities of success. In addition to introducing the much needed concept of flexibility into the financial model, it also provides an insight into how the drug development process can be managed to minimize risk.

Decision trees capture a set of possible outcomes for a project where probabilities can be defined at each node or decision point. This is especially useful in assessing drug development projects because each node or decision point can equate to the decision to enter a clinical stage of development or terminate the project. As the drug passes through the series of development phases/stages, practically all the costs associated with each stage can be incurred before it is known whether the drug has passed the stage successfully or failed.

Decision tree diagrams create representations of the drug development pathway and probability will be used to build models of the uncertainty inherent in the drug development process. Thus decision tree analysis is both mathematical and graphical, allowing the assessor (or investor) to find insights that may not be apparent on the surface. For example, the use of the decision tree may highlight an area of huge risk that a potential investor may wish to avoid and thus the investor can defer the decision to invest in the stock until that outcome has been determined. It is important to note that decision analysis is an iterative process and in the development of each model, a sensitivity analysis should be performed.

There are three kinds of nodes in decision trees:

1. Decision node is represented by a square. Branches coming from a decision node depict actions that can be taken. The action with the highest NPV is selected.
2. Chance node is represented by a circle. Each branch represents an individual state of nature that can occur when the uncertainty resolves (i.e. the clinical trial reads out and it can be either a success or a failure).
3. Termination node is where the project is discontinued.

Decision tree analysis is similar to the DCF approaches discussed previously in which a net present value is calculated. The NPV of a given project is calculated by using the expected value approach whereby the expected NPV is calculated by multiplying the cash flow value by the probability of its occurrence.

It is useful to think of the decision nodes as occurring in a time sequence. Beginning on the left side of the tree, the first thing to happen is typically a decision followed by other decisions or chance events in chronological order. On each node of the tree, certain projects can be attached. The options represented by branches from a decision node must be such that the decision-maker can choose only one option. Thus the tree portrays the future potential cash

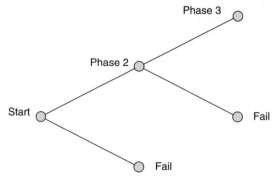

Figure 5.1   Example of a decision tree

flows as emanating from a series of decision points, or nodes, as in a decision tree, where the probabilities of both success and failure are multiplied by the cash flows associated with each particular outcome.

The decision tree exercise contains two critical lessons. First it highlights the value of being able to terminate a project at each point in its development which substantially reduces cost and risk. Second it highlights the distribution of value in various possible project outcomes, in particular the concentration of value in the upside scenarios. Many drug development projects have an asymmetric distribution of returns, reflecting huge potential upside with very limited downside exposure.

Figure 5.1 shows an example of a decision tree. The tree is started at a point that represents the decision that the company needs to make, i.e. continue development of the drug. From this decision node, draw out lines that represent each possible solution. In the case of drug development it is usually either to continue or terminate development, although sometimes the outcome will suggest that a delayed programme may be an alternative to termination.

Each chance node must have branches that correspond to a set of mutually exclusive and collectively exhaustive outcomes. (Mutually exclusive means that only one of the outcomes can happen. Collectively exhaustive means that no other possibilities exist and that one of the specified outcomes must occur). Putting these two specifications together means that when the uncertainty is resolved, one and only one of the outcomes occurs. Finally a decision tree represents all of the possible paths that the decision-maker might follow through time, including all possible decision alternatives and outcomes of chance events.

Once the tree is complete, assign a cash value to each potential outcome. Specifying the chances for the different outcomes requires us to use probabilities. At each circle, representing an uncertain inflection point, estimate the probability of each outcome, but remember that the percentages must add up to 100 %. Kellogg and Charnes (2000)[1] have used the conditional probabilities described in the table below. All the costs and revenues are stated in 1994 constant dollars (US$).

Figure 5.2 shows a decision tree for a drug in Phase 1. An investment of $ 5 million is required for the Phase 1 trials, $ 20 million for the Phase 2, $ 35 million for the Phase 3 and a further $ 20 million for the filing and pre-launch activities. The management team have also developed some scenarios highlighting a base, best and worse case for the commercial outcome if the project is successful. The advantage of using such an analysis is that it gives a perspective on the relative upside and downside to the project, assuming success.

Table 5.1   Conditional probabilities of success

R&D stage	Total cost ($ 000)	Years in stage	Conditional success
Discovery	2200	1	60 %
Preclinical	13 800	3	90 %
Phase 1	2800	1	75 %
Phase 2	6400	2	50 %
Phase 3	18 100	3	85 %
Filing	3300	3	75 %
Post approval	31 200	9	100 %

Source: Kellog, D. and Charnes, J.M. (2000) Real options valuation for a biotechnology company, *Financial Analysis Journal*, May/June.

A straightforward DCF analysis would suggest that this project has a positive NPV, assuming that the drug reaches the market. Yet in this example, management have initially used a high discount rate to counter their uncertainty regarding the drug development process. The NPV calculated using the hurdle rate of 15 % but assuming no technical risk is $ 102 million (Table 5.2). An assessment of technical risk for this early stage of drug development would warrant an overall probability of success of 5 % to 15 %. This adjustment makes NPVs derived using both hurdles rates (15 % and 50 %) negative. Using the 15 % hurdle rate, the management need to believe that this compound has a 40 % chance of reaching the market (NPV $ 4 million).

Decision trees can be solved by identifying optimal decisions in reverse chronological order, a procedure known as backward dynamic programming. Starting at the termination nodes, move backwards along the path to the chance node. At each encountered chance

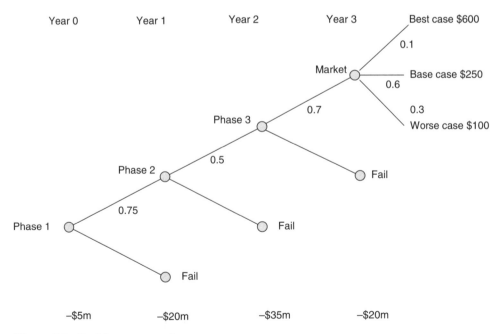

Figure 5.2   Decision tree example

Table 5.2 NPV derived by DCF

		0	1	2	3
	outflows	−5	−20	−35	−20
	inflows				250
		−5	−20	−35	230
NPV	50 %	34			
	15 %	102			

node, multiply the value of the outcome by the probability assigned to it occurring. Decision nodes are calculated by subtracting the cost of pursuing that option from the outcome already calculated. This yields a value that represents the benefit of that decision.

In the example portrayed in Figure 5.2, start at the far right of the decision tree and for each decision alternative calculate the expected NPV by multiplying the value of the outcome by its probability. Thus the Expected NPV (ENPV) of the market assumption equals $(600 * 0.1) +$ $(250 * 0.6) + (100 * 0.3)$ which yields an ENPV of $ 240 million. The conditional probabilities can be determined by management or from the literature. Now subtract the launch costs of $ 20 million which occur in year 3, which yields $ 220 million. This is the value of the cash flows at year 3, if the drug makes it to market, a scenario which management have assumed has a 70 % chance of success. This also means that there is a 30 % chance of not getting to market.

For the successful outcome the ENPV $= 0.7 * $ 220$ million $= $ 154$ million. For the unsuccessful outcome the ENPV $= 0.3 * \$0 = 0$.

Moving backwards to year 2 (i.e. the phase 3 investment decision), discount this value back for one year to calculate its present value at this node. In this example, I am using 15 %. The use of an appropriate discount rate will be discussed later.

$$\$ 154 \text{ million}/(1 + 0.15) = \$ 134 \text{ million}$$

Now calculate the NPV of the project at this node by subtracting the costs of doing the trials ($ 35 million), yielding $ 99 million. Calculate the ENPV of the payoff at year 2 by considering the mutually exclusive outcomes related to the product development.

The successful branch of the decision tree yields the ENPV $= 0.5 * \$ 99$ million $= \$ 49.5$ million. The branch that will be abandoned yields the ENPV $= 0.5 * \$0 = \$0$.

In a similar fashion, move back to year 1, and discount this value back for one year to calculate its present value at this node ($ 49.5 million$/(1 + 0.15) = \$ 43.04$ million). Subtract the costs of doing the trials to get the ENPV ($ 10 million) $= \$ 33.04$ million.

Calculate the ENPV of the payoff at year 1 by considering the mutually exclusive outcomes related to the product development. For the successful branch of the decision tree, the ENPV $= 0.75 * \$ 33.04$ million $= \$ 24.78$ million. For the branch that will be abandoned, the ENPV $= 0.25 * \$0 = \$0$.

Finally, move back to year 0, and discount this value back for one year to calculate its present value at this node ($ 24.78 million$/(1 + 0.15) = \$ 21.55$ million). Subtract the costs of doing the trials to get the ENPV ($ 5 million) $= \$ 16.55$ million.

The comparison of NPVs using a straight DCF with an adjustment for technical success and decision trees suggest that simple NPV analysis undervalues R&D projects because it excludes the value of flexibility. However decision tree analysis can overvalue a project if the discount rate is not chosen appropriately. The risk-adjusted discount rate used in decision trees can often differ significantly from the firm's hurdle rate used in DCF analysis. Decision trees offer additional information compared to the DCF analysis alone, especially with regard to identifying sources of uncertainty and providing an easily understandable graphic pathway for the decision process. However as I stated previously, the choice of discount rate and the use of probabilities need careful consideration.

Discount Rate

As ever the issue of which discount rate to use can be problematic. Some practitioners advocate the use of the risk-free rate using the argument that providing the probabilities are realistically assessed, one ends up with a probability weighted cash flow which, over the period up until commercial launch of the drug, should be discounted at the risk-free rate in order to avoid double counting of the risk involved. However as we have already demonstrated in previous chapters, it is not unusual to use different discount rates for companies and individual projects.

In my view it is better to use a discount rate based on the capital asset pricing model (i.e. WACC) if evaluating a company or use a hurdle rate that is in line with industry norms (in this book I have chosen 15 % as the typical hurdle rate). For a number of practical examples and some discussion on discount rates see Bogdan and Villiger (2007).[2] The development of decision tree analysis and real options analysis for financial options suggest that the risk-free rate should be used. However in the biotechnology industry I don't believe the capital required to fund any clinical development project can be raised at such a low rate. Furthermore, successful biotechnology companies should have a portfolio of drug assets and thus must also evaluate the opportunity cost of selecting a certain project above another project. This means that biotechnology companies implement capital rationing and must evaluate projects against each other with regard to the level of capital available. However any rate can be chosen and if the practitioner has a suitable proxy to provide a different hurdle rate, they should go ahead and use it.

In my view the commercialization phase of a successful drug faces the same commercial risks as any other drug in a similar market or therapeutic area. Thus the discount rates applied to the cash flows during the commercialization phase are likely to be more in line with normal rates, i.e. a discount rate based on the company's cost of capital. If the model assumes that the drug will be out-licensed, then the discount rates should reflect the licensor's cost of capital. However the use of such a discount rate should only apply at the start of the commercialization phase. In effect this means that as one moves from left to right, the discount rate transitions from a relatively high hurdle rate (15 %) or one derived from opportunity cost to a lower rate determined by the capital asset pricing model.

I acknowledge that discount rates can be contentious and there are views that a typical equity risk premium and a risk-free rate together should be sufficient when the clinical trial risks are accounted explicitly. When using the CAPM, the equity beta measures correlation between movements in an individual's company's stock return and the returns on the market as a whole. As I stated before, companies with a beta >1 expose their shareholders to a greater systematic risk compared to the average company; those that have lower systematic risk have a beta <1.

Some commentators suggest that CAPM is not a good substitute for risk assessment and CAPM may underpredict returns to low beta stocks and overstate the returns to high beta stocks. Industry betas are not static and therefore the beta should be evaluated within the framework of the broader market trends and adjusted accordingly. As an example, note that during the technology boom in the late 1990/2000 period, the pharmaceutical index (AMEX) beta ranged from 1 to 0.25, indicating a cost of capital variation of more than 3 % (using a 5 % equity risk premium). It is important to note that the cost of capital for pharmaceutical companies did not actually change due to changes in beta alone. Rather the relationship between the volatility of the pharmaceutical index and the market changed due to the increase in the volatility in the market, while the volatility of pharmaceutical companies remained relatively constant. As a consequence the cost of capital is understated because of the distortion of beta.[3]

Yet investors analyse specific risk that can affect cash flows generated by an investment, although they will not be compensated for taking those risks. Investors typically realize that how well an individual investment performs depends on how well a company manages its investments and specific risks.

Such specific risks (e.g. clinical trial failure) for which investors are not compensated should not be reflected in the discount rate, according to the International Federation of Accountants.[4] Risk that is specific to an investment should be reflected in an adjustment to the cash flows of the investment. This group also suggests that the discount rate used by an organization to assess an investment opportunity should be calculated separately; it should not necessarily be the same as the overall cost of capital for the company. It is worthwhile noting that a project with a high systematic risk will always be risky irrespective of the investor or the organization

Deriving Scenarios

The next challenge is to derive potential sales scenarios that reflect possible outcomes for the drug once it is in the commercialization phase. These scenarios can be chosen to reflect the level of anticipated competition, the utility of the drug in question based on achieving set target product profiles or changing clinical practices within the therapeutic area. Both Myers and Howe (1997)[5] and Kellog and Charnes (2000)[1] assume that a drug reaching the market would fall into one of five quality categories:

- Dog
- Below average
- Average
- Above average
- Breakthrough.

A marketed drug has a 60 % probability of being of average quality and a 10 % probability of being in each of the other four categories. One can follow this approach but it can be just as effective to assume three scenarios – base, good/high, bad/low – to obtain an expected NPV of sales at the launch year. One can then assign probabilities that these scenarios occur. The number of scenarios is not important but rather trying to capture an effective and realistic set of potential outcomes, without becoming mired in complexity. The same discount rate should be used for all commercialization scenarios. In general upside cases more than outweigh the downside cases, especially if the option for early termination of the project becomes part of the decision process.

Conclusion

The decision tree method is illustrative and computationally easy, but the method is very sensitive to the discount rate chosen and the conditional probabilities of success. It also has

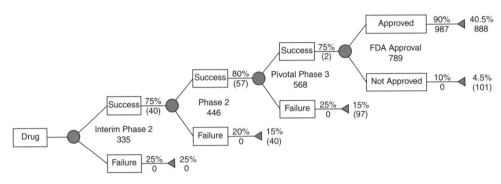

Figure 5.3 Worked example of decision tree

the notion of an abandonment option included. However the potential value of growth options is ignored and although multiple scenarios can be modelled to reflect potential commercial outcomes, the values of these are still discrete.

Decision Tree Example

The decision tree analysis works by estimating the NPVs as of today of all cash inflows and outflows of a project. At the end of the tree (far right) is the NPV of the project calculated as of today, should the product be ultimately approved and launched (C$ 888 million) or not approved (-C$ 101 million). These two values are calculated by taking the NPV of the cash flows generated by the product and subtracting all costs associated with the development of the product. A worked example is shown in Figure 5.3 using the decision tree software from Crystal Ball.[6]

Each node summarizes the value of the project ahead of the decision, taking into account the probability of each event (approved or not approved, for instance). The value of the project and the probability of each scenario happening is summarized at the end of each scenario. In this example, there is a 40.5 % chance that the product will be launched and that the project, as of today, will be worth C$ 888 million.

REAL OPTIONS

Real options combine the use of decision tress with the theory and insights developed for valuing financial options. The market-based valuation of a company can be divided into two parts, value from existing business and value of growth opportunities. Increasing amounts of studies agree that traditional valuation approaches struggle to capture the prospective growth opportunities and shareholder value creation potential of technology intensive companies. In the biotechnology industry, many companies have significant valuations long before they earn any profits from selling their products.

In biotech firms most of the value can be explained by future expectations. Drug development is inherently a stage gate process in which each successive phase depends upon the success of the previous phase. Each stage is similar to purchasing a call option and the entire process can be viewed as a series of call options. Many of these options are growth options whose values are affected by management's strategic investment decisions. It is obvious that options to commercialize the products of possibly successful R&D projects and to terminate R&D projects that prove failures, for example, are valuable in comparison with the situation where those opportunities were not available. As discussed in previous chapters, traditional methods of valuation can be considered inappropriate, especially if used as stand alone valuation tools. The motivation for using an options-based approach arises from its potential to conceptualize and quantify the option premium or flexibility component of value. Therefore real options analysis attempts to answer how much those options are worth.

Financial options have been around for quite some time (several decades) but real options have only developed relatively recently. Real options also differ in a number of respects from financial options. Real options are usually longer in maturity, with their time span usually measured in years. The underlying variable is free cash flow whereas a financial asset or equity underlies a financial option. Both types of option can be solved using similar approaches but in my reading of the literature, binomial lattices seem to be the favoured approach, possibly due to their ease of use. Binomial lattices can also be solved in two ways using either risk-neutral probabilities or market replicating portfolios.[7] Both produce the same result but the market replicating approach is more difficult to apply.

An option creates value by generating future decision rights. The theory of real options, in which the option in question is a real asset, is derived from theories originally developed in finance to account for the value of financial options.[8] A financial option conveys the right but not the obligation on the purchaser to either buy (call option) or sell (put option) an underlying asset at some point in the future at a pre-specified exercise (strike) price. Since the option is a right and not an obligation, the holder can choose not to exercise the right and allow the option to expire.

If the strike price of a call option is lower than the current market price of the underlying asset, the option would have a positive pay-off if exercised and the option is said to be in the money. If the option would have a negative pay off i.e. if at expiration the value of the asset is less than the strike price, it is out of the money.

The value of an option is determined by a number of variables including:

- Current value of the underlying asset. As the value of the underlying increases, values of call options will also increase.
- Variance in value of the underlying asset. As the variance or volatility of the asset increases both call and put options increase in value.
- Strike price of the option. In financial options this is a fixed value defined in the option contract. In real options this is the cost of buying or selling the underlying real asset.
- Time to expiration on option. Both call and put options decrease in value as the time to expiration gets closer. This is because the less time to expiration, the less opportunity for the value of the underlying asset to move.
- Risk-free interest rate, corresponding to life of option.

There are a number of ways to price options including dynamic programming (the calculations are similar to those used in the decision tree analysis) and contingent claims analysis. Dynamic programming can use two methods, the first using a binomial lattice method or as a continuous time diffusion process. The latter approach applies Black-Scholes – somewhat more complicated than the binomial approach, which is easy to build and can be structured to reflect most of the real options that biotechnology management teams may face. However, a quick summary of Black-Scholes is useful. Their model uses a replicating portfolio (a portfolio composed of the underlying asset and the risk-free asset that has the same cash flows as the option being valued). The formula is as follows:

$$V = SN(d_1) - Ke^{-rt}N(d_2)$$

S = current value of the underlying asset
K = strike price of the option
t = life to expiration of the option
r = risk-free rate corresponding to life of the option
$d_1 = [\ln(S/K) + (r + \sigma^2/2)t]/\sigma\sqrt{t}$
σ^2 = variance in the value of the underlying asset
$d_2 = d_1 - \sigma\sqrt{t}$

$N(d_1)$ and $N(d_2)$ are cumulative normal distribution functions that reflect the probability that the option will be in the money at expiration.

There is data[9] to suggest that the Black-Scholes formula is used sparingly by companies. Some of the limitations of the approach include:

- Corporate investments are much more complex than the European options the Black-Scholes formula is designed to value.
- The assumption of lognormal distributed project values is generally not appropriate.
- The formula is not intuitively easy to understand.
- Volatility as an input is difficult to measure in practice.

An important distinction between the Black-Scholes world of financial options and the corporate world of financial options is the link between real option value and the competence and motivation of the people managing the real options. The value of a financial option is basically the same no matter which institution owns it. But this is not true for real options. Exploiting real option value has everything to do with a company's managerial and operational competence. This could be a valid reason why biotechnology companies do not discuss real options analysis in public. Management teams of many biotechnology companies tend to be weighted towards people with scientific, not financial, qualifications. This lack of training may narrow their experience of valuation techniques. Furthermore, in revealing their real option analysis, their level of competence is revealed to a greater degree than with traditional methods, in my view.

Investing in real options can allow firms to analyse the above scenarios to a greater degree than would be possible if each option represented a full-scale launch. The cost of an option on an asset is small relative to the cost of purchasing the asset. Thus with the same resources to spend, more opportunities can be explored using options. Once uncertainty is reduced, management (or an investor) can then elect to exercise only those options that are "in the money" and allow the remainder to expire. By investing relatively small amounts in learning about several promising technical directions simultaneously, a firm can broaden the range of alternatives it can target.[10] Therefore R&D investments can be thought of as the price of an option on major follow-on investments.

Up to the moment of market introduction, management has the flexibility to react on unexpected events that change the NPV of the research project and hence to revise the decision to continue with product development and ultimately market launch. An options approach to valuation captures the flexibility of management to only invest the large sums of capital when things look promising and to avoid investment when the outlook is poor. The value of the development projects depend upon both the existence of real options (typically the right to structure the projects in stages, and then abandon or expand them depending upon future developments), and the assumption that management will exercise those options at the right time.

The existing literature provides six categories of real options based upon types of managerial flexibility. The fundamental idea underpinning these options is that flexibility has value. The option to abandon and the growth options are probably the most important options when considering biotechnology companies.

1. Option to defer. In some cases, the best course of action may be to defer investment until further data are available. This option can be valuable in the pharmaceutical and biotechnology industries because of the high uncertainties and long investment horizons.
2. Option to expand. This can provide a strategic advantage and can equate to a real world example of a biotechnology company committing more of its capital to a project that it has licensed, in order to capture a greater share of the future cash flows.
3. Option to contract. The option to contract may be useful if additional indications for a drug asset are deemed less attractive, either due to lack of effectiveness or a diminished commercial opportunity.
4. Option to abandon. This can also be a valuable option especially when the clinical development programme is segmented into different stages and the capital investment is planned according to the stage of development.
5. Option to switch. Can refer to the cost of restarting activities (for example manufacturing capability).
6. Option to grow. Very important option in biotechnology where products potentially can have multiple applications.

Thus within the pharmaceutical and biotechnology industries, real options can be used to justify the large investments in projects that appear to be unprofitable under DCF methods. The reason for this is that the investment in trials creates compounded expansion options in the future. This is reflected in everyday experience as hundreds of biotechnology management teams continue to invest in R&D which may return positive cash flows many years in the future. The real options analysis allows management to quantify their intrinsic "gut" feel. The ability to defer cost and proceed only if situations are permissible creates value. One issue with options analysis is that management tends to be optimistic even in the face of market failures. Thus management teams tend to look favourably upon growth options (expanding/increasing the commercial opportunity) whilst the option to discontinue is seldom exercised in practice.

Valuing Options

There are a number of ways to value real options as mentioned earlier but the most useful way, in my view, is to use binomial trees; I will however also use examples using the Black-Scholes formula. Binomial trees look like decision tress but subdivide the time to maturity in small time steps and assume that in each time step the market can go up or down, each scenario being associated with a certain probability. Binomial trees are similar to decision trees in that both are solved by the use of dynamic backward programming (i.e. starting at the end of the tree and working backwards). Obvious differences between the two approaches are that binomial trees always have two branches and the branches recombine with those of adjacent nodes. There are other lattices but the recombining binomial lattice is the method I shall use here. The fundamental mathematical differences between the two approaches are that the DCF-tree

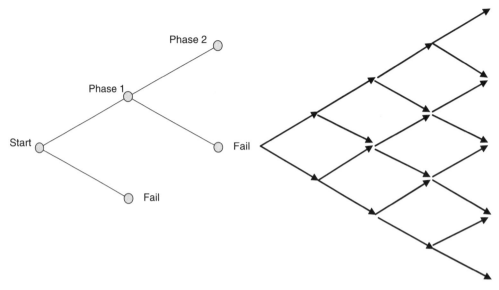

Figure 5.4 Schematic comparisons of a decision tree and a binomial lattice

weights cash flows by using subjective probabilities and a risk-adjusted rate for discounting, while the binomial lattice applies risk-neutral probabilities which allows for the use of the risk-free interest rate in discounting.

The binomial option pricing model uses an iterative procedure, allowing for the specification of nodes, or points in time, during the time span between the valuation date and the option's expiration date. The binomial model takes a risk-neutral approach to valuation.[11] It assumes that underlying security prices can only either increase or decrease with time until the option expires worthless. This assumption simplifies the calculations by eliminating the need to estimate the risk premium in the discount rate. Thus for valuation purposes future cash flows can be valued by discounting their expected values at the risk-free interest rate.

Due to its simple and iterative structure, the model presents certain unique advantages. For example, since it provides a stream of valuations for a derivative for each node over a span of time, it is useful for valuing derivatives such as American options which allow the owner to exercise the option at any point in time until expiration (unlike European options which are exercisable only at expiration). The model is also somewhat simple mathematically when compared to counterparts such as the Black-Scholes model, and is therefore relatively easy to build and implement with a computer spreadsheet.

The key inputs to the binomial tree are:

- Current value of the asset, S_0
- Standard deviation of the asset, σ
- Risk-free rate, r
- Amount and timing of exercise prices
- Probability of proceeding to next stage of development

Irrespective of the option to be valued, in each time period, the underlying asset can only take one of two possible values, the up movement, u, or the down movement, d. These factors represent the volatility of the underlying asset and can be described mathematically as:

$$u = e^{\sigma\sqrt{\Delta t}}$$
$$d = e^{-\sigma\sqrt{\Delta t}}$$

Where σ is the volatility (expressed as a %) and Δt is the time period for each step of the binomial tree. The volatility represents the standard deviation of the natural logarithm of the underlying free cash flow returns. The equation for d, the down step, can also be written as $d = 1/u$. It is this condition that makes the tree recombinant. It is worth noting that the choice of the time period influences the accuracy of the valuation, shorter steps improving the accuracy.

The risk-neutral probability (p) is defined as follows

$$p = (e^{r\Delta t} - d)/(u - d)$$

Where p is the risk-neutral probability and r is the risk-free rate corresponding to the life of the option. The probabilities associated with the value of p have no meaning and do not reflect a probability of financial or clinical success. Thus this value is very different from the probabilities of clinical success that were used in previous chapters.

An n-period binomial lattice of asset values is constructed period by period. In the first period there are two possible outcomes, Su and Sd. In the second period there are three possible outcomes, Su_2, Sdu and Sd_2. Note that the tree recombines in the sense that an up movement followed by a down movement leads to the same stock price as a down movement followed by an up movement.

The tree widens out the further into the future it extends, reflecting our increasing uncertainty regarding potential outcomes (Figure 5.5). The process of considering all possible combinations of up and down movements of asset value for each period is continued until the nth period, which has end branch values $Ek, k = 1, \ldots n + 1$. Some of these end nodes may have negative values, reflecting that the expected revenues do not cover the required capital

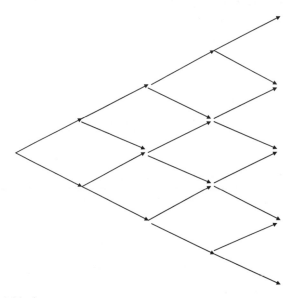

Figure 5.5 Binomial lattice

outlay to get the drug to this stage. These negative values are set to zero, which corresponds to the option to abandon.

Consider the example of a biotechnology patent which can be viewed as a call option where the product is the underlying asset. BioDream is a therapeutic-focused biotechnology company that has just identified a new lead compound and has established a patent estate around this molecule. The estimated cost of developing the product through clinical trials is $ 85 million. The internal evaluation of the compound suggests that the NPV of the drug over the life of the patent is $ 120 million. However a large pharmaceutical company is interested in the intellectual property and has offered to pay $ 60 million to acquire the patent at any point over the next three years. Yet, in my view, one of the most difficult aspects of the use of real options is how to frame the problem, i.e. the problem needs to be configured in a structure that works for real options analysis. Furthermore it is worth remembering that the risk is comprised of both technical and market (commercial) risk. Framing this issue suggests that the management of BioDream have created a strategic abandonment option and now need to estimate the value of the option.

The input parameters are as follows:

S_0 = $ 120 million, the current expected NPV of the asset over its life
X = $ 60 million, the offer from the large pharmaceutical company equates to the strike price of the option
T = Three years which is the time to expiry of the option corresponding to the timeframe outlined by the large pharmaceutical company
σ = The estimate of the volatility. In this example I use 25 %
r = Risk-free rate corresponding to the time of the option. In this example, I use 5 %
Δt = Incremental time step which is one year in this example.

The next step is to calculate the option parameters.

$$u = e^{\sigma \sqrt{\Delta t}}$$
$$= \exp(0.25 * \sqrt{1})$$
$$= 1.284$$
$$d = 1/u$$
$$= 0.779$$
$$p = (e^{r \Delta t} - d)/(u - d)$$
$$= [\exp(0.05 * 1) - 0.779]/(1.284 - 0.779)$$
$$= 0.539$$

Table 5.3 Building a binomial lattice (1)

Year 0	Year 1	Year 2	Year 3
			254
		198	
	154		154
120		120	
	93		94
		73	
			60

Table 5.4   Building a binomial lattice (2)

Year 0	Year 1	Year 2	Year 3
			254
			154
			94
			60

The next step is to build a binomial tree over three years. Start at the left with S_0 ($120 million) and use the up and down steps to calculate the asset value at each node until the terminal nodes are reached.

Options are evaluated by starting at the end of the tree. Each node represents the value that maximizes abandon versus continuation. The value of the option is known at time T, in this case Year 3. For example, the value of the option can be calculated at the expiration by the following formulas:

$$\text{Option} = \max(St - X, 0)$$

Thus in Year 3 the option values are shown in Table 5.4:

At each terminal node, the value is maximized or abandoned. Thus in the bottom node, the option value is $60 million. This is because the value of the asset in this node is less than the value of the strike price of the option ($57 million versus $60 million). For management it makes financial sense to sell the patent for $60 million rather than continue with a project that is estimated to be worth $57 million.

The value of an option in the previous period (Year 2) can be calculated as

$$[p(\$254\,\text{million}) + (1 - p)(\$154\,\text{million})] * \exp(-r\Delta t)$$
$$= [(0.539 * \$254\,\text{million}) + (0.461 * \$154\,\text{million})] * \exp(-0.05 * 1)$$
$$= [136.906 + 70.994] * 0.951$$
$$= \$198\,\text{Million}$$

The remainder of the table is filled in this way. The DCF analysis would suggest that the NPV for this project is $35 million ($120 million less the development cost of $85 million). The real options analysis shows that there is additional value in the abandonment option ($2 million). This example was used to show the mechanisms of the calculations but it should

Table 5.5   Calculating the option values in the lattice

Year 0	Year 1	Year 2	Year 3
			254
		198	
	156		154
122		124	
	96		94
		74	
			60

highlight the importance of real options as a means of quantifying, within a NPV framework, the value of options.

The same option can be valued using Black-Scholes:

$$V = SN(d_1) - Ke^{-rt}N(d_2)$$

This equation needs a slight modification to value a put option:

$$\text{Put option} = Ke^{-rt}N(-d_2) - SN(-d_1)$$

    S = current value of the underlying asset ($120 million)
    K = strike price of the option ($60 million)
    t = life to expiration of the option (3 years)
    r = risk-free rate corresponding to life of the option (5 %)
    $d_1 = [\ln(S/K)+(r+\sigma^2/2)t] / \sigma\sqrt{t}$
    σ^2 = variance in the value of the underlying asset
    $d_2 = d_1 - \sigma\sqrt{t}$

$N(d_1)$ and $N(d_2)$ are cumulative normal distribution functions that reflect the probability that the option will be in the money at expiration. Putting the values in the equations yields an option value of $2.5 million. This value is very close to the value of the option derived using the binomial lattice approach. It would get closer if the number of time steps were increased. However the Black-Scholes approach lacks the intuitive graphical nature of the binomial lattice method.

Using the same company, BioDream, let's work through another example. The company has a compound about to enter Phase 3 pivotal trials. Two Phase 3 trials have just completed successfully but these trials were not pivotal (i.e. the drug would not get approved with these trials alone). Two further trials costing approximately $50 m would be required for registration, if successful, and management hope to start these shortly. The approximate timelines for the drug development process of the asset are detailed in Table 5.6.

BioDream's guidance is that the trials will last approximately two years and could require investment of up to $50m. If these trials are positive, the process for filing a NDA (New Drug Application) is estimated to take about twelve months at a cost of approximately $10m. The estimate of $10m in management's model also assumes a significant level of pre-launch activities. Finally, the company anticipates launching the drug in Year 4 (2012) for the treatment of patients with moderate to severe rheumatoid arthritis. The ENPV at launch is estimated to be $720 million.

The very last decision that the management of BioDream will need to make is in Year 4, when the management will need to assess whether it's worth spending the $25 million to launch

Table 5.6 Timeline of development

	2008 Year 0	2009 Year 1	2010 Year 2	2011 Year 3	2012 Year 4
Clinical trials					
Filing					
Launch					
Costs	−50			−10	−25

the drug on the market or to abandon it for commercial reasons. Although this seems unlikely, it has been reported that up to 33 % of drugs are abandoned due to economic assessments of the potential return they could generate.

As with decision trees, move backwards in time to the next decision that management need to make. In Year 3 (2011) management need to invest $ 10 million dollars in order to file the drug with the regulators or abandon the project. Thus if management spend the $ 10 million they obtain the option to make another decision, when they can decide to launch the drug. Remember the option is the right but not the obligation to launch the drug. In the period between filing and launch, management have the opportunity to learn more about the market, i.e. a clearer idea of competitive threats but also more about the prospects for their own drug. For example, is the label likely to be advantageous given the competitive state of the external market?

Thus the management of BioDream have a call option which they can buy for $ 10 million (the cost of filing the drug with the regulators). The time to maturity is one year and the strike price is $ 25 million (the cost of launching the drug). The risk-free rate is 5 % (in this example). The underlying asset is what management receives in return for exercising the option, namely the expected present value of the cash flows associated with the drug over the course of its lifecycle.

Using the same approach, move backward in time to the Phase 3 investment decision. The trials are expected to last two years, reading out in 2010. The decision is similar to the previous one: management can invest the $ 50 million or abandon the project. As before this investment buys a call option with a time to maturity of two years. The risk-free rate remains the same but what has changed is the nature of the underlying asset. In this instance management are buying a call option on an option, not the projected cash flows associated with the drug. The starting value of this option is what management expect this drug to be worth at the time of its expected launch ($ 720 million). This is the value that management expect if the drug successfully completes the technical phases of the drug development process. Take the expected NPV in Year 4 and discount it back to the current date.

This is the starting value for our binomial lattice that the management team will use to value the asset. The starting value of the underlying asset is the current value of this option and the volatility is the uncertainty regarding the value of this option. In any option application, the volatility of the underlying asset is a measure of how much the underlying asset's value can change (per unit time) between the initiation of the option and the expiration. In a real options context, the volatility can be interpreted as the uncertainty about the initial estimate of the value of the underlying asset. A volatility of 0 corresponds to an asset that is 100 % predictable. As a corollary, the higher the volatility the less predictable the asset.

How can the volatility of the underlying asset be estimated? The volatility underlying the majority of biotechnology shares concerns the uncertainty regarding the outcomes of future clinical trials. Biotechnology companies can have volatilities ranging from 20 % to 80 %. This

Table 5.7 ENPV discounted to current year

		Year 1	Year 2	Year 3	Year 4
NPV	15 % $ 412 million	0	0	0	$ 720 million

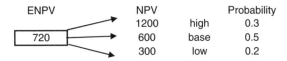

ENPV		NPV		Probability
		1200	high	0.3
720		600	base	0.5
		300	low	0.2

Figure 5.6 Probabilities associated with each commercial scenario

is a large range and aside from plugging in the middle value (50 %), is there a way of estimating the volatility?

In determining the ENPV, three scenarios were evaluated and probabilities assigned as shown in the table as detailed in Figure 5.6.

Management's assumptions at this point suggest that the expected value of the new drug is $720m. I have already incorporated probabilities of certain commercial outcomes and will use these to provide an estimate of the volatility using the formula below. These could be derived from management expectations or one could use the probabilities in the literature. The perceived inability to calculate the underlying assets volatility is a key hurdle to the use of real options analysis in biotechnology valuation. The three estimates can be viewed as representing a distribution that reflects a range of forecasts and thus the uncertainty underlying the cash flows. Spreadsheet add-ins such as Crystal ball or @Risk that make use of Monte Carlo analysis can be used to build the distributions.

The probability that the underlying asset exceeds value Z on the exercise date is:

$$N((\ln(S_0/Z) + (\mu - 0.5\,\sigma^2)T/\sigma\sqrt{T})$$

From the table above it can be seen that volatility estimate of between 35 and 45 % reasonably correlates with base case and high sales scenarios but does not correlate very well with the low case scenario. However the exercise shows that the volatility can be estimated. Also note that these numbers were generated as an example and a real management team would have other experience from developing their drug assets to refine this estimate further.

Another method that is often used to estimate volatility is publicly available stock market data for a set of comparable firms. The issue is the same when using any comparable data. There are concerns that the risks inherent in the sample of firms chosen do not reflect the risk inherent in the project under assessment. However a proponent of the real option analytic framework is Merck, the US pharmaceutical company.[12] Merck uses the capital investment to be made at the time of option expiry as a proxy for the strike price and the present value of the cash flows associated with the project as the underlying asset. Volatility is derived from the standard deviation of biotechnology stocks and the risk-free rate based off Treasury bills. For those readers more used to analysing equity, increasing volatility decreases the value of the firm but conversely, increasing volatility increases the value of an option. In practice it is worth using a broad range of cases for both σ and t.

Table 5.8 Estimating volatility

	15 %	25 %	35 %	45 %	55 %	65 %	75 %	85 %
1200	0.04	0.12	0.15	0.17	0.16	0.16	0.14	0.13
600	0.72	0.58	0.49	0.42	0.36	0.32	0.27	0.24
300	1.00	0.94	0.83	0.71	0.61	0.52	0.44	0.38

Table 5.9   Worked example of a binomial lattice

2008 Year 0	2009 Year 1	2010 Year 2	2011 Year 3	2012 Year 4
				2042
			1368	
		917		917
	615		614	
412		412		412
	276		276	
		185		185
			124	
				83

Using the underlying value of the asset currently, build a binomial lattice. This initial value can either move up or down within a time period.

$$u = e^{\sigma \sqrt{\Delta t}}$$
$$d = 1/u$$

Using the above formulas to calculate the up and down steps one gets:

$$u = e^{\sigma \sqrt{\Delta t}} = e^{40\% \sqrt{1}} = 1.492$$
$$D = 1/u = 0.67$$

The value of the asset at the time of the decision is estimated to be $412 million. This is the starting point. Using the calculated values for u (1.492) and d (0.67) expand the tree along the time points. In this example, the time jumps are at one year intervals and the volatility is estimated at 40 %. The result is a tree as shown in Table 5.9.

Now work backwards calculating the value of the option in Year 4 as the expected present value of the Year 4 payoffs discounting at the risk-free rate. As I stated earlier the launch will only go ahead if the cash flow associated with launching the drug is greater than the cost of launching the drug (in this example $25 million). The rationale is that each of the values at the end nodes represents the present value of the drug if launched in a number of different states. Each state gives the potential of the project if this state were actually achieved. Remember at the end nodes there are no more decisions to be made.

Another binomial lattice is now constructed, starting in Year 4. The expected value as one goes down this column is the maximum value of the underlying asset minus the launch costs ($25 million) or zero. Thus the first state in the new binomial lattice would be calculated as:

$$Max[2042 - 25, 0] = 2017$$

I have used the maximum as I am trying to select the optimal allocation across states that will maximize the returns with the minimum amount of risk. Once this column (Year 4) is complete, the next task is to calculate the steps backwards using the risk-neutral probabilities to account for risk and to discount using the risk-free rate to account for time. Given a risk-free rate of 5 % and one-year intervals, the risk-free time value factor is $e^{r\Delta t} = e^{0.05/1} = 1.05$. Using

Table 5.10   Binomial lattice with capital costs and technical risks

| | 2008 | 2009 | 2010 | 2011 | 2012 |
	Year 0	Year 1	Year 2	Year 3	Year 4
	89	348	528	798	1613
	0	148	226	346	713
	0	55	94	144	309
	0	12	27	61	128
	0	0	0	0	46
Costs	50			10	25
Probability	0.5			0.75	0.8

this value to calculate the risk-neutral probabilities

$$p = (e^{r\Delta t} - d)/(u - d)$$
$$= (1.05 - 0.67)/(1.492 - 0.67)$$
$$= 0.462$$

Table 5.10 shows the calculations. Note that some nodes have an important difference; they are modified by a success factor to account for the technical success associated with moving onto the next decision point. It is only required at the nodes where the drug compound transitions from one phase or tollgate to another. The remainder of the tree is filled out accordingly. For example the Year 4 value of 1613 is derived by subtracting the cost of launch ($25 million) from the value calculated (2042) and adjusting for the technical probability at the node (0.8). The value of 528 in year 2 is calculated as follows

$$((798 * 0.462) + (346 * 0.538))/1.05$$

You will note that there are negative values appearing in the lattice as the costs of running the trials are factored in. Remember though that at each calculation we take the maximum value so these values go to zero and the project is discontinued.

Completing the last step to the time before the decision needs to occur shows that the investment in the Phase 3 trials allows management to purchase a compound option that is worth $72 million. Since the trial requires $50 million investment, the net NPV is positive and management should go ahead with the trial.

In the example, I have used many approximations and assumptions to simplify the concept. I am also an outsider to a company and therefore will have much more limited information regarding costs, timings and target drug profile compared to the company's management. Thus the use of binomial lattices will differ depending on whether you are inside or outside the company.

Estimation of the Input Variables

Discount Rate

When one starts reading up on real options analysis, there appear to be two schools of thought regarding the appropriate discount rate, risk-free or risk-adjusted. The cash flows underlying any biotechnology asset are risky and therefore that risk should be accounted for. In real options analysis I think that it is better to adjust the probabilities leading to the cash flows and then discount them at a risk-free rate. This method avoids having to estimate project specific discount rates at different nodes along the binomial lattice. Others may disagree, specifically highlighting that the use of the risk-free rate in financial options is justified because financial options are valued as part of a risk-free portfolio. In real options analysis the business opportunity is not hedged.

Volatility of the Underlying Asset

This is perhaps the most difficult input parameter in terms of implementing real options. The two approaches that I have used are the management assumption approach and the market proxy approach. The latter is simple to use but all the caveats of finding a truly comparable proxy company for your asset remain.

Conclusions

Both decision tree analysis and real options analysis are incomplete as a stand alone in complex situations and neither are substitutes for DCF analysis. Both methodologies approach the same problem from different perspectives. Taking the advantages of both approaches and melding them into an overall valuation strategy, decision trees should be used to frame the problem, real option analysis should be used to solve any existing options and the results presented back on a decision tree. A distinct weakness of the pNPV approach is that it ignores return distributions (e.g. a 50 % chance at $ 100 is the same as 10 % chance of $ 500 is the same as $ 50 cash). The distribution analysis provided by decision trees is valuable to a company and (to a lesser extent) an investor. The distribution histogram allows management to determine likely results and the associated risk. The wider the distribution the greater the uncertainty.

Although the development process looks as if it were tailor-made for the application of real options, one of the most difficult aspects of the valuation is how to frame the problem appropriately. In order to do this, the problem must be set with far greater structure than in the DCF analysis, especially defining:

- What the flexibilities are
- When do they occur in time.

The real options analysis integrates traditional valuation tools into a more sophisticated framework and is a means of quantifying in an explicit manner the real options that management implicitly recognize in their business planning.

6

Biotechnology Investing

In the past few chapters I have tried to go through the underpinnings of the biotechnology industry and have attempted to provide tools and pointers on how to analyse the industry in both a subjective and objective manner. The next step is to put that hard work into practice and try investing in the industry.

As I have demonstrated in this book, the valuation of biotechnology companies is fraught with difficulties. The diverse nature of the business models, limited financial histories and spectacular growth forecasts make it demanding on anyone trying to estimate value. Various valuation tools can be used to assess the potential of a biotechnology company but there is no one correct way to value the sector, given the diversity of the companies and markets in which they operate.

Investment is about value and that is why you the reader have slogged to this point in the book. The focus on valuation should help prevent the novice investor chasing momentum stocks, i.e. stocks that have high returns over a recent period. However there are other lessons that can be applied when thinking about investing in a biotechnology company.[1] The aim of this chapter is to help you, the investor, learn the questions you should ask when assessing biotechnology stocks.

TYPES OF HEALTHCARE INVESTMENT

The creation of novel medicines is the main thrust of the industry and the predominant focus of this book. However other areas of healthcare are also potential areas for investment and I'll briefly review the opportunities and the risks associated with this. The figure on next page highlights the key areas of healthcare investment.

It attempts to highlight that healthcare investment can occur across a spectrum of sub-sectors. Biotechnology represents one of highest reward areas of investment but also one of the riskiest. This risk-reward spectrum impacts upon the sentiment of generalist investors towards biotechnology stocks which in turn influences the attractiveness of the sector as a whole. In times of market downturns the asset rich portion of healthcare, notably services and, to an extent, pharmaceuticals, rise in investors' minds, possibly reflecting their diminished appetite for risk. Conversely when the emphasis is placed on future growth prospects and the market as a whole has an increased tolerance for risk, the biotechnology stocks tend to do well.

Large pharmaceutical companies appear to have been out of favour with investors over the past few years and this sub-sector has lost some of its gloss as a "defensive play". The sector in recent years has significantly underperformed for a number of reasons including:

- Concerns about increasing generic competition
- Lack of new product flow
- A deterioration in the legislative and regulatory environment for drugs.

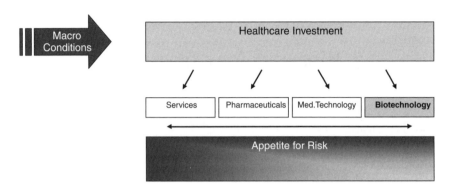

Figure 6.1   Spectrum of healthcare investment

The way in which stocks are analysed is also somewhat cyclical and appears to vary in accordance with market conditions. In the late 1990s momentum/news flow driven investing frequently showed scant regard for valuation, but recently this has been replaced by a much greater appreciation of downside risk and the justification of prospective earnings. Notably this has manifested itself by investors' willingness to heavily discount stocks because of patent expiration risk, while the failure of many high profile drugs in development has substantially increased the risk discount placed on pipelines. However as market multiple returns over time to long-term norms, the need to justify higher than historical asset values diminishes, as does the need to justify medium to long-term growth projections.

As depicted in Figure 6.2, 2006 and 2007 were very volatile for the biotech sector globally, with both years marked by depressed periods over the summer, followed by a recovery. Unfortunately the phenomenon of a late Q4 rally did not materialize. The fourth quarter is traditionally the strongest performing quarter for the biotech sector as investors look forward to the medical conference season and a higher number of clinical and regulatory milestones.

Figure 6.2   Nasdaq Biotechnology Index performance against the market, last two years
Source: Datastream

Since 1992, the AMEX Biotechnology Index (BTK) has risen 11 % on average in every fourth quarter, and the NBI has risen 10 % on average. However 2007 posted a measly 2.4 % as investors became increasingly risk averse.

Developments such as the sequencing of the human genome provide a foundation that will support decades of research and discovery. An important issue in the biotechnology industry is intellectual property – some argue that the scope of patent protection actually defines the industry. Because many biotechnology companies must partner with larger firms to complete product development, merger and acquisition activity is monitored to gauge the maturity of the industry. Recently the biotechnology sector has been hit with a wave of M&A deals, reaching peaks in terms of both numbers of transactions and valuations. Across the pharmaceutical industry there is a lack of high profile late-stage products which in the absence of in-house pipeline development forces the large pharmaceutical companies to build their drug portfolio through in-licensing from (or acquisition of) biotechnology companies.

BIOTECHNOLOGY SECTOR EVOLUTION

The founding of Genentech in 1976, and possibly more importantly its initial public offering in 1980 on NASDAQ in the US, marked the start of the modern drug-based biotechnology industry. This event demonstrated that a firm with no product revenues could raise significant amounts of capital in the public markets. That year, 1980, also provided two other contributing factors in the emergence of the biotechnology sector. The US Supreme Court ruled in *Diamond v. Chakrabarty* that genetically engineered organisms can be patented, thereby paving the way for biotechnology companies to protect their inventions. The Bayh-Dole Act and an associated piece of legislation, the Stevenson-Wydler Act, in the US increased universities' incentives for technology transfer, commercialization and start-up formation, providing incentives for scientists to look upon their work in a more entrepreneurial way.

In Europe, London was, and is, the largest financial market but the rules of the London Stock Exchange meant that only companies with significant revenues, profits or trading histories could become public companies. It was not until 1992 that the London Stock Exchange changed its listing rules to allow biotechnology companies to list when the exchange developed its "Chapter 20" listing rules. British Biotechnology Limited was the first British biotechnology company to be publicly listed when it was floated on 1 July 1992. European exchanges implemented similar rulings in 1996. In the intervening period, the biotechnology sector has witnessed the entry of hundreds of newly formed biotechnology firms, although the pattern of entry has being highly cyclical.

These developments proved an inspiration to others and the number of biotechnology start-ups increased dramatically – the US by 1987 was averaging about 75 per year.[2] In 1982 the first genetically engineered drug, Humulin, was approved. This drug is manufactured using recombinant DNA technology and is identical in chemical structure to human insulin. This event heralded the interaction of genetic engineering with complex pharmaceutical production. The drug had been developed by Genentech but commercialized by large pharmaceutical partner, Eli Lilly. This alliance has had a significant influence on the way the remainder of the biotechnology industry has evolved and signalled that R&D collaboration could provide an alternative means of funding for biotechnology companies. In 1985, Protropin (human growth hormone) was the first biotech product to be launched by the biotech company that developed it. This was another first from Genentech.

The development of the industry over the next 20 years can be assessed through the annual Ernst & Young biotechnology report, first published in 1986. In that year, the US had 150 publicly traded companies and approximately 700 private companies whilst the industry was emerging in Europe and Japan. By 2008, the number of US publicly traded companies had reached 386, with a further 412 companies listed across the globe.

In the 1990s the US industry shifted its attention from the science towards commercialization and the level of M&A increased as companies balanced the need to spend on R&D with the increasingly large budgets required to develop and maintain marketing infrastructures. In Europe the sector had initially focused on technology processes but in the later half of the 1990s various European governments began to support ambitious programmes to develop a therapeutic focused biotechnology industry in their own regions.

The public euphoria that enveloped the biotechnology sector in the years 1999–2000 is unlikely to return for the foreseeable future. The promise of the immediate translation of the sequence of the human genome and platform technologies into products helped drive the genomics bubble. The science that underpinned the sequencing endeavour was spectacular but it also had additional factors which compounded the impact. The bubble was driven in part by a race to sequence the human genome (the academic collaboration, and the company, Celera) and this race had personalities. The media attention that focused on the sequencing of the human genome drove valuations of public stocks up to extreme levels, especially as certain industry observers thought that genomics would have the potential to redistribute the wealth of the pharmaceutical industry back through the value chain to the smaller players who were "mining" this huge resource. Company overstatement of the power of the tools that they had may have been a factor in raising valuations. The excess led to an investor frenzy in biotechnology stocks. On 3 March 2000, the bubble burst, and soon the sector was back at more traditional levels.

The downside with this return to rational thought was that many generalist investors got burnt and this contributed to the perception of the sectors' inherent riskiness. The plethora of companies following indistinguishable business models also led to a general apathy amongst investors regarding any business model, resulting in the entire sector suffering. On the positive side the biotechnology industry directly benefited from the bubble in its ability to raise an unprecedented amount of capital. In 2000, the biotechnology industry raised an amazing US$ 39 billion with US$ 8.5 billion being raised through IPO. In the US alone, $ 4.9 billion was raised through IPO and $ 14.9 billion through follow-on offerings.

Post the genomics boom, investors have favoured biotechnology companies with late stage, lower risk products and also look for near term revenues. This is especially so in Europe. However, discovery platform companies still exist but only those with revenues from services or licensing and a clearly validated platform will survive.

The premise of the early financiers and investors in the biotechnology sector was akin to a potential gold rush, vast riches would be found by everyone who ventured into the space. In a way, it was this somewhat irrational view that allowed the sector to attract the private and public capital to create its establishment. However despite the obvious success of the industry as depicted in the previous figures, some claim that the biotechnology industry has not demonstrated an inherent ability to provide an economic return.[3] In fact data suggests that financial returns vary dramatically across firms and time and by investment stage. Although revenues have grown, proxies for cash flow have been close to zero over the same period.

In 2006, the vast majority of publicly held biotech firms were cash flow negative and of the profitable firms 89 % is accounted for by only five firms. Despite the growth of the industry, two firms, Amgen and Genentech alone accounted for 64 % of the profit generated by the sector. Indeed the sad message is that the vast majority of biotechnology companies have never generated positive cash flows. The fact is that the number of profitable therapeutic focused biotechnology companies remains rather low and in 2006 reached a peak of 23 companies, compared to 19 in 2001.

Nonetheless there have been spectacular returns from biotechnology investing and people and institutions will continue to invest in biotechnology stocks as long as that promise holds true, for some, if not for all. This suggests that investing blind into the sector is probably not a winning strategy and instead a more thoughtful approach based on careful stock selection is what is required by investors. This book sets out to enable investors to do just that.

Biotechnology Investment Cycles

Currently there are more than 2300 drugs and vaccines in human clinical trials in the United States and there are many more being evaluated in the discovery phase.[4] There are more than 400 biotech drug products and vaccines currently in clinical trials targeting more than 200 diseases, including various cancers, Alzheimer's disease, heart disease, diabetes, multiple sclerosis, AIDS and arthritis.[5] Even allowing for technical failure and an average development time of six years, these figures suggest that the industry should be able to deliver significant numbers of new drugs to the market over the 2010–2015 period. The biotechnology industry offers tremendous potential for improving the quality of life and the standard of care of patients all over the globe. The proportion of GDP devoted to healthcare will continue to increase, and healthcare continues to capture a large part of the broad economy. In 2004, total US national health expenditures rose 7.9 %, which was over 3× the rate of inflation, accounting for 16 % of GDP. To put it in perspective, this amount is 4.3× that spent on defence. This healthcare expenditure is not just a US phenomenon.

The basic drivers that make healthcare investing in general, and biotechnology investing in particular, appealing remain the same:

• Increased consumer demand, fuelled by factors such as proliferation of information on medical treatments and Direct To Consumer (DTC) advertising in the US.
• New medical treatments, new imaging technologies, new biologics and lifestyle drugs, all of which are costly options.
• More intensive diagnostic testing, also termed defensive medicine. Changing clinical thresholds for treatment that have increased number of patients managing chronic diseases.
• Ageing population, baby boomers approaching retirement.
• Increasingly unhealthy lifestyles, obesity, smoking, drug abuse and physical inactivity.

The essential value proposition of biotechnology companies is to develop applications based on proprietary technologies, granting them monopolies on the products of their R&D investments. Management is responsible for identifying commercial possibilities for the markets a company wishes to target and positioning the company to realize them. Capital is required to fund research and development and ultimately enable commercialization.

Management is one of the most important items in a biotechnology company and investors should take into account the strength, quality and experience of the management team. Factors such as their ability to do deals, the ability to manage risk, rather than simply avoid it and the ability to make the correct business development choices are key attributes. Perhaps most important of all, especially in the early stages, is their ability to raise money for the company.

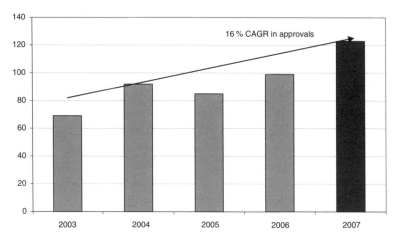

Figure 6.3 FDA approvals, 2003–2007
Source: www.fda.gov

Naturally, depending upon the maturity of the company, different skill sets will be required in management teams. At the beginning, as I mentioned, fund raising is very important and this needs to be coupled with a level of scientific leadership. Note that I am talking about the team and not necessarily one individual. As the company enters into clinical development, it requires clinical and regulatory expertise coupled with a strong background in business development in order to deliver and maximize any potential corporate partnerships. Finally, as the company garners product approval, sales and marketing skills come to the fore. While technological abilities and market opportunities can gauge how successful a company may be, skilled management is essential to realizing commercial goals. For investors the obvious point is to ensure that the experience of the management team is suitable for the current phase of development of the company.

However, the pharmaceutical investment environment continues to be turbulent as the regulatory environment remains focused on drug safety issues. Despite an increase in the number of drugs being approved by the FDA, as shown in the chart below, a significant number of these (18 in 2005, 27 in 2006 and 52 in 2007) were new indications for existing agents.

In my view the FDA has become increasingly conservative with a greater emphasis on safety than ever before. The depth of Advisory Panel discussions and the outcome of the panels have also been very difficult to predict. Regulatory risk aversion is making drug development more risky and increasing the cost of drug development.

Furthermore late-stage product failures appear to have been increasing in recent years, and have placed the development pipelines of the pharmaceutical companies in sharp relief. Across the industry there is a lack of high profile late-stage products, which in the absence of in-house pipeline development, forces Big Pharma to build its drug portfolio through in-licensing from (or acquisition of) biotech companies. Beyond whole company M&A, which looks to be on the rise, product by product in-licensing has been a major theme and, in my view, is set to continue to be so. It appears that biotechnology assets will continue to play an important role in filling the pipeline gaps in the pharmaceutical industry. It could be argued that it may be cheaper for potential pharmaceutical partners to buy the licensor outright. However, in-licensing continues to be attractive to pharmaceutical companies as it is a flexible option – in essence a real option that can add value – coupled with the aforementioned growth of the number of products in the biotechnology pipeline.

As stated earlier the pattern of company entry into the biotechnology sector has been highly cyclical and three distinct waves of company formation can be readily identified:

1. 1976–1985. This period was characterized by companies focusing on recombinant biotechnology techniques to develop human versions of therapeutic proteins and monoclonal antibodies. The early companies tended to have quite a broad range of discovery and development programmes, unified by the use of recombinant technologies to achieve their aims. Although scientifically exciting, these drugs were not therapeutically innovative. In many ways the early companies picked the "low hanging fruit". Initially this approach was perceived as low risk but as more challenging targets were chosen, the risks intensified.

2. 1986–1992: This period tended to focus on certain disease areas and also moved into developing small molecule drugs, in addition to biologics. Alliances with partners became an increasingly important component of the funding strategy as companies realized that gaining access to capital to form fully integrated pharmaceutical companies (FIPCOs) was going to be increasingly difficult.

3. 1992–2000: The genomics wave driven by the human genome project and also fuelled by a huge push to transform the productivity of R&D. The industrialization of biotechnology had begun and brought to the market a wave of platform companies. The business model was also significantly different in that it relied upon getting a (very) small slice of a broad number of commercialized drugs.

The period that we are currently in is rather interesting. There does not appear to be any emerging technology that is capturing the public's imagination and more importantly the leading US biotechnology companies are now at a stage where their major products are maturing and this has been associated with a decline in EPS growth. Analysts have suggested that revenue growth rates (market cap weighted) could fall from 26.3 % in 2006 to 9.5 % in 2010.[6] It's a similar story for earnings with an anticipated decline from 37.2 % in 2006 to 12.8 % in 2010. Clearly historical P/E multiples of over 50× earnings can not be supported by this trend in earnings.

Nonetheless while biotechnology stocks are clearly volatile, the sector has shown a remarkable ability to rebound and attract fresh capital, despite its poor track record. I believe that this is because there have been, and will continue to be, stellar individual stock successes. As in any area of investing, timing is everything. The sector has undergone significant peaks and troughs since its inception as an investable sector. The lessons from the past suggest that playing the sector as a whole is less likely to be as successful a strategy compared to the approach of being a selective stock picker.

Figure 6.4 shows how great the year 2000 was in terms of financing, especially in terms of follow-on financing. Follow-on offerings are increasing but the "other" category is the key growth segment in 2006. This includes significant debt financings undertaken by the larger biotechnology companies, including Amgen, Gilead and MedImmune, taking advantage of attractive terms on offer. The appetite for follow-on offerings dropped off in 2007. Interestingly most companies issue follow-on offerings when the stock is trading at a high price. The decline in sentiment towards biotechnology in 2007 obviously dented investors' appetites. The cyclicality of the financing window can be seen in Figure 6.5.

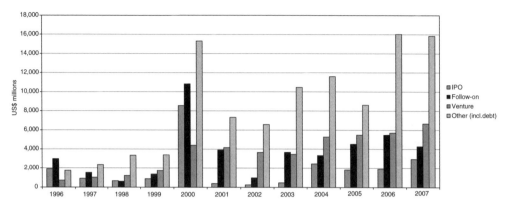

Figure 6.4   Financing by year and by type (1996–2007)
Source: Biocentury

The biotechnology sector is similar to other industries in that it has sought and received backing from venture capital to facilitate the formation of new firms. However no venture capitalist will be able to fund a biotechnology company through from discovery to launch. Despite the global nature of the biotechnology sector, the US remains the global biotech leader by a significant margin, raising approximately 80 % of the funding. The number of life science companies receiving venture funding has hovered between 150 and 175 per quarter, or about 650 per year, since 2000 in the US.[7] That year, 838 investments were made, the highest ever. The median size of a venture investment in healthcare also has remained relatively steady. It has increased on an annual basis from $ 7 million in 2000 to $ 8 million in 2006. The findings also show that US biotech companies tend to have a larger amount of investment received per VC firm, a larger number of investing VC firms and greater biotech investment experience of the investing VC firms. Biopharmaceutical, biotechnology and pharmaceutical companies consistently represent almost half of the recipients and are awarded about 60 % of the dollars from healthcare venture capital firms.

In order to augment their financial resources, biotechnology companies tend to seek corporate partnerships and strategic alliances as a source of non-dilutive financing or seek a listing

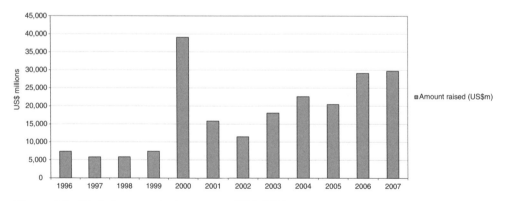

Figure 6.5   Total of money raised per annum 1996–2007
Source: Biocentury

on a stock exchange through an initial public offering (IPO). I view the development of the industry as a sequence of steps each with its own set of investors. As companies progress across stages they need to interact with different gatekeepers who, at different times in a cycle, may have different agendas.

Although the number of private companies continues to grow, the volume of IPOs, in my view, is set by the success of the companies currently public. It is important to note that biotechnology funding can be cyclical and seasoned investors often refer to the funding window being "open" or "shut". Thus if the sector is successful, it will act to pull companies through the IPO window. Conversely, if the public markets are poor and the biotechnology sector is out of favour, it is difficult for private companies to push their way into the public sphere, at least without getting their valuation slashed.

It is not clear that investors will do well by investing in biotechnology companies at IPO. There are a lot of financial papers on the topic of the "winner's curse" which suggests that in an auction where the item (the stock wanting to go public) is roughly of equal value to all bidders but the bidders don't know the stock's value when they bid. Each investor has to provide an independent value of the item before bidding. The winner is cursed because he has paid the highest price and is likely to overpay. Move away from game theory though and the caution is still warranted. The charts below show the performance of US and UK biotechnology stocks in the year they went public. Stock picking is obviously required to make the investor a winner.

The historical trends suggest that the volume of IPOs is both cyclical and also declining, possibly reflecting the flat trend in VC funding for the sector. One should note the relatively low percentage of money raised from IPO (10 % in 2007 versus 7 % in 2006). Nonetheless public funding plays a hugely significant role in capitalizing the biotechnology industry. This is also reflected in the fact that over the past 18 months, there has been a shift in the exit routes

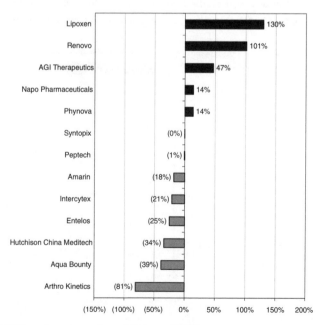

Figure 6.6   UK IPO performance – from IPO to end 2006
Source: Datastream

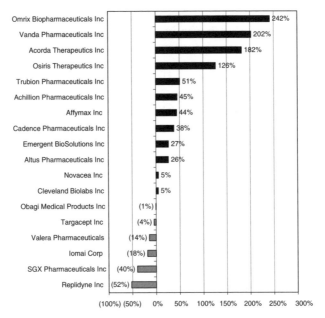

Figure 6.7   US IPO performance – from IPO to end 2006
Source: Datastream

favoured by private companies, most notably for product focused companies. I anticipate that companies that have interesting late-stage pipelines and/or a significant and therapeutically relevant platform technology will continue to be a target for both large biotechnology and pharmaceutical companies. Some private companies are facing an increasingly uncertain

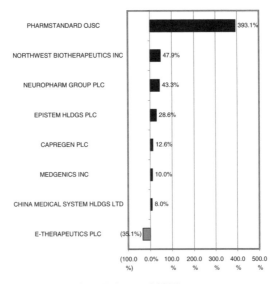

Figure 6.8   UK IPO performance – from IPO to end 2007
Source: Datastream

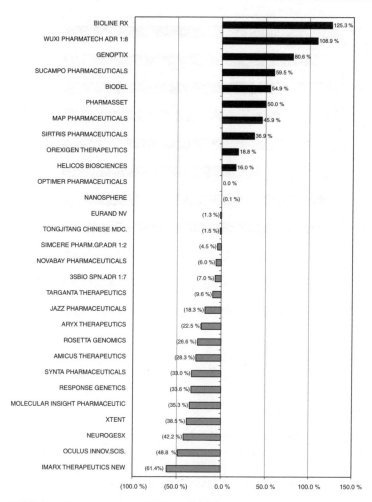

Figure 6.9 US IPO performance – from IPO to end 2007
Source: Datastream

future in that cash reserves are running low and the longer the window remains shut to them, the higher the likelihood that a trade sale or merger occurs.

I also believe that M&A is now the preferred exit route for VCs and as Figure 6.10 shows, there has been a significantly larger proportion of exits through M&A since 2000. In the period from 2000 to 2007 there were 162 biotechnology IPOs compared to 1234 completed M&A transactions.[8] The premia paid for publicly listed companies remain a healthy average of almost 60 % one day before the deal and over 60 % a month before the announcement. For private companies a trade sale may offer a higher return on investments in a shorter time than an IPO.

When overlaid on the continued decline in R&D productivity from the pharma industry, the prospect of M&A continues to be a key driver of performance of the biotech sector, in addition to the evergreen attraction of later stage clinical programmes under development.

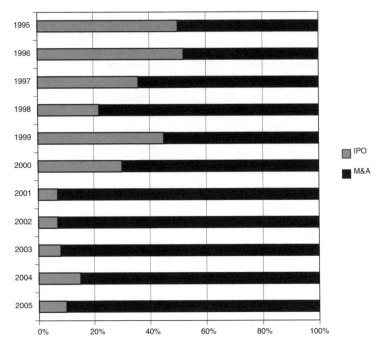

Figure 6.10 Exit routes for private investments in all sectors

Biotechnology Business Models

A common danger for both investors and analysts is to become overly fixated on the technology/drug in question. It is important that investors are able to step back and look at the company in terms of a sustainable model. Inevitably there are issues and instances when a certain level of expertise will be required but in the main, biotechnology companies can be assessed by using common sense, i.e. does the business model make sense and can management deliver on their promises?

The traditional biotechnology business model is based upon start-up companies sustaining themselves through successive rounds of financing until IPO and this still remains at the core of most biotechnology business strategies. However as more data becomes available on the potential increased returns available through the route of a trade sale, biotech companies and their backers need to become more flexible throughout the company life cycle and be able to evaluate all opportunities. What I am advocating is similar to what already happens with young medical device companies.

In order to attract investors and build a biotechnology company, a commercial idea must exist with the potential to generate revenues. Innovative technologies and ambitious goals may attract press attention and early investors, but continued success requires profitable commercial execution.

Biotechnology business models can be segmented into a few discrete types, each with unique advantages and weaknesses that make them suited for specific contexts. Factors such as technical challenges, barriers to entry, and the level of competition in a sector may dictate the best model for a new entrant or incumbent firm. As the biotechnology company develops, moving from the research and development phase to the product approval and marketing phase, the management will be faced with the question of whether to increase vertical integration or alternatively license the products to someone else. Many biotechnology companies tend to license their products at the end of Phase 2 when the ratio between the market value and development expenses is at its maximum.[9]

This latter strategy is often suggested as the dominant one and can be termed a fully integrated discovery company (FIDCO). Another strategy would be to increase vertical integration either incorporating manufacturing or marketing. This type of model can be termed a fully integrated pharmaceutical company (FIPCO). The former is generally easier to implement from a cost perspective. In an environment where barriers to entry are relatively low – no "gatekeepers" controlling markets through broad patents or domination of marketing channels – and the financing climate is amenable, dedicated product development may be a good strategy. As markets mature, the control of markets through patents and ownership of key infrastructure or sales and distribution channels limits the ability of start-ups to reach customers, making tool or platform approaches preferable.

The processes of selecting a business model and attracting funding are linked. Indeed the type of model that is in favour often depends on the market and as I have highlighted, the different waves of biotechnology investing had different drivers. One of the differences was the business model. Investors initially embraced the FIPCO model but soon realized that the scale required demanded significant upfront investment of cash. This investment did nothing to alter the risk profile and as drug failures increased, the model declined in popularity. The genomics boom highlighted the fact that very small commercial royalties of assets that would remain chemicals or peptides (and not drugs) for a long time was not a less risky model. The rush to streamline and maximize the efficiency of the drug discovery process resulted in a focus on throughput, which persuaded many small biotechnology companies to concentrate their resources on a small part of the drug discovery chain. It soon became apparent that limited value is created with this approach and therefore any such business model is likely to place a cap on company valuations. Technology-based business models appear to have appealed to investors who knew little about drug development. In an attempt to minimize risk, investors focused on technology plays with no product development expertise. The thought being, I assume, that they believed technology-based biotechnology companies would offer the upside potential of biotechnology without the drug development risk. Commoditization risk replaced technical risk, however.

There are often several modes by which a drug can be commercialized. Some of these can be more lucrative than others, but attracting funding may ultimately require crafting an opportunity that suits market trends and the interests of investors. The market has tended to prefer the out-licensing model as many companies have floundered by being too ambitious too early. Investors prefer to get an endorsement of the drug or technology by a partner and when this is seen to be making significant progress, more integrated strategies can be considered. Furthermore, if a company signs too good a deal early on, it may restrict strategic choices later on (i.e. the company may be less attractive as a M&A target).

It is generally assumed that all financial investors want to maximize return while minimizing risk, although they may have different profiles regarding how much risk they are willing to tolerate. Biotechnology can be arbitrarily split into companies that have a therapeutic focus, a platform model or a hybrid of both. Hybrids usually combine the technology platform approach with a product story in an attempt to maximize reward and minimize product-specific risk.

Focus on People

Management continues to be a key variable in determining the success of a biotechnology company. Sustainable success can only be achieved by those companies led by individuals who can manage risk and not merely avoid it. The requirements for management also differ as the company evolves through its different stages. Indeed one of the key tasks of the management team is to continue to source funds for the company and thus management need to be able to create a number of different strategic options for the firm. Furthermore the management team must demonstrate an ability to generate and communicate relevant information.

A key hurdle facing biotechnology companies is finding a suitable CEO at an early stage who knows that he/she will need to bring in more experienced management as the company grows. Potential investors should spend some time going through the background of the key management team and become comfortable with their range of skill sets. The timing of management transition can also pose problems for biotechnology companies and again it is worthwhile for potential investors to ask the current team how they intend to manage succession.

While there is a high level of scrutiny on the management team, it is important, in my view, that investors do not overlook the board of directors. Their role is to direct the company so that shareholder value is maximized. The directors should add substantial value to the company, in terms of contacts, experience, advice and business acumen. Investors looking at a potential investment should look at the board to see whether they are there as window dressing or whether they will really help the company flourish. Experience of doing business development or previous management experience is useful.

Most biotechnology companies have a Scientific Advisory Board (SAB), which advises the management on any technical aspect that the company needs guidance over and, specifically, provides perspective, contacts and advice on all areas of science that might be relevant to the company. Many companies in their presentations highlight the experience of their scientific advisory board but it is usually worth probing the extent of their involvement as there have been cases where management teams disregard the SAB. Although examples are not occurring every week, biotechnology has its fair share of scandals, which act to remind us that management are key to the success of a company.

In 1998, scandal hit the UK biotechnology bellwether, British Biotechnology PLC when the head of clinical research was dismissed and subsequently made allegations regarding unfounded optimism amongst management executives regarding the potential success of their clinical development drug programmes. Investigations from financial regulators (SEC), the stock exchange (LSE) and drug regulators (FDA & EMEA) on both sides of the Atlantic found that the company had wilfully misled the public about the progress of some drug programmes.

On 28 December 2001, US biotechnology company, Imclone failed to get its cancer drug, Erbitux, approved by the FDA and the share price declined dramatically. It later emerged that numerous executives had sold stock before the announcement that the drug had failed. Further investigations highlighted a culture of corruption that dated back to 1986.

Both of these examples show that utmost faith has to be placed in the reputation of the management team. Given the long drug development timeframes and the asymmetric nature of information (management know the details of correspondence with the regulators, investors and the public do not), one must be very systematic in monitoring management, especially by recording what they say they will deliver and what actually takes place. Investors have to rely on management for credible updates regarding the progress of drug assets through the regulatory process. Disclosure is important because the level of disclosure (or rather the interpretation of the information disclosed) impacts valuation. Unfortunately a knock-on (incidental) effect of these scandals has made it difficult for companies that are conducting their duty appropriately to refute criticisms and innuendo due to the lack of transparency of the development process. This disadvantage is further exacerbated by the high level of rumour generation in the sector. It is surprising that there is so much reticence to disclose, when data suggests that increased disclosure of R&D can actually have a positive effect on the market values of biotechnology companies.[10] Until companies adopt this strategy and disclose more data, more frequently, investors must learn to do their own homework and trust their own instincts.

Cash

For many biotech companies, as we have seen, the release of a commercial product is often many years away and requires millions of dollars. Thus, a company's burning of cash in ongoing research and development or "burn rate" is a critical measure of a company's longevity. Many industry observers suggest that investors should look for companies that have a minimum of two years' cash on the balance sheet. I agree with this view. In my experience it takes a company about nine months to raise cash and it is rare that investors who specialize in the sector will invest in a company that has less than six months' cash.

Public companies have two main sources of cash, the markets and deals. The availability of cash from the markets changes over time and this appetite (or lack thereof) to fund biotechnology is referred to as the "financing window".

The financing window remains relatively selective and thus partnering assets can provide an important source of additional funding. Because of the central importance of funding, a balance must be maintained between supporting long-term commercial goals and meeting the relatively shorter term needs of investors. The primary causes of biotechnology company failure are mismanagement and undercapitalization. Accordingly, biotechnology companies should secure able investors and ensure that milestones are consistently met. It is a truism in biotechnology that well funded companies have a competitive advantage over their less well funded peers. Companies with two years' cash on the balance sheet can develop a number of drug assets across multiple areas and more importantly can endure the failure of individual products.

A counter argument can be made if one believes that a biotechnology company has too much cash. A report demonstrated that smaller biotechnology companies with relatively higher levels of cash move drugs from Phase 1 to Phase 2 at a much higher rate than firms with less cash but in doing so, they experience a much higher rate of failure.[11] The study suggests that firms with high levels of cash tend to make poorer decisions compared to their peers with less strong balance sheets.

Investors should look to management teams that have shown that they are able to tap the capital markets when the stock is high and the financing window is open. Having sufficient funding does not ensure success but the opposite (i.e. being cash constrained) certainly restricts options and reduces prospects.

Product Pipeline

Investors should look for companies with at least two drugs in clinical trials. If, for some reason, the product proves to lack efficacy, then at least the company has something to fall back on. Another approach is to look for companies diversified around a specific disease class or that have a niche technology that can be used as a platform for a range of different drugs. The more advanced these products are in clinical trials the better in terms of risk/reward. Investors are advised to re-read the chapter on drug development and assess whether the company is doing the right trials and also to benchmark the development programme against companies that have successfully or unsuccessfully passed through the regulators. For example if the FDA seems to be looking at a safety database in the order of 1500 patients based on recent approvals (or non-approvals) it would be prudent to check with the company in question if they are likely to have this level of safety data at the time of filing.

Companies that fail to link up with a corporate or academia partner can have trouble surviving. As mentioned previously biotechnology companies tend to sign collaborative agreements with various pharmaceutical companies for research or marketing. These deals, even if early-stage, can act as a validation for the technology or therapeutic approach. However it is worth checking to see if the partner has expertise in this area. This clearly acts as a stronger signal of validation compared to the case where the pharmaceutical company has no experience in the area and has signed the deal to get a presence. The later situation is not necessarily bad news but it may not be the risk mitigation that the investor is looking for.

The obvious advantage of any deal is that it can provide non-dilutive financing. Investors should look for substantial milestone payments and cash commitments when the deal is announced, not just "talk" about a research alliance. They should also look beyond the top line "bioworld dollars" value of the deal and assess how much cash will be transferred to the biotechnology company in the near term.

Post the 2000 boom, there has been a demand for investors to see companies take a more rapid, less risky approach, to getting revenues. This has resulted in companies in-licensing drugs that require reformulation or are just a few years further ahead of the assets that prompted the company's formation in the first instance. Although product breadth and depth is required, investors should be cautious when evaluating companies that have adopted this approach. Firstly when large pharmaceutical companies give up a drug, there is generally a good reason, either technical or commercial, and thus investors need to be sure that the company's assessment of the compound's timelines and commercial opportunity are realistic. Furthermore, even if successful, the remainder of the pipeline needs validation in its own right. The lesson is to keep focused and not to carry value from the in-licensed programme and apply it to other non-related programmes that may have a different level of risk involved.

Furthermore, deciphering a biotech firm's research methodology is not an easy task. When evaluating a biotech company, the individual must look to see if the research and development can do what it needs to do and supposedly solve a medical problem or problems. This has become more obvious as companies have gone public with earlier programmes. In my view it is almost impossible on a consistent basis to predict how successful a drug will be until there is enough Phase 2 data available to be able to draw up a therapeutic product profile (TPP). This allows one to compare the attributes of the drug one has with those on the market, and in development, and assess whether it is addressing an unmet medical need or whether it is just a "me-too" drug showing a small incremental improvement.

Commercial Risks

It is probably stating the obvious but successful biotechnology companies must match their scientific creativity with market need. Investors must focus as much on commercial success as technical probabilities. Products being developed should be valued in accordance with the size of the market they serve. Investors should also assess the level of protection afforded to intellectual property. This is always a difficult area to assess but at the very least the company should have the freedom to operate without incurring punitive charges from a third party. Ultimately technical risks can be reduced to a binary decision; is the drug approvable or not? In contrast, the commercial risks are much broader and consist of a spectrum of possible outcomes. Once a therapeutic is on the market, it may face a number of threats that prevent it from achieving its sales potential. These may be pricing- or marketing-related or from unforeseen competitive pressures.

Investors should consider issues such as: are there other drugs on the market, or perhaps even more importantly, are there drugs in development now, that if they reach the market may change its dynamics to such a degree that the current therapies (and possibly the drug in development at your company) are rendered obsolete? Does the drug address a generalist or specialist market? Generalist markets almost always require a marketing deal with a large pharmaceutical company due to the size of sales force required. With biotechnology, the product is only part of the story and investors should assess whether the company has the relevant commercial strengths to be successful.

Biotechnology companies are now facing more competition, both from development stage and commercial products. Although there is currently no clear pathway to the regulatory approval of generic biologic products such as insulin, growth hormone and other therapeutic proteins, I believe that it is only a matter of time until one is instituted in the US and in Europe.

It is estimated that over \$40 billion in current biopharmaceutical sales will be exposed to generic competition over the next 10 years.[12] The first biogeneric products were approved in Europe in 2006 (Novartis' Omnitrope and BioPartners' Valtropin). In the US, Omnitrope was approved in July 2006 under Section 505(b)(2) but this process was not extended to generic biologics. The EU regulatory agency has published guidelines for the approval of the following biogenerics:

- Growth hormone, launched 2006
- Insulin, biogenerics possible from 2008
- G-CSF, potential in the 2009–2010 period
- Erythropoietin, potential in the 2007–2008 period

Amgen states in its regulatory filings that its US patents with claims relating to the manufacture and use of epoetin alfa expire in 2012 and 2013, respectively. Recently Teva[13] announced that it had received a positive opinion from the CHMP in Europe for its G-CSF product, which is mainly indicated for the treatment of chemotherapy-induced neutropenia. The innovator product, Neupogen (Filgrastim), had annual sales of approximately \$300 million in the EU for the twelve months ended 30 September 2007, based on IMS sales data.

The EMEA guidelines require comparative efficacy trials, clinical safety and 12-month immunogenicity data, all of which add at least two years to the timelines and significant capital expense.

However, the US has no regulatory pathway and I do not envisage biogenerics in the US until after 2010. Nonetheless the Democratic majority in Congress has accelerated efforts to provide a regulatory framework for follow-on biologics. The key driver appears to be a hypothesis that follow-on biologics could save the government substantial sums through lower expenditure on government programmes such as Medicare and Medicaid, according to BioCentury.[14]

In July 2006 the Access to Life Saving Medicines Act was filed and includes a pathway to approve follow-on biologics. The bill requires the FDA to determine the data needed to support approval on a product by product basis. The legislation also provides six months of market exclusivity to the first follow-on biologic.

For the foreseeable future, it is probable that biogeneric products will be approved on an individual case-by-case basis, but with a continuous focus on cost containment. I expect both insurers and governments will push for the expanded use of generic drugs, especially for the expensive biologics. While biogenerics are likely to become a reality in the coming years, the generic competitors will probably be few in number, and will face significant sales and marketing challenges. Additionally, they are not likely to offer massive discounts, as we have seen with many small molecule pharmaceutical products, because biogenerics require significant investment in terms of clinical work up and manufacturing.

Newsflow

We have attempted to take the analysis a little further in the UK, plotting the gain/loss in market capitalization (in US$) against significant news flow triggers. The chart shows that in Europe, at least, there is a general trend towards increasing valuations at time of IPO as one progresses through the clinical phase. However valuation at this stage can be rather arbitrary and relative valuations play a significant part in the post money valuation, especially for the medical device companies. However, post IPO there is a clear differentiation between the winners and losers in terms of performance.

The winners consistently deliver on investor expectations and provide significant news flow across a number of key parameters (clinical, business development, financial and personnel) to clearly demonstrate to the market that the business strategy is on track. The under-performers continually fail to set realistic investor expectations, disappoint the market shortly post IPO or just have "light-weight" news flow.

The importance of news flow on stock can be highlighted in the following examples.

Figure 6.11 shows a share price graph over a two-year period for Genmab from May 2005. The rapid rise in the share price from August 2006 through to the end of 2006 has been highlighted. Genmab is a Danish-based biotechnology company that has used its human monoclonal antibody technology to build a pipeline of therapeutics. The investment case is built on its three late-stage assets that are targeted at indications in inflammatory disease and oncology.

Genmab's stock performed remarkably in 2006, rising 180 % in the year and almost 50 % in Q4 alone, driven by a mix of clinical and business development news flow, and possibly spurred by intense media speculation regarding M&A. Genmab and GSK announced in late December 2006 a global development and commercialization agreement for HuMax-CD20. In addition to payment of licence fees and royalties on global sales, the agreement includes the purchase by GSK of ∼10 % of Genmab's share capital.

The total value of the agreement could exceed DKK 12 billion (∼US$ 2.1 billion), of which DKK 9 billion (∼US$ 1.6 billion) would be paid directly to Genmab. The deal was a very good deal for the company but what drove the share price was that management had highlighted that they would deliver a deal in 2006. It is often dangerous for management teams to outline fixed timeframes because timelines for business development are often hard to predict. However investors believed in the management team, especially CE Lisa Drakeman, who had an excellent background in business development within the biotechnology industry.

As is often the case with biotechnology stocks, the shares traded down after the deal on the back of profit taking, possibly accentuated by the news breaking ahead of the end of year

Figure 6.11   Share price chart for Genmab from May 2005 to May 2007

holiday period. This a great example of how investors can make significant returns by careful stock picking based on believing in a management team that can deliver upon their promises.

Figure 6.12 illustrates some of the regulatory hurdles that have faced Labopharm over the past few years while trying to commercialize once-daily tramadol. Although the US partnership deal with Purdue Pharma was clearly a positive for the company (signed in August 2005),

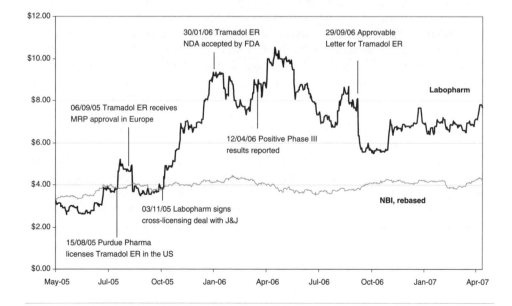

Figure 6.12   Share price chart for Labopharm from May 2005 to May 2007

challenges relating to a three-year Hatch-Waxman exclusivity for competitor Biovail/Johnson and Johnson (J&J) led to volatility until a cross-licensing deal was struck in November 2005. At that time, Biovail and marketing partner J&J waived their FDA-granted market exclusivity in exchange for an exclusive licence to Purdue's patent portfolio covering once-daily formulations of tramadol.

Anticipation of the European commercialization and the potential US approval of tramadol resulted in significant share price gains in Q3 2005. The potential for a positive decision from the FDA was further enhanced following the disclosure of additional Phase 3 results in April 2006. However, the company received an approvable letter from the FDA on its 29 September 2006 PDUFA date, which (surprisingly) requested additional statistical analysis on Labopharm's clinical trials despite the fact that a Special Protocol Assessment was in place.

LESSONS FROM BIOTECH INVESTING

Fledgeling biotech companies can market niche products and they can collaborate with large pharmaceutical companies to reach larger markets. And despite twenty years of speculation and market mood swings, biotech companies do not appear to be on the verge of being swallowed up en masse by large pharmaceutical companies. Small biotech companies can become big biotech companies on the back of one blockbuster product. The goal of biotechnology companies is to produce products and services that satisfy market needs and generate profits. Biotechnology companies by their very nature can be technical but do not need to be overwhelmingly so. Yet it can be difficult for investors to get to grips with the science. Furthermore in many cases, the scientific leader is also a key part of the management team and thus the inherent technical difficulty of the subject matter can be further confused with the enthusiasm (or natural bias) that the scientific originator has for her hypothesis. A first step is to focus on the market, not the science. The second is to check that the company in question has freedom to operate, because a competitive advantage is central to commercializing biotechnology. Without control of a competitive advantage, it will be difficult to attract talent and funding.

The 2006 performance data presented earlier in this chapter has shown that partnering can have significant impact on the stock involved. However, as we have also argued above, it is difficult to recommend the sector as a whole, based on M&A opportunities, as management teams often lack the skill and experience necessary to deliver upon deal expectations.

Furthermore, many investors continue to believe that it is better to travel than arrive – to follow the momentum in anticipation of the deal but exit ahead of the event being realized. This approach is mostly driven through an active trading stance, but can also be linked in to a general stock picking approach.

The downside of investing on the basis of partnering is that biotech companies can only do a certain number of deals in a year and therefore in some cases the news flow can tail off. That being said, I expect M&A to continue in 2008 and I look for companies with late stage un-partnered drug assets and strong management teams to rise to the fore of investor interest.

7
Early-stage Valuation

Early-stage investment is fraught with difficulty reflecting the limited amount of data available on the assets underpinning the company. For biotechnology companies, the assets may be chemical or biological entities that are being tested in a laboratory or even just a patent estate. Product launch and sustained profitability are many years away. Furthermore there is both a lack of readily available financial data and a less liquid market.

The majority of investors at this nascent stage of a business tend to be venture capitalists (VCs). For a review of the process of raising venture capital, see Pearce and Barnes.[1] In this chapter I will highlight some of the issues that VCs face. I believe that this is important because the perspective of the person doing the valuation and the objective of doing the valuation will alter the outcome based on some of the subjective inputs. For example a strategic buyer will usually place a higher value on a company compared with an investor. I have adapted the perspective of a VC in this chapter to highlight different methods of approaching private company valuation, although there are increasing numbers of other non-VC sources of cash for early-stage biotechnology companies. These include foundations such as the Michael J. Fox foundation (provides funds for research into Parkinson's disease) and the Cystic Fibrosis Foundation, as well as incubator companies being formed within big pharmaceutical companies. The benefit of these additional sources of cash is that they extend the runway facilitating the ability of companies to hit inflection points. Another key advantage is that the financing is less dilutive and less expensive than equity. However in my view, these alternate sources provide only a small percentage of what is required for biotechnology funding. Irrespective of the sources of finance, at this stage of maturity, valuation is definitely in the form of art rather than science!

Venture capitalists are professionals who manage venture capital funds. Their goal is to invest money in promising companies in return for equity. Venture capital organizations finance these high risk potentially high reward projects by purchasing equity or equity linked stakes while the firms are still privately held. The VCs hope to generate substantial gains by exiting their investments at a later date. The exit event can be either selling the shares at some point post the company going public (through an initial public offering) or by the selling the company to another party. In order to produce the return on investment that their investors seek, venture capitalists make a number of risky investments in the hope that some of them will do phenomenally well.

Most new ventures will need a cash injection at some stage in their early development. As we have seen in previous chapters, most biotechnology companies will require several hundreds of millions of dollars before a product gets launched. Venture capitalists can act as a pool of capital and thus allow firms to receive financing that they cannot raise from other sources. VCs scrutinize the firms very carefully before investing and then monitor them closely afterwards. The tools that VCs use to monitor firms include:

- Staging finance over time
- Syndicating investments with other VC firms

- Taking board seats
- Compensation arrangements including stock options

To produce high returns VCs must take a large amount of equity in a developing company in exchange for their investment. Venture capitalists also lend their experience in corporate development.

Staged capital infusion may be the most potent control mechanism a VC can employ. The VC can increase the duration of funding and reduce the frequency of re-evaluation as the company becomes better established and conflicts with the entrepreneur become more likely.

Two common exits for investors are the sale of private companies (through merger or acquisition) and initial public offerings. It is also important to consider the timelines of investors. Venture capitalists raise new funds every few years and need high value exits in order to demonstrate their ability to deliver outstanding returns for investors. Since the bubble burst in 2001, there has been a steady increase in both the number of venture financings and the aggregate amount invested. The biotechnology venture financing environment has been generally positive and ticking upward since 2001. The median amount invested per median investment rose in 2007 after several years of stagnation.

When the outlook for biotechnology companies is positive, companies can raise significant amounts of money, enabling them to fund operations and foster growth. When public markets turn against biotechnology, public and private companies can find themselves challenged to raise funds. Public firms may find that trading equity for cash when markets are down will overly dilute company ownerships and hurt existing shareholders. Weak public markets can also affect private companies, as investors lower their exit expectations and demand a relatively greater share of equity in exchange for funding.

PRIVATE VALUATION

As with investing in public companies, private company investment has a lot of qualitative factors that influence the decision. However valuation is still a key parameter. Private company valuation can be even more challenging. It is not just the VC community that needs to value private companies but situations such as divestiture of a business. Private equity investors also merit some discussion on valuation. It is worth remembering that the number of private companies in existence far exceeds the number of public companies. Thus it should come as no surprise that the number of private company transactions occurring is much larger than the number of public transactions. Three methods that can be used include:

1. Discounted cash flow (NPV) methods
2. Comparable valuation
3. Venture capital method

Whichever approach one favours, it will always require a significant amount of judgement in application, which will introduce some degree of subjectivity into the process. As a result, at some point, business valuation becomes much more of an art than a science. This is especially true for private company valuation.

All Industries Venture Financings: Quarterly Since 2001

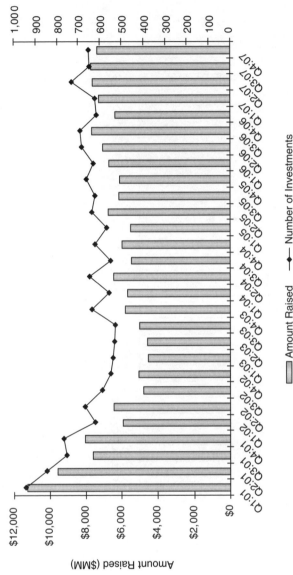

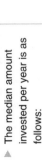 The median amount invested per year is as follows:

- 2001 – $6.6MM
- 2002 – $6.0MM
- 2003 – $6.0MM
- 2004 – $6.5MM
- 2005 – $6.5MM
- 2006 – $7.0MM
- 2007 – $7.6MM

Source: VentureSource as of 1/28/08

Figure 7.1

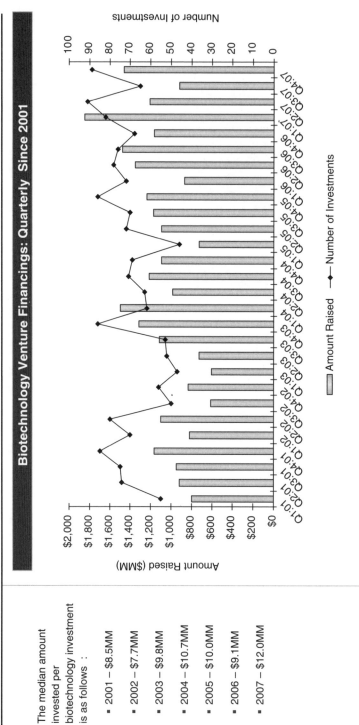

Figure 7.2

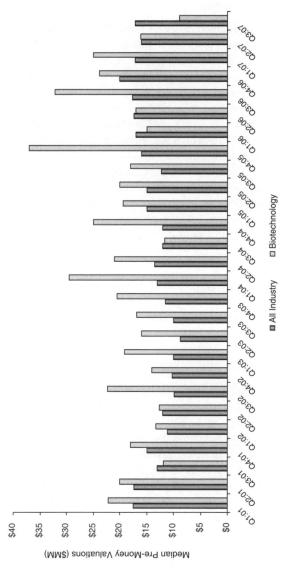

Median Pre-Money Valuations : Quarterly Since 2001

▲ Generally, the median pre-money valuations for biotechnology investments since 2001 has been greater than the all industries averagey

Source: VentureSource as of 1/28/08

Figure 7.3

Discounted Cash Flow Method

Although in theory the discounted cash flow methods should lead to the best estimate of the true value of a project or company, there are challenges in the practical application of these models, especially for biotechnology companies. The maturity of the drug development pipeline of private companies tends to be early-stage and thus the initial issue is that there will be several years before the drug could potentially reach the market, assuming that the technical hurdles of drug development are overcome. Thus the generation of revenues and cash flows many years into the future for a company that may not have been in existence for very long is problematic.

The fact that the information which is publicly available tends to be much less for a private company compared to a public company also highlights the importance of management. Yet as discussed previously, the management team may be incomplete and the current team may have little experience in business or entrepreneurship.

Using the techniques covered in Chapter 2, in order to derive a discount rate, an investor may use the weighted average cost of capital (WACC) which accounts for industry risk, the company specific risk and the financial risk of the target company.

$$WACC = K_E (E/(E + D)) + K_D (D/(E + D))(1 - t)$$

WACC = the weighted average cost of capital
E = amount of equity in the company
D = target amount of debt in the company
K_E = cost of equity
K_D = cost of debt
t = corporate tax rate because debt is tax deductible

The cost of debt for private firms can be estimated by assuming that the private firm can borrow at the same rate as similar firms in the industry. However, most private biotechnology companies will not have debt on the balance sheet. The debt to equity ratio for a private firm can be estimated based on the assumption that the private firm will move to the industry average debt ratio. In this case the beta for the private firm will converge on the industry average beta.

Estimating the cost of equity is more challenging than estimating the cost of debt and is especially problematic in terms of private company valuation. To determine the cost of equity, investors can use various models, one of the most widely used being the capital asset pricing model (CAPM) shown below. The CAPM has become the standard tool for calculating the equity cost of capital and although it has limitations, it is relatively simple to use and the assumptions can be based on logic and reality checked in the public market, another example of the art in valuation. The CAPM says a company's cost of equity equals the risk free rate plus the product of the equity risk premium and beta.

$$K_E = R_F + B_L {}^* (R_M - R_F)$$

R_F = Risk free rate
R_M = Market risk premium
B_L = levered beta of the comparable company

As with public stocks, R_F can be determined using the appropriate risk free rate and R_M can be determined in the same manner, using public data. When valuing a public company, a historical beta can be observed, because actual returns can be calculated for both the stock and the market portfolio (generally using a relevant index as a proxy) over a certain time period. This historical beta is usually used as an estimate of the future beta. In terms of valuing a private company, historical returns cannot be calculated. The best solution is to use data from similar public companies or the biotechnology industry overall and use this as an estimate for the company in question. Investors should note that the use of this comparable derived estimate can introduce significant error into the valuation if there are few really comparable public companies. Common sense is also required and some thought should be given to the cyclical nature of the particular firm and whether risk can be diversified away.

The use of the CAPM also assumes a reasonable level of liquidity, such that investors in assets can buy and sell the shares easily and at a low transaction cost. Even among public companies there are differing degrees of liquidity, with the stocks of smaller companies trading less often than those of larger companies and generally having larger bid-ask spreads. Private company liquidity is at an extreme end. This implies that the owner of equity in a private company bears more risk than the owner of equity in a public company. This increased amount of risk is not captured by the beta, as determined by CAPM, and is therefore not priced into the cost of capital.

Given the many assumptions and estimates that have been made during the valuation process, it is unrealistic to arrive at a single valuation. Different assumptions should be evaluated under a number of scenarios, potentially using different discount and terminal growth rates to derive a likely range of valuations. If probabilities are assigned to each scenario, a weighted average will determine the expected value of the firm. The use of CAPM also entails a number of other assumptions which do not hold up well for private company valuation. These include unique risk and bankruptcy risk. Items of unique risk – the CAPM assumes that investors hold a fully diversified portfolio but this assumption is probably not true for the owners of private companies, either entrepreneurs or small VCs. Thus these investors are not protected from the unique (non-systematic) risk of the investment. The CAPM assumes that this risk is diversified. The CAPM also requires the assumption that the business being valued will operate indefinitely. To the extent that many private companies are smaller and do not have access to public markets for financing, it is possible that they have a higher risk of bankruptcy, which is not being reflected by using the CAPM. In the case of biotechnology companies this is a real risk as often the drug development pipeline will lack depth and any setback on the lead programme could have disastrous consequences.

The above suggests that the discount rate implied by the use of CAPM when applied to private company valuation will underestimate the risks involved. This leads to the question of how to adjust the valuation to reflect this potential underestimation? A number of studies have been conducted in an attempt to estimate how large a discount should be applied to the initial valuation of a private company in order to take into account the illiquidity of the investment, as well as the unique risk and the bankruptcy risk. These have looked at restricted stock and pre-IPO discount studies.[2]

Restricted stocks are shares which, although owned in a public company, cannot be traded to the general public for some period of time. They usually arise as a result of a public company making a private placement, a condition of which is restricted sale for a period. From time to time these shares can be sold to another informed party but not to the public at large. Thus they are considered to have a discount for marketability. The discount varies within the sample but larger companies had discounts of around 14 % while small companies with no earnings had discounts in the region of 50 %.

Other studies have looked at the price paid by purchasers who acquired stock privately in the period before an IPO with the IPO price and found discounts with a mean value of 47 % from the IPO price.[3] Some academics have utilized the findings of such studies to postulate a formula for valuing private companies which attempts to take into account the illiquidity of the investment.[4]

This latter approach involves using a 30 % discount for illiquidity in a firm with negligible revenues. This discount is then adjusted to reflect the size of the firm. Although the relationship is not linear, it is suggested that the discount be adjusted to reflect the size of the firm. For example a firm with revenues of $ 100 million would receive a discount of 6 % resulting in an illiquidity discount rate of 24 % while a firm with revenues of $ 1 billion would have a reduction of 11 %. This would yield an illiquidity discount of 19 %. Finally the discount should be increased by approximately 10 % if the firm has negative earnings. Thus for many of the biotechnology companies that are in existence, there is a rationale to use a discount rate up to 40 % compared to the calculated NPV.

Comparable Valuation

As in the case of public company valuation, comparable company analysis is often used. It involves collecting data on public companies that are comparable to the private company being valued to enable the development of valuation benchmarks that can be applied to the private company. A major challenge with this methodology is that the companies being compared should ideally be identical in terms of such aspects as timings of cash flows, business risk, financial risk and growth prospects. The use of comparables often provides a quick and easy way to obtain a "ballpark" valuation for a firm.

However the use of public company data to perform comparable data does not address many of the issues addressed earlier such as the illiquidity premium and the premium associated with unique risk. A discount compensating for illiquidity and other factors may need to be applied to a private company valuation derived from a quoted multiple. Indeed in the UK one can look at the Private Company Price Index (PCPI)[5] which tracks the average price paid (as measured by the P/E multiple) in private company acquisitions. Although an acquisition valuation is not directly comparable with a valuation of an equity stake in a quoted company, the PCPI demonstrates that private companies are usually valued at a discount to quoted companies and that the size of the discount fluctuates over time. At the time of writing the four-month average P/E for the FT Index (non financials) was 14.0× compared to the PCPI of 13.4×.

A way round this is to look at comparable transactions. Therefore it is important to look at the valuation of companies recently sold or companies that have recently gone public. In the case of the former, one must be aware that some transactions will have occurred for strategic reasons and thus the multiples so derived may not accurately reflect the value of the company and, in the latter case, the valuation at IPO reflects the maturity of the company but also market sentiment and indeed, possibly, even the market's perception of the management team.

Biotechnology companies are notoriously difficult to value using conventional metrics, such as earnings or earnings growth. The valuation of initial public offerings is also problematic. Combining both elements gives rise to some challenging problems. There are two broad approaches in the valuation literature. The first is a direct valuation approach in which the firm is valued from its fundamentals without considering the price of other firms and we have discussed this previously. However of the various financial measures that one could examine, only R&D expenditures turn out to be a consistent driver of IPOs.[6] This is consistent with the finding that firms that are most likely to pass through rounds of financings and achieve success are those with the deepest scientific base,[7] suggesting that predictors of biotechnology company success might include R&D expenditures and the active involvement of star scientists. Other major drivers are the stage of development, the number of assets in the pipeline and the level of intellectual property protection. Surprisingly the authors of this study find that there appears to be a negative association between IPO prices and the issuer's numbers of alliances. This may be a reflection of investors' assessment that the firm has transferred too much value to the alliance partner at too early a stage in the asset's development.

The second approach is a relative valuation in which the firm is estimated indirectly by reference to the prices of comparable firms. Similarly to the direct valuation results, the study found that the stage of product development is a significantly positive factor and the level of alliances a significantly negative factor in determining a firm's relative value. Interestingly, when the three performance indicators post IPO were assessed, patent protection led to excessive optimism of investors, indicated by long-term returns, whereas alliances, which are negatively perceived by investors at the IPO stage, in fact turn out to be value creators in the long term.

Thus peer group comparisons are useful because they factor in what the market is willing to pay for stocks; it is very much an external view. Below I have undertaken a comparative analysis based on a peer group of other antibody companies to assess the potential valuation range of a private antibody company in 2007.

The data presented suggests that investors seem to value companies with Phase 2 assets as their most advanced clinical compound in a range from US$ 120 million to $ 380 million.

These companies tend to raise amounts between $ 45 million and $ 75 million at the time of IPO.

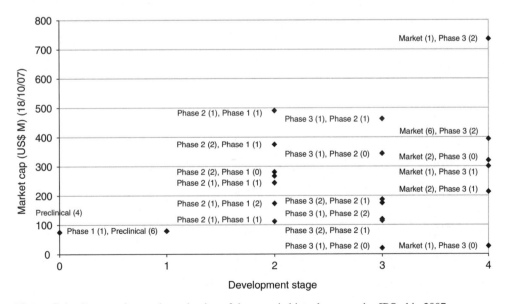

Figure 7.4   Comparative market valuation of therapeutic biotech companies IPOed in 2007

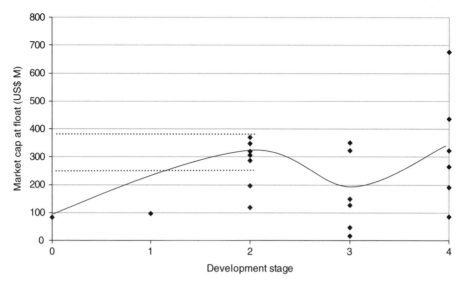

Figure 7.5 Valuation of companies with Phase 2 assets

Venture Capital Method

The venture capital method is commonly used in the venture capital community and is underpinned by a number of concepts

1. The valuation is in terms of total company value rather than in a price per share.
2. The value of the company depends upon the perspective of the person doing the valuation and may differ if the person is a strategic or financial investor.
3. The realization that implicit value is ascribed to a company when investment occurs.

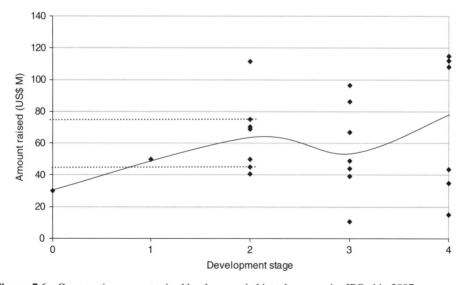

Figure 7.6 Comparative amount raised by therapeutic biotech companies IPOed in 2007

The VC will estimate the time at which it is likely that they will want to exit the investment. The VC will then attempt to put a value on the company at that exit date. Note that VC money is not long-term money and typically the VC plans to exit after a few years. This period determines the forecast period required. Typically this value is calculated by estimating the company's earnings or other valuation metric. The value at this point is taken as the "terminal value" of the investment. This value is then discounted back to the present using a high discount rate, typically between 25 % and 75 %. The lower rate is for investments in later stage or more mature businesses and the higher rate for early-stage or seed investments. Instead of using a traditional cost of capital as the discount rate, VCs typically use a target rate of return, which is the yield the VC feels is required to justify the risk and effort of the particular investment using the formula below:

$$\text{Discounted terminal value} = \text{terminal value}/(1 + \text{target})^{\text{years}}$$

As an example, imagine a private biotechnology company. It has 1.6 million shares outstanding and is seeking a \$ 4 million investment. The VC thinks that the company can go public in five years and for the moment assume that it will not require any additional equity investments. The VC assumes the exit value to be \$ 150 million, on the basis of similar stage companies that have recently gone public via an IPO. For this type of investment the VC has a target rate of return of 50 %.

The pre-money valuation is thus \$ 16 million, i.e. the valuation prior to the VC's investment. If the VC invests the \$ 4 million, the post money valuation is \$ 20 million (the pre-money value plus the investment). Thus the post money valuation includes the cash that has just been invested in the company. However the process also factors in the experience of the VC in dealing with other similar investments. These rules of thumb will contribute to the VC assessment of the company and will influence her final valuation. The factors that contribute to this analysis can range from the strength and completeness of the management team to the evaluation of the potential competitive advantage of the drug. The net impact of these rules of thumb may be to set a ceiling valuation for a company at a certain stage of development.

The next step for the VC is to calculate the required final per cent ownership. The amount of the proposed investment is divided by the discounted terminal value (post money) to determine the ownership necessary for the venture capitalist to earn his desired return, assuming that there is no subsequent dilution of the investment. In this case the VC will ask for a 20 % stake (4/20).

The final step is to calculate to estimate future dilution and calculate the required current ownership, known as the retention ratio. This ratio quantifies the expected dilutive effect of future rounds of financing on the VC's ownership. Using the example above, one could assume that if additional senior staff needed to be recruited, options may be required amounting to approximately 10 % of the common stock outstanding. If one also assumes that the exit in

Table 7.1   Pre-money valuation

		Year 0	Year 1	Year 2	Year 3	Year 4	Year 5
cash flow		−4	0	0	0	0	150
Discount rate	50%						
PV	16						

question is an IPO, additional shares equivalent to 30 % of the common stock will be issued. The retention ratio is calculated as

$$1/(1 + 10\%)/(1 + 30\%) = 70\%$$

This implies that in order to maintain the initial stake (assuming no dilution) of 20 %, the VC needs to own 29 % today assuming that the common stock will be diluted by 10 % to attract management and a further 30 % at the time of IPO.

The post financing valuation is important because it sets the baseline for future valuations and the challenge of management is to use the fresh capital to build greater value in the company. Subsequent financings use the same process as above. When an early-stage company is seeking an additional round of financing, investors have to decide what the current valuation is (i.e the pre-money valuation). The investors providing the new money have a large say in determining the pre-money valuation. If management have delivered and value has been created then an increase in valuation should be obtained. Once the valuations have been made, one should focus on the pattern of valuations. However it is misleading to look only at the post financing rounds.

The company in Table 7.2 has raised four rounds of capital. If only the post financing valuations are used, one could easily conclude that the value of the company has been increasing. Yet for any given round of financing, one should compare the pre-financing valuation with the post financing valuation of the prior round.

At the time of the fourth round of financing, the post money valuation is $ 150 million, a steady rise from the $ 100 million post money valuation in Round 1. Yet the pre-money valuation in Round 4 ($ 115 million) is less than the post money valuation in Round 3 ($ 135 million). Thus the value of the company has declined. One can also see that there was no increase in value between Round 1 (post money valuation of $ 100 million) and Round 2 (pre-money valuation of $ 100 million).

Although the venture capital method is useful, one should be cautious. The method establishes a valuation for a company at a particular moment in time as the result of a specific transaction. Thus it allows one to compare different rounds of financing. It should not be interpreted as a method for calculating what a company should be worth.

I have outlined the theoretical approach to the venture capital method above but add a note of caution. A VC (practically) never asks for a 20 % stake unless they have co-investors who together take control of the company. In reality, VCs have a fund of a certain size and from this fund they decide to make some investments (say 15) that the fund believes it can manage with, say, 40 % as first-stage investments and the remaining to be held back for additional financial rounds. The VC wants each round to get about 50 % of the company. Also VCs often want co-investors involved so that additional follow-on funds are available (and probably for a sense of security in numbers). The key point is that these factors and "where the pre-money valuations

Table 7.2 Pre and post financing valuation comparison

	Round 1	Round 2	Round 3	Round 4
Total cash raised	25	25	10	36
Post money valuation	100	125	135	150
Pre-money valuation	75	100	125	115

are" drive investment size and pre-money valuations as much or more than anticipated returns. If the going rate of pre-money valuations for similar deals is at a $ 15 million level, then no early-stage company is going to get a pre-money valuation of $ 50 million, regardless of the internal rate of return (IRR) the VC thinks (hopes) to get. If the VC is getting a good deal, the VC does not take less of the company.

In summary the real method of VC valuation is:

1. Knowing where pre-money deals are from a market perspective
2. Making a more or less fixed investment with a number of co-investors with the fixed investment sized to enable the fund to make 15–25 investments (and still have some dry powder available for additional financing)
3. Taking about half the company to get control.

The VC compares this going rate investment schedule to the expected exit value (using comparable analysis) after anticipated dilution to determine if the investment exceeds some level of return (e.g. rules of thumb, internal rates of return).

Discount Rates

The venture capital industry has come to rely on the use of risk-adjusted premiums in evaluating potential investments. The underlying risk faced by venture capitalists is that the companies in which investments are made have at best only a short trading history and if capital is invested at a very early stage there will be no history of revenues.

A number of rationales have been provided to account for why these discount rates are so high, including compensating the VC for the illiquidity of the investment, and also a compensation for the assumption that the forecasts are optimistic. The forecasts provided by companies at this stage tend to be over optimistic and it should be remembered that the majority of early-stage businesses fail. VCs also provide considerable experience and other resources to fledgeling firms and the large discount rate could be viewed as a way (albeit crude) to compensate VCs for these services.

Conclusion

The venture method is another tool that facilitates the evaluation of early-stage investments. Similar to the conclusion with decision trees and real options, I do not see it as an alternative to DCF methods of valuation but rather an additional tool that helps crystallize the return that the VC is looking for in an investment, given that these investments are made at very early stages in the company's evolution.

Glossary

I have included this glossary of technical terms, not all of which occur in this book but which potential investors may find useful. It is not intended as a replacement for a good medical dictionary.

Absorption, Distributions, Metabolism, Excretion and Toxicology (ADMET): an element of preclinical trials used to measure the effects of a drug on animal and human physiology.

Adenine: one of the four basis units making up DNA. It binds to (T). In RNA adenine binds to Uracil. Therefore, the DNA pairing is AT and RNA pairing is AU.

Adjuvant: a compound that increases the effectiveness of another drug or antibody.

Affinity: affinity refers to the strength of binding between a drug and its receptor. The number of cell receptors occupied by a drug is a function of an equilibrium between a drug which is bound to receptors and a drug that is free. A high-affinity agonist or antagonist is less likely than a low-affinity drug to dissociate from a receptor once it is bound.

Agonist: drugs which alter the physiology of a cell by binding to plasma membrane or intracellular receptors. Usually, a number of receptors must be occupied by agonists before a measurable change in cell function occurs.

Amino Acid: building block of proteins. Proteins consist of amino acids linked end-to-end. There are 20 different amino acid molecules that make up proteins. The DNA sequence that codes for a gene dictates the order of amino acids in a given protein.

Amplification: increasing the number of copies of a gene.

Aneuploidy: the addition or deletion of parts of a chromosome.

Angiogenesis: used in reference to an agent that promotes the growth of new blood vessels.

Antagonist: antagonists inhibit or block responses caused by agonists.

Antiangiogenesis: use of an agent to block the formation of new blood vessels.

Antibiotic: a chemical substance that can kill or inhibit the growth of a micro organism.

Antibody: immune system protein produced by humans and higher animals to recognize and neutralize bacteria, viruses, cancerous cells and other foreign compounds.

Antigen: a molecule on the surface of an invading organism that the body identifies as alien and then uses to target an immune system attack.

Antisense: a natural or synthetic DNA or RNA molecule that specifically binds with messenger RNA to selectively inhibit expression of a single gene.

Apoptosis: genetically programmed cell suicide, a natural process that biotechnology is attempting to harness in order to induce the death of cancer cells.

Apparent volume of distribution: is a calculated value that describes the nature of drug distribution. It is the volume that would be required to contain the administered dose if that dose was evenly distributed at the concentration measured in plasma.

Assay: laboratory technique to search for a biological response to an agent.

Autoimmune disease: an attack by the immune system on the body's own tissues.

Autoradiography: the imaging of radioactive labelled substances that are placed in the body and targeted to regions of interest.

Autosome: a chromosome that has no role in sex determination.

Bacteriophage: also known as a phage, this is a virus that attacks bacteria.

Base: a key component of DNA and RNA molecules. Four different bases are found in DNA: adenine (A), cytosine (C), guanine (G) and thymine (T). In RNA uracil (U) substitutes for thymine.

Base Pair: two bases that bond together to form one rung in the spiral (or twisted ladder formation) of DNA. Base Adenine can only pair with Thymine. Cytosine can only pair with Guanine (the pairs are joined by weak bonds).

Base sequence analysis: a system to determine the sequences of bases.

Biochemistry: the study of the processes involved in the chemical reactions of living organisms and their application. The study of structure and reactions of proteins, nucleic acids, carbohydrates and lipids.

Bioinformatics: the application of information technology to manage and analyse the vast amounts of data generated from biological research.

Bioluminescence: the emission of light by a biological material, useful in genetic analysis and high throughput screening.

Bioreactor: a tank used for large-scale fermentation of biological materials such as bacteria that have been engineered to produce a medicinal protein.

Biotechnology: the application of molecular biology for useful purposes.

Blood brain barrier: Larger molecules are prevented from reaching the brain through this defence system. It protects the brain from toxins but it also stops drugs from reaching important targets. Crossing this barrier is a major threshold in delivering medicine to the brain.

B-lymphocytes: these are attack cells that are produced to combat invading organisms. They are produced in lymph nodes, in blood and in the spleen.

Cancer cells: cells that multiply and do not respond to the body's usual instructions to regulate cell division. These can appear as solid tumours and nonsolid tumours.

Carrier: a carrier holds one copy of a mutant gene that may cause inherited disease. The carrier may not manifest this disease because two copies of a "recessive" mutant gene must be combined to create a disorder. Offspring of the carrier may develop disease from this "recessive gene" if both parents are carriers.

Catalyst: a chemical agent that facilitates a reaction without undergoing change.

cDNA (complementary DNA): DNA synthesizes from mRNA (messenger RNA); often used in DNA probes to find complementary strands.

Cell: the basic unit of life. A membrane-bound unit capable of processes associated with life.

Cell biology: the study of the processes inside a cell.

Cell culture: special preparations used to grow isolated cells in a test tube in the hopes of maintaining their specific characteristics alive for research or therapy.

Cell cycle: the stages of cellular reproduction.

Cell fusion: the fusion of a sperm cell and an egg.

Cell line: cells that grow in a lab rather than a living organism.

Cell membrane: the outer shell of a cell, which regulates everything entering and leaving the cell.

Centromere: a portion of the chromosome that anchors spindle fibres during cell division. It is centred between two telomeres that mark the end of a chromosome.

Chimera: an organism that carries information from two different organisms, created by grafting part of an embryo from one species onto an embryo from another.

Chirality: Chemically left-handed and right-handed proteins may be exactly the same but they behave differently because of their chirality, just as left and right hands are essentially the same but often cannot perform tasks in the same way.

Chromatid: a strand created by the duplication of a chromosome (in mitosis or meiosis).

Chromatin: the basic material of chromosomes, created when strands of DNA are joined in a matrix by organic compounds.

Chromosome: the DNA protein complexes that contain all the genes in a cell.

Clone: an exact copy of an organism or part of an organism such as a length of DNA.

Cloning vector: a DNA molecule that has been genetically engineered to allow the insertion of cloned DNA. Using a cloned vector, it is possible to make enormous quantities of cloned DNA.

Codon: a sequence of three DNA or RNA bases that specifies an amino acid in the synthesis of a protein.

Coenzyme: a molecule needed by an enzyme to trigger its action.

Collagen: the protein that give fullness or firmness to skin cells. As it breaks down, wrinkles form.

Combinational chemistry: a product discovery technique that uses robotics and parallel chemical reactions to generate and screen as many as several million molecules with similar structures in order to find chemical molecules with desired properties.

Competitive antagonist: competes with agonists for receptors.

Complementary sequence: a sequence of DNA base pairs that will match with and join with another DNA sequence. In a sense, it is a molecular mirror image.

Conserved sequence: a sequence of base pairs in DNA that has remained stable throughout the evolutionary process. For example, a sequence that is the same in a fruit fly and a human.

Contig: pieces of cloned DNA that overlap and give a picture of the whole chromosome.

Cosmid: a vector, or delivery vehicle, that allows for the insertion of large amounts of DNA into a target.

Crossing-over: during reproduction (meiosis) chromosomes from the mother and father line up in pairs and the two chromosomes may swap genes. Some paternal genes may wind up on the mother's chromosome and vice versa.

Cystic fibrosis: an inherited condition in which a missing enzyme does not allow the lungs to clear mucus.

Cytokine: the name for a family of immune system proteins, including interleukins, interferons, tumour necrosis factor (TNF) and colony-stimulating factors (CSF).

Cytology: the study of cells, including function, appearance and behaviour.

Cytoplasm: the internal contents of a cell excepting the nucleus.

Cytosine (C): one of the four bases of DNA and RNA. Cytosine always pairs with guanine (C-G).

Data mining: using computers to analyse masses of information to discover trends and patterns.

Diagnostic: a product used for the diagnosis of a disease or medical condition.

Diploid: an organism or cell having two sets of chromosomes.

Dissociation constant: the dissociation constant is the measure of a drug's affinity for a given receptor. It is the concentration of drug required in solution to achieve 50% occupancy of its receptors. Units are expressed in molar concentration.

Distribution half-life: reflects the rapid decline in plasma drug concentration as a dose of drug is distributed throughout the body.

DNA (deoxyribonucliec acid): the primary source of genetic information in cells. DNA is comprised of nucleotides and is composed of two strands wound around each other, called the double helix.

DNA fingerprinting: a DNA analysis method that measure genetic variation among individuals. This technology is often used as a forensic tool to detect differences or similarities in blood and tissue samples at crime scenes.

DNA probes: small sequences of the base units (A,T,C,G). They are tagged with a radioactive or fluorescent label and merge with complementary DNA sequences. Because the sequence of the probe is known, the sequence of a DNA fragment that pairs with it can be inferred.

DNA replication: use of existing DNA to synthesize multiple copies.

DNA sequencing: the process of determining the exact order of bases in a segment of DNA.

Domain: any part of a protein that has a discrete, identifiable function.

Dominant disease: if a disease is dominantly inherited, only one copy of the gene is needed to express the disease in the child who receives the mutation (recessive diseases require two copies).

Dominant gene: unlike a recessive gene, a dominant gene from either parent is always expressed in the next generation (one copy is enough). With recessive genes, two copies are needed to express this gene in offspring.

Double-blind: an experimental protocol whereby neither the experimental subjects nor the administrators know whether a drug or placebo is being administered. Double-blind protocols are used to eliminate bias.

Double helix: the pattern of a DNA molecule. It resembles two entwined circular staircases.

Drug delivery: the process by which a formulated drug is administered to the patient.

Drug development: the process of taking a lead compound, demonstrating it to be safe and effective for use in humans, and preparing it for commercial scale manufacture.

Drug receptors: receptors are generally proteins or glycoproteins that are present on the cell surface, on an organelle within the cell, or in the cytoplasm. There are a finite number of receptors in a given cell. Thus, receptor-mediated responses plateau upon (or before) receptor saturation.

Duration: is the length of time for which a drug is therapeutic. The duration usually corresponds to the half-life of the drug (except when the drug binds irreversibly to its receptor) and is dependent on the metabolism and excretion of the drug.

Effective concentration 50%: the concentration of drug which induces a specified clinical effect in 50% of the subjects to which the drug is administered.

Efficacy: the degree to which a drug is able to induce maximal effects.

Electrophoresis (or gel electrophoresis): the system that creates the familiar DNA finger-print, a ladder of bars or varying thickness. A gel containing DNA fragments is electrically charged and the smaller pieces move toward the attracting pole faster than the bigger ones. They spread out in a consistent way and a characteristic pattern is laid out.

Electroporation: the use of pulsed electrical charges to open pores in cell walls, allowing drugs or genetic material to be inserted.

Elimination half-life: reflects the metabolism and excretion of the drug. Note that several half-lives pass before the serum concentration of drugs read steady state.

Embryo twinning: a developing embryo (bigger than one cell but not too big) physically split at an early age. These two embryos or zygotes may grow into distinct but identical creatures.

Endoplasmic reticulum: a membranous system of tubes and sacs found in eukaryotic cells. Its function is to store proteins made by ribosomes.

Enzyme: a functional protein that catalyses (speeds up) a chemical reaction. Enzymes control the rate of naturally occurring metabolic processes such as those necessary for growth and reproduction.

Escherichia coli (E coli): a common gut bacterium that is a workhorse and model organism for molecular biology.

Eukaryote: any cell with a self-contained nucleus. Cells that store DNA without protection from the wall of a nucleus (like bacteria) are called prokaryotes.

Excipient: an inactive ingredient (there are no absolutely inert excipients) added to a drug to give it a pill form or otherwise aid in delivery.

Exon: the section of a gene that codes for (or helps express) a given protein (see intron).

Expression: a highly specific process in which a gene is switched on at a certain time and its encoded protein is synthesized, resulting in the manifestation of a characteristic that is specified by a gene. Genetic predispositions to disease arise when a person carries the gene for a disease but it is not expressed.

Factor VIII and Factor IX: proteins for blood clotting. A shortage results in haemophilia.

False negative: an experimental outcome that incorrectly yields a negative result. False negatives can complicate disease diagnosis.

False positive: an experimental outcome that incorrectly yields a positive result. False positives can frustrate assessing the performance of lead compounds.

Fermentation: a scientific process commonly known as brewing. In the context of biotechnology, it refers to the placement of organisms and nutrients in large vats with an optimized environment. The organisms then produce material that is filtered in order to obtain the desired product, which could be a medication or even protein used to make food.

First pass effect: blood from the gastrointestinal tract passes through the liver before entering any other organs. During this first pass through the liver, a fraction of the drug (in some cases nearly all) can be metabolized to an inactive or less active derivative. The inactivation of some drugs is so great that the agents are useless when administered orally.

Functional foods: foods containing compounds with beneficial health effects beyond those provided by the basic nutrients, minerals and vitamins.

Functional genomics: the use of biological experiments and genetic correlations to establish what each gene does, how it is regulated and how it interacts with other genes.

Gamete: a complete reproductive cell: sperm or egg.

Gene: the fundamental unit of heredity, a segment of DNA which encodes a defined biochemical function. Some genes direct the synthesis of proteins, while others have regulatory functions.

Gene amplification: laboratory technique in which selected portions of DNA from a single cell can be duplicated indefinitely until there is a large enough quantity to analyse. This is made possible by a process called polymerase chain reaction.

Gene expression: the complex process which a gene's code is expressed (or converted) into chemical structures such as proteins or mRNA.

Gene family: a group of genes believed to be related by their ability to make similar products in the body.

Gene mapping: establishing the positions of genes on DNA molecules.

Gene pool: the grand total of all genetic information held by all members of a breeding population.

Gene product: the final materials that a gene expresses (or codes for). When a gene has been associated with a product, it's easier to determine if the gene is overactive or underactive.

Gene therapy: the replacement of a defective gene in a person or organism suffering from a genetic disease.

Genetic code: the language in which DNA's instructions are written. The genetic code consists of triplets of nucleotides (codons), with each triplet corresponding to one amino acid in a protein structure, or a signal to start or stop protein production.

Genetic disease: a disorder caused by a defective or partially defective gene or chromosome. There are 3000 known genetic diseases in humans, including cystic fibrosis and Down's syndrome.

Genetic disorder: a condition or mutation that results from one or more defective genes.

Genetic drift: random fluctuations in gene frequency in a small population.

Genetic engineering: the manipulation of genes to create heritable changes in biological organisms and products that are useful to people, living things or the environment.

Genetic equilibrium: a gene pool with no mutations or outside influences.

Genetic predisposition: a susceptibility to disease that is related to a genetic condition, which may or may not result in actual development of the disease.

Genetic screening: the use of a specific biological test to screen for inherited diseases or medical conditions.

Genetics: the study of patterns of inherited traits.

Genome: the sum total of an organism's genes.

Genomic library: a collection of DNA clones used for reference and analysis.

Genomic sequence: the exact order (or sequence) of nucleotides that make up any given section of DNA.

Genomics: the study of genes and their function.

Genotype: the actual genetic composition of a patient. Discovering a patient's genotype may provide valuable information about the nature of disease and the kind of medicine most likely to be safe and effective (see also phenotype).

Germ cells: reproductive cells that, when mature, can participate in fertilization.

Germ line gene therapy: genetic manipulation of germ cells.

Globulins: blood proteins that do not dissolve in water: alpha, beta and gamma types.

Good Manufacturing Practice (GMP): guidelines ensuring the quality and purity of chemical products that are intended for use in pharmaceutical application and controls ensuring that methods and facilities used for production, processing, packaging and storage result in drugs with consistent and sufficient quality, purity and activity.

Guanine (G): one of the DNA base units. Guanine pairs with cytosine (GC).

Half-life: is the amount of time required for the plasma concentration of a drug to decrease by 50% after discontinuance of the drug.

Haploid: any organism that has only one complete set of chromosomes.

Haemoglobin: the blood protein responsible for carrying oxygen.

Hedgehog protein: an important protein that appears to stimulate nerve regeneration.

High throughput screening (HTS): the highly mechanized and computerized process of checking thousands of different molecules to see which interact with a target molecule.

Histocompatability complex: the spot on Chromosome 6 that allows the body to distinguish between self and non-self.

Hormones: chemical messengers that direct bodily processes. According to type they can influence the growth of various cells and organs (i.e. beard, breasts).

Human Genome Project: the international research effort which identified and located the full sequence of bases in the human genome.

Human Growth Hormone: one of the first proteins created artificially by the biotechnology industry, used to stimulate growth in hormone-deficient children. May also have properties to slow down the ageing process.

Hybridization: the creation of a double-stranded DNA molecule by joining two complementary strands of DNA (or a strand of DNA with an RNA strand).

Hybridoma: a highly specific antibody derived from a single clone. Hybridomas are used to produce highly reliable monoclonal antibodies, thus reducing the amount of contaminants in the desired product.

Immune system: the cells, biological substances (such as antibodies) and cellular activities that work together to recognize foreign substances and provide resistance to disease.

Immunology: the study of the immune system. The immune system makes up the body's defences against foreign bodies, whether microscopic or not. Its main defences are in the form of proteins called antibodies. The immune system can also make antibodies against itself and cause diseases classified as autoimmune.

Imprinting: a peculiar phenomenon of inheritance. A gene mutation received from the father can cause one disease and the same mutation from the mother causes another. Positioning of the gene in the genetic sequence of offspring is believed to be the cause.

Inducer: any substance that stimulates an increase in the amount of enzymes required to metabolize the substance (e.g. sugar stimulates insulin that leads to metabolization of sugars).

Inhalation administration: generally rapid absorption. Some agents, marketed in devices which deliver metered doses, are suitable for self-administration.

Irreversible antagonist: irreversible antagonists are insurmountable. These agents compete with agonists for the agonist-binding domain. In contrast to competitive antagonists, however, irreversible antagonists combine permanently with the receptor.

In silico (**'in computer'**): computer-based predictions that can complement *in vitro* and *in vivo* procedures.

In situ hybridization: finding the location of DNA or cDNA in a tissue sample to locate which part is expressing a certain gene or harbouring a virus. Probes perform this function by binding to complementary targets only.

Insulin: hormone that regulates blood sugars.

Interferons: three proteins called Alpha, Beta and Gamma defend the body against disease such as viruses and tumours.

Interphase: the period between cell divisions when a cell performs its intended functions.

Intramuscular (IM) administration: drug passes through capillary walls to enter the blood stream. Rate of absorption depends on formulation (oil-based preparations are absorbed rapidly). May be used for self-administration by trained patients.

Intravenous (IV) administration: rapid onset of action because agent is injected directly into the blood stream. Useful in emergencies and in patients that are unconscious. Insoluble drugs cannot be administered intravenously.

Intron: a segment of a gene that does not code for a protein. See exon.

Inversion: reversing the order of genes in a chromosome.

*In vitro***:** experimental procedures carried out in test-tubes, beakers etc.

*In vivo***:** experimental procedures carried out on living cell lines or in living animals.

Keratin: an inert protein that makes up hair and nails.

Kilobase (kb): shorthand for 1000 nucleotides. Used as a unit of DNA length.

Lead compound: in preclinical trials and clinical trials, a potential drug being tested for safety and efficacy.

Lethal dose 50%: the concentration of drug which induces death in 50% of the subjects to which the drug is administered.

Ligand: a name for a molecular structure that binds to another molecule (such as antigens that antibodies are designed to attach themselves to).

Ligase: an enzyme that can break down fats.

Linkage: a prediction based on the distance between two (or more) units such as genes on a chromosome. The theory holds that the closer together these units or "markers" are, the greater the likelihood that they will be inherited together.

Lipids: a family of fatty molecules.

Liposome: an artificial membrane. Can be used to encapsulate drugs and aid in drug delivery.

Loading dose: is an initial dose of drug that is higher than subsequent doses for the purpose of achieving therapeutic drug concentrations in the serum rapidly.

Locus: the position of a gene or other point of interest on a chromosome.

Lymphocytes: white blood cells.

Lymphokines: substances produced by T-cells to assist in immune reactions to foreign agents.

Lysis: the destruction of a bacterium by a bacteriophage (virus).

Mapping: charting the position of a gene or marker along the chromosomes.

Margin of safety: the margin between therapeutic and lethal doses of a drug.

Marker: a genetic variation found on a chromosome. This variation points the way to a specific gene that may show an important mutation.

Megabase (Mb): one million nucleotides. Used as a standard of measure.

Meiosis: a form of cell division. The chromosomes in sex cells are duplicated, and then the resulting structures are split in half. The result: four sex cells, each with half chromosomes.

Messenger RNA (mRNA): a molecule shaped by DNA that directs the creation of proteins.

Microarray: a tool that permits the identification of DNA samples and examination of gene expression in individual tissues and different conditions.

Microbiology: the study of micro organisms, including bacteria, viruses, fungi, protozoa and yeasts.

Micro organisms: also known as microbes. Living organisms invisible to the naked eye but visible under a microscope.

Mitochondria: cell organelles that produce energy for the cell.

Mitosis: the full version of cell division. When chromosome are duplicated and the cell is divided, each resulting cell has a full copy of genetic information. There are five important phases of mitosis: interphase, prophase, metaphase, anaphase and telophase. These describe the process after interphase (normal cell life) when a cell replicates its information, confirms its suitability, organizes itself into position and splits in two.

Molecular biology: a branch of biology that deals with molecules, such as proteins and DNA.

Molecular evolution: the process of making discrete changes in genes to improve the functional characteristics of proteins and enzymes.

Molecular farming: using biotechnology to produce useful products from domesticated plants and animals.

Monoclonal antibody: an antibody that recognizes a single target. Polyclonal antibodies recognize several related targets.

Monogenic disease: a disease caused by a mutation in a single gene versus polygenic disease, multiple mutations that are expressed as disease.

mRNA (Messenger RNA): a ribonucleic acid molecule that transmits genetic information from DNA to the protein synthesis machinery in cells, where it directs protein synthesis.

Mutagen: an environmental element that can cause mutation, for example, some elements of cigarette smoke.

Mutant: a cell or organism harbouring one or more mutated genes.

Mutation: a change in the base sequence of a gene that results in it not performing its normal task.

Non-competitive antagonist: binds to a site other than the agonist-binding domain. Induces a conformational change in the receptor, such that the agonist no longer "recognizes" the agonist-binding domain. Even high doses of agonist cannot overcome this antagonism.

Non-Hodgkin's lymphoma (NHL): unregulated growth of the defenders, called B-lymphocytes, which usually repel invasion by foreign organisms.

Nuclear transfer: the process of cloning Dolly the sheep that began by placing chosen DNA matter in an empty (nucleus removed) egg casing. This egg, after growing, was implanted into a host sheep that gave birth to Dolly (see embryo twinning).

Nucleic acid: a chain of nucleotides.

Nucleotide: one of the structural components, or building blocks, of DNA and RNA. A nucleotide consists of a base plus one molecule of sugar and phosphoric acid.

Nucleus: the sac inside a cell that carries genetic material.

Nutraceuticals: foods that have a health benefit beyond simple nutrition.

Oligonucleotide: a short, custom-made strand of DNA.

Oncogene: a gene that helps regulate cell growth but may cause cancers.

Oncogenic: viruses, chemicals, genes, proteins etc. that cause the formation of tumours.

Onset: is the amount of time it takes a drug to begin working. Drugs administered intravenously generally have a more rapid onset than drugs taken orally because oral agents must be absorbed and pass through the gut before entering the bloodstream.

Oral administration: most compatible with drugs that are self-administered. Oral agents must be able to withstand the acidic environment of the stomach and must permeate the gut lining before entering the bloodstream.

Organelle: a component of a cell. Some commonly known organelles are the mitochondria, the ribosomes and the Golgi apparatus. Organelles are found only in eukaryotic cells, which are the type of cells found in humans.

Partial agonist: a drug which fails to produce maximal effects, even when all the receptors are occupied by the partial agonist.

Pathogen: a disease-causing organism.

Peptide: small protein molecules, usually composed of fewer than 20 amino acids. They are easily synthesized and have a wide variety of uses including medicinal applications.

Phages: viruses that attack bacteria.

Pharmacogenomics: examination of the genetic basis for variation in response to therapeutics by different individuals.

Phase I reactions (non-synthetic): drugs are oxidized or reduced to a more polar form.

Phase II reactions (synthetic): a polar group, such as glutathione, is conjugated to the drug. This substantially increases the polarity of the drug. Drugs undergoing phase II conjugation reactions may have already undergone phase I transformation.

Phenotype: the characteristics of a genetic trait as expressed or as observable in a living organism. See genotype.

Physiological antagonism: two agonists, in unrelated reactions, cause opposite effects. The effects can cancel one another.

Physiology: the study of the function of cells or organisms.

Placebo: a mock-treatment used in single-blind or double-blind experiments to eliminate bias from experimental subjects or administrators respectively.

Plasmid: a circular DNA molecule, found in bacteria but not a part of the bacterial chromosome. Plasmids can be self-replicating and may be used as tools for cloning.

Platform technology: a technique or tool that enables a range of scientific investigations. Examples include combinatorial chemistry for producing novel compounds, microarrays for gene expression analysis and bioinformatics programmes for data assembly and analysis.

Point mutation: these occur when one nucleotide ATCG is incorrectly copied.

Polygenic diseases: caused by several gene mutations working together. See monogenic.

Polymer: a long molecule characterised by a repeating pattern of components. Plastics are the best-known polymers but biotechnology is now joining proteins together to form polymer chains.

Polymerase Chain Reaction (PCR): a method to produce sufficient DNA for analysis from a very small amount of DNA.

Polymorphism: a variation in the sequence of a segment of DNA among individuals.

Potency: the amount of drug required to produce 50% of the maximal response that the drug is capable of inducing.

Preimplantation genetic diagnosis: the testing of a single early-stage embryo cell for genetic disease.

Primer: a short sequence of nucleotides (ATCGs) that kick-start or prime the copying of DNA, allowing polymerase to go to work.

Prion: a naturally occurring protein that can be converted into a disease-causing form. Prion diseases can be transmitted in the absence of DNA or RNA.

Probe: a known single-stranded DNA or RNA molecule that can be used to probe or search for complementary sequences in a given sample. For example, a probe for a genetic mutation would signal the presence of a complementary strand of DNA or RNA, indicating the sample in question contained the mutation in question.

Prokaryote: an organism with no cellular nucleus.

Promoter: a DNA sequence preceding a gene that contains regulatory sequences influencing the expression of the gene.

Proof of principle: demonstration of the commercial potential of a discovery or invention.

Proteases: a form of enzyme that breaks up proteins.

Protein: a long-chain molecule comprised or amino acids that folds into a complex three-dimensional structure. The type and order of the amino acids in a protein is specified by the nucleotide sequence of the gene that codes for the protein. The structure of a protein determines its function.

Proteomics: the study of the protein profile of each cell type, protein differences between healthy and diseased states and the function of, and interaction among, proteins.

Purines: the "two-ringed" base units of DNA: adenine and guanine.

Rational drug design: using the known three-dimensional structure of a molecule, usually a protein, to design a drug that will bind and have a therapeutic effect on it.

Recessive gene: a variation that appears in offspring only when two copies are present – both the mother and father must contribute the recessive gene. Recessive disease is expressed or suppressed based on this criterion. See dominant gene.

Recombinant DNA: the DNA formed by combining segments of DNA from different sources.

Rectal administration: useful for unconscious or vomiting patients or small children. Absorption is unreliable.

Restriction enzyme: a protein that cuts DNA molecules at specific sites, dictated by the nucleotide sequence.

Retrovirus: a type of virus that reproduces by converting RNA into DNA.

Reverse transcriptase: a viral enzyme that sparks the synthesis of DNa from a retrovirus's RNA pattern.

Ribosomes: cellular factories that synthesize proteins as directed by RNA.

Ribozymes: these are RNA molecules that can destroy other RNA molecules. They may be useful against RNA-dependent retroviruses.

RNA (ribonucleic acid): a nucleic acid, similar to DNA, which has roles in gene expression.

RNA interference: using antisense techniques to selectively inhibit expression of a gene.

Selective breeding: crossbreeding pairs of organisms with desirable traits.

Sequencing: the process of determining the nucleotide sequence of a DNA or RNA molecule. Shotgun sequencing involves the reduction of a genome to fragments, learning their structure and determining how the tiny pieces fit back together. Directed sequencing involves the sequencing of DNA from adjacent stretches of DNA.

Silent mutations: usually dormant mutations in DNA. They have no apparent effect and can go unnoticed.

Single Nucleotide Polymorphism (SNP): a single base difference in the sequence of a gene which alters the structure and function of the gene product.

Small molecule: denotes a molecule that is small enough to be absorbed by the body in pill form. Larger molecules must be injected or delivered by novel system.

Somatic cell: any cell in the body other than the gametes (sexual reproductive cells).

Spacer DNA: DNA that has no apparent function in protein expression. It is found between genes.

Stem cell: an undifferentiated cell that can multiply and become any sort of cell in the body.

Subcutaneous (SubQ, SC) administration: drug is injected beneath the skin and permeates capillary walls to enter the blood stream. Absorption can be controlled by drug formulation.

Sublingual administration: good absorption through capillary bed under tongue. Drugs are easily self-administered. Because the stomach is bypassed, acid-lability and gut-permeability need not be considered.

Tandem repeats: DNA sequences that repeat again and again. They have been compared to a stutter.

Telomeres: the tips of chromosomes. Telomeres are key to the replication of DNA molecules. They may be important factors in ageing and in the uncontrolled replication of cells characteristic of cancer.

Testosterone: the male sex hormone.

Therapeutic index: a measure of the safety of a drug. Calculated by dividing the lethal dose 50% by the effective concentration 50%.

Thymine (T): one of the base nucleotides, which pairs with adenine (TA).

Tissue engineering: the production of natural or synthetic organs and tissues that can be implanted as fully functional units or may develop to perform necessary functions following implantation.

Topical administration: useful for local delivery of agents, particularly those which have toxic effects if administered systemically. Used for most dermatologic and ophthalmologic preparations.

Transcription: the synthesis of an mRNA molecule as a copy of a gene. In gene expression, transcription precedes translation.

Transdermal administration: a few drugs can be formulated such that a "patch" containing the drug is applied to the skin. The drug seeps out of the patch, through the skin and into the capillary bed. Very convenient for self-administration.

Transgenic: an organism with one or more genes that have been transferred to it from another organism.

Transgenic animal: an animal that has received genetic material (inserted into its DNA) from another organism. For example, a goat with human DNA might express insulin in its milk. A transgenic animal can also be used to test therapies that act on a specific portion of inserted DNA.

Transgenic plant: as above.

Translation: the synthesis of a protein based on the nucleotide sequence of an mRNA molecule, which corresponds to the sequence of a gene.

Transposons (jumping genes): these DNA segments move from one position on a chromosome to another. They are incapable of self-replication.

Tumour necrosis factor: a so-called "biological response modifier", produced naturally in small amounts to enhance response to disease.

Uracil: a base that is part of the make up of RNA but not DNA. It pairs with adenine (UA).

Vaccine: a preparation of either whole disease-causing organisms (killed or weakened) or parts of such organisms, used to confer immunity against the disease that the organisms cause. Vaccine preparations can be natural, synthetic or derived by recombinant DNA technology.

Vector: a way of delivering genetic information or codes to target cells. For example, a patient requiring gene therapy may be infected with an engineered virus (the vector) that will deliver new DNA sequences to cells. As much as possible, the viral vector will be rendered harmless before the subject is infected with it.

Virus: an extremely small carrier of genetic information. In the presence of a host, it takes over the genetic machinery and instructs the host to reproduce new viral copies. If the host develops resistance to this infection, the virus will evolve its surface to become undetectable.

X-chromosome: the chromosome believed responsible for sex determination during reproduction. A female usually carries two of them and a male only one.

X-ray crystallography: an essential technique for determining the three-dimensional structure of biological molecules.

Xenotransplantation: transplanting a foreign tissue into another species.

Y-chromosome: usually joined with an X chromosome in males.

Yeast artificial chromosome (YAC): a vector (tool) to clone large DNA pieces.

Zoology: the study of animals.

Zygote: the original cell formed by the union of two sex cells, sperm and egg, the gametes. A zygote is sometimes used to describe the very early stages of an embryo when a few stem cells are all that exist.

References

Chapter 1

1. Davies, K. (2002) *Cracking the genome: Inside the race to sequence human DNA*, Johns Hopkins University Press: Johns Hopkins Paperbacks.
2. Craig Venter, J. (2007) *A Life Decoded: My Genome: My Life*, Allen Lane Science.
3. Shreeve, J. (2005) *The Genome War: How Craig Venter Tried to Capture the Code of Life and Save the World*, Ballantine Books.
4. Spinks, A. (1980) *Biotechnology*, Report of a joint working party. HMSO, UK.
5. Drews, J. (1998) Biotechnology's Metamorphosis into a Drug Discovery Industry, *Nature Biotechnology* 16: 22–24.

Chapter 2

1. Alexander, D., Britton, A. and Jorissen, A. (2003) *International Financial Reporting and Analysis* Thomson Learning (UK).
2. Brealey, R. and Myers, S. (2003) *Principles of Corporate Finance*, 7th edition, McGraw-Hill/Irwin (USA).
3. Damodaran, A. (2001) *Corporate Finance: Theory and Practice*, 2nd edition, John Wiley & Sons, Inc.
4. Moscho, A. (2000) Deals that make sense, *Nature Biotechnology* 18: 719–722.
5. DiMasi, J.A. and Grabowski, H.G. (2007) The cost of Biopharmaceutical R&D: Is Biotech Different? *Managerial and Decision Economics* 4–5: 469–479.

Chapter 3

1. Tufts Center for Drug Development.
2. Pharmaceutical Research and Manufacturers of America (PhRMA) 2007. Pharmaceutical Industry Report 2007.
3. Pharmaceutical Research and Manufacturers of America (PhRMA) 2007. Burrill and Company analysis for PhRMA reported in the Pharmaceutical Industry Report 2007.
4. DiMasi, J., Hansen, R.W. and Grabowski, H.G. (2003) *Journal of Health Economics* (22): 151–185.
5. DiMasi, J. and Grabowski, H.G. (2007) The Cost of Biopharmaceutical R&D: Is biotech different? *Managerial and Decision Economics* 28: 469–479.
6. PhRMA.
7. DiMasi, J. (2001) New Drug Development in the United States from 1963 to 1999. *Clinical Pharmacology & Therapeutics* 69 (5): 286–296.
8. Center for Medicines Research International 2006/2007 *Pharmaceutical Factbook*.
9. PBM & Generic Pharmaceutical Issues Symposium, 18–19 June 2007.

10. Grabowski, H.G. and Kyle, M. (2007) Generic Competition and Market Exclusivity Periods in Pharmaceuticals, *Manage. Decis. Econ.* 28: 491–502.
11. CanaccordAdams: Initiation of Coverage. 23 July 2007. Basilea Pharmaceutica "Success is already in the price".
12. Lou, K. and de Rond, M. (2006) *Nature Reviews: Drug Discovery* (5): 451–452.
13. Abrantes-Metz, R.M., Adams, C.P. and Metz, A.D. (2005) Pharmaceutical development Phases: A Duration Analysis, *Journal of Pharmaceutical Finance, Economics & Policy*, 14 (4): 19–37.
14. CanaccordAdams Daily Letter, 20 February 2007. CeNeS "M6G: equivocal phase 3 results".
15. Newron, 22 August 2007. Press release Merck Serono Announces 18-month Safety and Efficacy Data of Phase III Trial of Safinamide in Parkinson's Disease.
16. Merck, 22 August 2007. Press release Merck Serono announces 18-month Safety and Efficacy Data of Phase III Trial of Safinamide in Parkinson's Disease.
17. Canaccord Capital Daily Letter, 19 October 2005. UCB "Cimzia fine but market shifting".
18. www.humira.com.
19. Schwartzman, S. and Morgan, G.J. (2004) *Arthritis Res Ther* 6 (Suppl 2): S19–23.
20. http://www.healthpromoresearch.com.

Chapter 4

1. Grabowski, H.G. and Vernon, J. (2000) The distribution of sales revenues from Pharmaceutical Innovation, *Pharmacoeconomics* 18 Suppl. 1: 21–32.
2. CanaccordAdams, 22 August 2007, "The Slings and Arrows of Outrageous Fortune: The Biosimilar Debate".
3. *MedAdNews*, June 2006.
4. Humphreys, A. (2004) Future Blockbusters, *MedAdNews*, January, 1–12.
5. Bonifant, B. (2007) 11 Missteps in valuation and how to avoid them, *SpecialtyPharma*, 3 (1): 52–55.
6. http://www.ncbi.nlm.nih.gov/pubmed/. PubMed is a service of the US National Library of Medicine that includes over 17 million citations from MEDLINE and other life science journals for biomedical articles back to the 1950s. PubMed includes links to full text articles and other related resources.
7. www.cms.hhs.gov.
8. www.micromedex.com/products/redbook/.
9. BioCentury. The Bernstein Report on BioBusiness, 2 July 2007, A10.
10. Poterba, J.M. and Summers, L.H. (1995) A CEO survey of U.S. companies time horizons and hurdle rates, *Sloan Management Review* (Fall): 43–53.
11. Grabowski, H., Vernon, J. and DiMasi, J.A. (2002) Returns on research and development for 1990s new drug introductions, *Pharmacoeconomics* 20 Suppl. 3: 11–29.
12. Grabowski, H.G. and Vernon, J. (2000) The distribution of sales revenues from pharmaceutical Innovation, *Pharmacoeconomics* 18 Suppl.: 21–32.
13. Stuart, T.E., Hoang, H. and Hybels, R.C. (1999) Interorganisational endorsements and the performance of entrepreneurial ventures, *Administrative Science Quarterly*, 44: 315–349.
14. Stewart, J. *et al.* (2001) Putting a price on biotechnology. *Nature Biotechnology* 19: 813.
15. Arojärvi, O. (2001) *How to value biotechnology firms: a study of current approaches and key value drivers*, Helsinki School of Economics and Business Administration.
16. Ekelund, A. (2005) Valuating Biotech project portfolios using crystal ball and real options – case: Natimmune. Proceedings of the 2005 Crystal Ball User Conference.
17. Reichert, J. (2001) Monoclonal antibodies in the clinic, *Nature Biotechnology* 19: 819.
18. Biotechnology Industry Organization, "A Brief Primer on Manufacturing Therapeutic Proteins" April 2003.
19. Brealey, R.A. and Myers, S.C. (2000) *Principles of Corporate Finance* (6th edition). Irwin/McGraw-Hill: Burr Ridge, IL.
20. DiMasi, J.A., Hansen, R.W. and Grabowski, H.G. (2003) The price of innovation: new estimates of drug development costs, *Journal of Health Economics* 22 (3): 141–185.
21. DiMasi, J.A. and Grabowski, H.G. (2007) The cost of biopharmaceutical R&D: is biotech different, *Managerial and Decision Economics* 28: 469–479.

22. Grinblatt, M. and Titman, S. (2002) *Financial Markets and Corporate Strategy*, McGraw-Hill Higher Education, New York.
23. The index is a collection of stocks from 23 countries in the developed world and is maintained by Morgan Stanley Capital International.
24. Myers, S.C., and Shyam-Sunder, L. (1995) Measuring pharmaceutical industry risk and the cost of capital, in *Competitive Strategies in the pharmaceutical industry*, Helms, R.B., (ed). American Enterprise Institute for Public Policy: Washington DC.
25. *Fortune Magazine* 17 April 2003.
26. CannacordAdams 12 June 2007, Merck KGaA "Hybrid model captures the mood".
27. Canaccord Capital 3 June 2004. "US Multiple Sclerosis market".
28. Taylor and Leitman (Harris Interactive) Vol. 1, issue 15 (2001).
29. The Red Book.
30. Tremlett, H.L. and Oger, J. (2003) Interrupted therapy: stropping and switching of the β interferons prescribed for MS, *Neurology* 61: 551–554.

Chapter 5

1. Kellog, D. and Charnes, J.M. (2000) Real options valuation for a biotechnology company, *Financial Analysis Journal*, May/June.
2. Bogdan, B and Villiger, R. (2007). *Valuation in Life Sciences: A Practical Guide*, Springer.
3. McCord, C.M.K. (2006) Pitfalls in Pharmaceutical Capital Allocation: the case of the beta bias, *Specialty Pharma* 2 (5): 36–39.
4. International Federation of Accountants. June 2007. International management Accounting Statement: project appraisal using discounted cash flow, www.ifac.org.
5. Myers, S.C. and Howe, C.D. (1997) A life-cycle financial model of pharmaceutical R&D. Program on the pharmaceutical industry, Massachusetts Institute of Technology.
6. Crystal Ball.
7. Mun, J. (2002) *Real options analysis: Tools and techniques for valuing strategic investments and decisions*, John Wiley & Sons, Inc.
8. Black, F. and Scholes, M. (1973) The pricing of options and corporate liabilities. *Journal of Political Economy*, 81: 637–654.
9. Triantis, A. and Borison, A. (2001) Real options; state of the practice, *Journal of Applied Corporate Finance*, 14 (2): 8–24.
10. McGrath, R.G. and Nerkar, A. (2004) Real options reasoning and a new look at the R&D investment strategies of pharmaceutical firm, *Strategic Management Journal* 25: 1–21.
11. Cox, J., Ross, S., and Rubenstein, M. (1979) Option pricing: a simplified approach, *Journal of Financial Economics* 7 (September): 229–263.
12. Nichols, N.A. (1994) Scientific management at Merck: An interview with CFO Judy Lewent, *Harvard Business Review*, January/February.

Chapter 6

1. Keegan, K. (2001) The Biotechnology Sector in *The Global Investor Book of Investing Rules* ed. Jenks, P. and Eckett, S., Harriman Publishing, London, UK, pp. 227–230.
2. Ernst & Young (2006) "Beyond Borders: The Global Biotechnology Report".
3. Pisano, Gary P. (2006) *Science business: the promise, the reality, and the future of biotech*, Harvard Business School Press.
4. www.PhRMA.org Adis R&D Insight database, 8 February 2007.
5. www.BIO.org.
6. UBS Investment Research. 18 January 2008. "2008 Biotechnology Sector Preview".
7. Dellenbesch, R. "VC funding trends for Life Science Firms", *Genetic Engineering & Biotechnology News*, 1 September 2007, Volume 27 No. 5.
8. Dealogic database.
9. Gustafsson, J. (2000) *Risk Management in Finnish Biopharmaceutical Companies*, Helsinki University of Technology.

10. Lev, B. (2004) Sharpening the Intangibles edge, *Harvard Business Review*, (June): 1–9.
11. Guedj, I. and Scharfstein, D. (2004) "Organisational Form and Investment: Evidence from Drug Development Strategies of Biopharmaceutical Firms", NBER 10933.
12. Teva Pharmaceutical Industries Ltd Strategy Overview, 21 February 2008.
13. Teva Pharmaceutical Industries Ltd Press Release, 21 February 2008.
14. BioCentury 29 January 2007.

Chapter 7

1. Pearce, R. and Barnes, S. (2006) *Raising Venture Capital*, John Wiley & Sons, Ltd.
2. Silber, W.A. (1991) Discounts on Restricted Stocks; the impact on illiquidity on Stock Prices, *Financial Analyst Journal* July–August: 60–64.
3. Emory, J. (1994) The value of marketability as illustrated in Initial Public Offerings of Common Stock-February 1992 through July 1993, *Business Valuation Review*, March: 3–7.
4. Damadaran, A. (1996) *Investment Valuation. Tools and Techniques for determining the value of any asset*, John Wiley & Sons, Inc., New York.
5. Compiled by BDO Stoy Hayward LLP, UK, www.bdo.co.uk.
6. Guo, R.-J., Lev, B. and Zhou, N. (2005) The valuation of science based IPOs, *Journal of Accounting Auditing and Finance*, 20 (4): 423–459.
7. Darby, M.R. and Zucker, L.G. (2002) Going Public when you can in Biotechnology. National Bureau of Economic Research Working Paper, No. 8952.

Index

Index compiled by Terry Halliday